DYNASTY

WEBSTER
CLAIBORNE
UNION
MOREHOUSE
BOSSIER
CADDO
HOMER
FARMERVILLE
BASTROP
OAK GROVE
EAST CARROLL
WEST CARROLL
LAKE PROVIDENCE
BENTON
SHREVEPORT
MINDEN
LINCOLN
RUSTON
ARCADIA
OUACHITA
MONROE
RICHLAND
RAYVILLE
MADISON
TALLULAH
BIENVILLE
JACKSON
JONESBORO
CALDWELL
DE SOTO
RED RIVER
FRANKLIN
WINNSBORO
TENSAS
WINN
COLUMBIA
COUSHATTA
MANSFIELD
ST. JOSEPH
WINNFIELD
LASALLE
CATAHOULA
NATCHITOCHES
HARRISONBURG
NATCHITOCHES
SABINE
GRANT
JENA
MANY
COLFAX
VIDALIA
CONCORDIA
ALEXANDRIA
RAPIDES
VERNON
AVOYELLES
MARKSVILLE
LEESVILLE
WEST FELICIANA
EAST FELICIANA
CLINTON
POINTE COUPEE
BEAUREGARD
ALLEN
EVANGELINE
ST. FRANCISVILLE
DE RIDDER
VILLE PLATTE
ST. LANDRY
NEW ROADS
E. BATON ROUGE
OBERLIN
BATON ROUGE
OPELOUSAS
W. BATON ROUGE
PORT ALLEN
JEFFERSON DAVIS
ACADIA
ST MARTIN
CALCASIEU
IBERVILLE
LAFAYETTE
PLAQUEMINE
CROWLEY
LAFAYETTE
LAKE CHARLES
JENNINGS
ST. MARTINVILLE
DONALDSONVILLE
ABBEVILLE
ASSUMPTION
CAMERON
VERMILION
NEW IBERIA
IBERIA
NAPOLEONVILLE
PART OF ST. MARTIN PARISH
ST. MARY
FRANKLIN
CAMERON
TERR

DYNASTY

The Longs of Louisiana

BY THOMAS MARTIN

G. P. Putnam's Sons New York

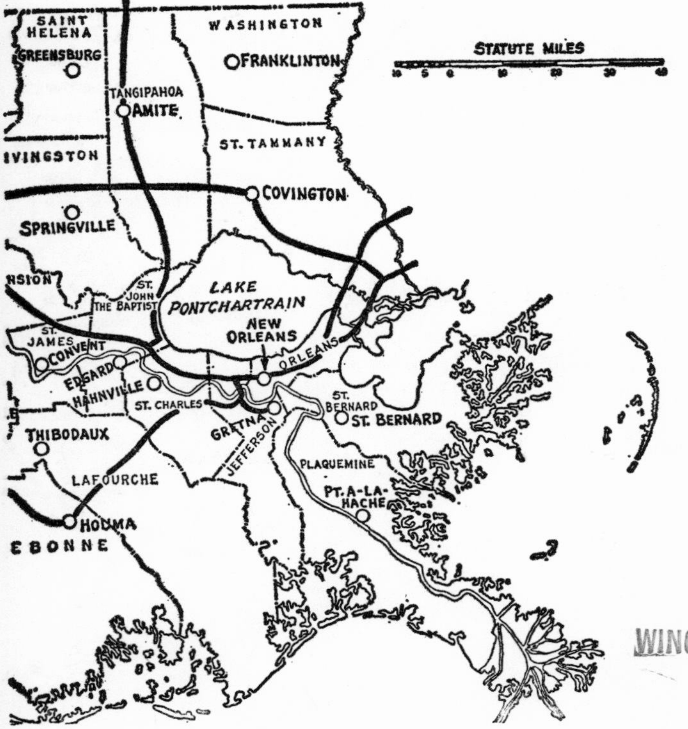

Library of Congress Catalog
Card Number: 60-8475

MANUFACTURED IN THE UNITED STATES OF AMERICA

VAN REES PRESS • NEW YORK

To Mary Lou, with love . . .

. . . the difficulty of maintaining hereditary states accustomed to a reigning family is far less than in new monarchies; for it is sufficient not to transgress ancestral usages, and to adapt oneself to unforseen circumstances; in this way such a prince, if of ordinary assiduity, will always be able to maintain his position, unless some very exceptional and excessive force deprives him of it; and even if he be thus deprived, on the slightest mischance happening to the new occupier, he will be able to regain it.

Of Hereditary Monarchs,

THE PRINCE—Niccolo Machiavelli

CONTENTS

PROLOGUE:
The Stage

PRESIDENT JEFFERSON was troubled.

"Every eye in the United States," he told his minister, "is now fixed on this affair of Louisiana. Perhaps nothing since the Revolutionary War has produced more uneasy sensations through the body of the nation." [1] His instructions to Diplomat Robert Livingston at Paris were explicit: To give America a deepwater outlet to Gulf commerce, the United States must buy the "Island of New Orleans." Livingston and his fellow diplomat, James Monroe, did even better. They bought Louisiana—from Canada to the Gulf.

The incident is symbolic and revealing. Seldom in the four centuries since the white man arrived has the territory been without crisis. Frequently, the eyes of the nation have been fixed on Louisiana with amusement, wonder, anxiety. At times, shock, disbelief, even perverse fascination have occasioned the stares. And in the present an incredulous nation fastens its gaze on the state as Louisiana finishes an experiment. A political dynasty (the very word is repugnant to the American conception of free politics) is ending. Twenty-five years after the death of its founder, Huey Long, it may indeed be over.

But the end of the dynasty—if not of Longism, the philosophy that nurtured it—may well be the beginning to an understanding of how it came to be. Basically, the Longs and Longism appeared as the answer to decades of discontent at the grass roots—discontent on the part of the rural white, the poor farmer, the hill-country redneck. Before Huey's ascendance

[1] President Jefferson to Robert Livingston, April 18, 1802, Official Correspondence.

these were the disenfranchised elements, the political lower class, the have-nots. They asked little, got less. They expected the worst—and got it.

It was Huey Long who galvanized their chronic frustration into a political force, a potent voice that, having been heard, would no longer be silent. It was the voice of protest—against big business, against big-city domination of the Legislature, against legislative indifference to rural pleas. In the beginning, in short, the dynasty arose as a protest against what previously had passed as representative democracy in Louisiana. In this respect, perhaps, the Longs were not unique. For the history of Louisiana began with a protest.

The first organized white men to reach Louisiana came there by accident, then left quickly. Hernando de Soto's explorers, in search of the Florida treasures, determined to return to the Old World in gold-laden ships. They found little to loot in the Everglades, but they were adamant in their goal. On foot and on horseback, they slogged their way westward across Dixie and became the first organized white band to set foot in Louisiana.

They were dismayed by what they found. There were no fabulous cities, no glittering temples. Instead, Louisiana—lush and verdant, a land of cypress and moss, of mosquito-filled swamps and unbearable humidity, through which flowed the majestic Mississippi. When de Soto died, dissension broke out in the ranks. To a man, the conquerors rode the river to the Gulf, leaving Louisiana behind them.

The French followed, with the English close on their heels. But trickery came early to Louisiana. An English sea captain, sent to explore the mouth of the Mississippi, came upon a band of French, who told him that he had entered the wrong river, that the French were already there in numbers. The sailor gave up the search. The spot where he executed his retreat is still referred to, with some amusement, as the "English Turn."

By 1700 the French were establishing permanent colonies in Louisiana, but the new territory quickly became the center of Europe's boldest confidence game. In France, a canny Scotsman named John Law persuaded the French government to let him operate Louisiana much like an overseas branch office. By promoting the new territory's resources, the stock of Law's company shot upwards. In Paris, there was frenzied buying, followed by the inevitable crash. John Law fled France. The first Louisiana swindle—the "Mississippi Bubble"—burst. Despite the notoriety, the territory's population swelled. The company's charter expired and the French reclaimed the land as a crown colony. New France grew.

In the beginning, the trappers pushed their skiffs and pirogues up the muddy river in search of pelts for the fur trade. In other sections cotton and sugar cane crops were introduced. The city at the river's mouth—New Orleans—became a melting pot and a crossroads for the region. As its activity diversified, so did its population. New Orleans became not only a center of commerce but a citadel of vice. Thieves, low-lifers, harlots and shady adventurers concentrated there. The French government, disturbed at the number of prostitutes in the new settlement, sent boatloads of proper women to the New World. They were called *filles à la cassette*—casket girls—for each got from the government a small casketlike box containing a trousseau. The delighted settlers married them and called for more.

By 1730 the territory's population had increased tenfold, from the original 500 settlers to more than 5,000, with new groups arriving monthly. Waiting for them were easy trapping, fishing, cotton and sugar planting, shrimping along the lazy Gulf. With them they brought their Old World customs and language, and a rigid and established social order. When France lost Canada a new breed arrived in Louisiana. From Nova Scotia, bent on escaping the new English tyranny, came the enigmatic Cajuns—4,000 of them—who settled in the areas adjacent to the Gulf and the city.

The Treaty of Paris in 1763 abruptly changed the new way of life in Louisiana. Suddenly, Louisiana was no longer French, but Spanish, bartered off in a flicker of international courtesy. A new flag and a new culture appeared—the first suddenly, the second more gradually. By losing the Seven Years' War, France lost the magnificent empire she had acquired in North America. Canada went to England, New Orleans and the rest of the Louisiana Territory to Spain. Overnight, the hated Spaniards were established as masters.

The hearty, buccaneering French spirit that predominated in Southern Louisiana at the time took less than kindly to the Spanish interlopers. In New Orleans, the first contingents of

Spanish garrison troops found their weapons sabotaged by the local residents; rebellion became the password and the cry *"Liberté"* tumbled passionately from defiant lips. Passion, however, was no match for cold steel. Mustering an army led by an Irish soldier of fortune with the unlikely name of Don Alejandro O'Reilly, Spain suppressed the conspiracy, executed the ringleaders and established a new peace along the bayous.

The Spanish flag flew over Louisiana for thirty-five years while the French—and Germans, Italians, English and Irish—who arrived assimilated their Iberian overlords. Frenchmen and Spaniards, thrown together by a common religious bond and Latin temperament, merged, married, assimilated, and produced the proud Creole strain that even today is regarded as the genuine aristocracy. Spain, mindful of its prerogatives as master of the territory, sometimes balked at granting the privileges of the Port of New Orleans to the traders who trooped in from the north country. As late as 1795, Charles III of Spain concluded a peace treaty with the United States allowing Yankee traders to use the port for their fur, lumber and grain businesses. At the end of three years, the treaty specified, His Majesty would review the situation to see if this paternal and benevolent policy was inimical to the best interests of his country.

By 1800, however, the indulgences of Spain's king had become unnecessary. In Europe, conniving in his own sphere, Napoleon longed to re-establish French rule in the Louisiana Territory. By assuring Spain that a million French citizens would be settled in the Duchy of Parma, ruled then by a Spanish prince, Napoleon persuaded Charles to cede Louisiana back to France. France's dictator, operating *in absentia,* had retaken Louisiana without firing a shot. And a scant three years later, absorbed with the coming war with England, facing a depleted treasury, Napoleon quietly invited the United States to take the whole of Louisiana off his hands. President Jefferson, anxious to secure the unchallenged Mississippi outlet for westward bound colonists and traders, approved the purchase for a trifling fifteen million dollars. For the third time in less than half a century, Louisianians woke to find themselves shuffled or sold to someone else. Now, with Gallic sighs and upturned palms, they resigned themselves to new roles. They were Americans.

By 1812, the territory (its boundaries reduced to present-day size) had become a state. Three years later, New Orleans was attacked by the British. Although the War of 1812 had already ended, the news was late reaching the British commander, who pressed his siege. Andrew Jackson, who led the defense, was acclaimed the city's savior. The business of building Louisiana continued anew.

The first slaves had come to Louisiana almost a century before —about 1719—to labor on the cotton and, later, the sugar plantations. For all—save, perhaps, the hapless blacks—the plantations became the symbol of European aristocracy, transplanted to the rough New World. Quickly the landed gentry took hold of politics to lay the foundations of that uniquely nineteenth-century southern tradition, "government by gentlemen." What did it matter if, to the north, in the rougher, hardier hill country, Yankee *émigrés,* pushing across the Allegheny Territory, had begun to hack out a meager, agrarian existence on substandard land? Louisiana was now a way of life and it would be preserved. Slavery was a part of that way of life.

By 1830, the Abolitionist voice was heard in the South. From South Carolina, proud citadel of southern class demarcations, came the first rumblings that bespoke rebellion, then secession. As in other crises, the planters glanced uneasily around them, condemned (by the popular vote they controlled) South Carolina's hasty nullification ordinance, talked co-operationism rather than secession.

But the spark of secession that flickered into life in South Carolina soon engulfed the South, Louisiana included. By 1860, while the dissident parishes (the Louisiana equivalent of counties) of the north grumbled about fighting for the gentry and sent delegations to the capital to protest Louisiana's affiliation with the Confederacy, the die was cast: Louisiana stepped out of the Union and into the Confederacy. Not until the late 1870's, after Louisianians had tasted bitterly of the Reconstruction, did the state re-enter the Union and re-establish white supremacy.

Federal troops left Louisiana in 1879, but now the restless land reacted to new dissensions. From the northern parishes, filling with the small tenant farmers and sharecroppers—sturdy Protestants who settled in the red-tinged hill country—came a persistent plea for agrarian aid and reform. For the most part, the late-comers looked down from their northern perches with distrustful Puritan grimness, seeing in the easygoing, moral free-wheelers to the south all that bespoke corruption and decay. Stolidly, sullenly, they wrestled with the land, farmed their parcels, stuck to the Scriptures, damned the plantations and their owners. When foreign land reform movements like the Farmers' Alliance moved in to beckon them to brighter futures, they responded eagerly. Turning their backs on the traditional political virtues (for example, white supremacy) they joined in protest against the *status quo*. Cannily, the older, more sophisticated elements employed the first order of politics: soothe a dissident, promise him what he wants, then forget to deliver.

To the rebellious country folk, the Democrats—controlled for the most part by plantation and cotton interests—promised agrarian reform, relaxations of the crop lien, easier overseer managements. The hill folk listened, then bought. By 1890, they knew they had been duped; there was precious little for the poor farmer. Looking about, the have-nots thought they heard a rallying cry in the Populist movement. In a body, they welcomed it as a political panacea. By 1896, they had been disillusioned again. Although William Jennings Bryan carried Louisiana and the Populists packed solid political weight, the country at large rejected the silver-tongued orator. The tangible promise of a brighter tomorrow became another faded illusion. By 1900, for all practical purposes, the Populist Party ceased to exist, although the Populist philosophy continued to attract adherents for several years thereafter.

Now, new forces were at play. On the heels of Populism's death, industrialization appeared in the form of the railroad and lumber industries. With industrialization appeared the Socialists headed by Eugene Debs, then the Wobblies with the railroad gangs, promising a new economic day for the downtrodden. But to the south, in burgeoning New Orleans, the "Ring" was born—the first big-city political machine to come to awakening Louisiana.

Big-city machine politics came to Louisiana just three years before the end of the century. The machine grew in prestige, power and numbers (save for a factional fight in the early 1920's) for the next quarter of a century—or until Huey Long successfully challenged it. In effect, it became the dominant political force in Louisiana.

Prior to 1898 the plantation, then later the industrial interests, had played the prime political role in Louisiana's politics. But the constitution of 1879 put much of the business of running Louisiana at the local level in the hands of the governor and the Legislature. With its population increasing dramatically, itself the only really urban area in the state, New Orleans had an immediate and natural advantage in seeing that it was well represented at the state level. By 1879 a coalition of big-city politicians, industrialists and some planters (who, as a group, had been losing influence) formed the first New Orleans Ring, or Choctaw Club of New Orleans, as it was originally known. Its purpose was simple: to dominate, as much as possible, politics at the state level. With twenty of the hundred House members, and eight of the thirty-nine members of the Senate allocated to the city (a number sufficient to influence legislation and constitutional amendments) and with the biggest single identifiable vote in the state, the Ring, which took control of the city's political machinery, soon became a formidable political influence across Louisiana.

Under the Ring, New Orleans became a center of vice. With benign and benevolent Mayor Martin Behrman in office for the biggest part of the first quarter of the century, the fusion of officialdom and vice was complete. Gambling, whoring, pimping, and illegal night clubs flourished under the indulgent eye of the Ring's police officials, while state authorities, fearful of the loss of bloc vote support, kept a strict hands-off policy in local matters.

At the state level, the Ring played the political game in the style of a veteran but cautious madam; she would survive if only she jumped in the right direction at the right time. The Ring rarely endorsed a gubernatorial candidate at the outset. It was only after battle lines were drawn, and after a meeting of minds between candidate and the Ring, that the quiet endorsement came. In those days, the game was a "you scratch me, I'll scratch you" proposition. Nobody got hurt and nobody was unhappy.

The Ring lost no time in aligning itself solidly with big business. Voting as a unit, the city's legislators (supported by friendly governors) stalled child labor law amendments, labor law reform, bills that would have exempted rural homesteads from burdensome taxes. Direct taxes on industry were overlooked or kept to a minimum.

While New Orleans householders paid exorbitant rates for artificial gas, the Ring-directed politicians refused to allow cheap natural gas in the city, kept the city's electric rates at a scandalously high level, the local utility under the supervision of the city, rather than a state regulatory agency. Big business opposed a federal income tax, so the Ring opposed it too. The city became the "Paris of America"—gay, light, cosmopolitan, enjoying a perpetual Mardi Gras. Dissent was out; rocking the boat was unpopular and unprofitable.

As the voice of the Ring grew more strident in state affairs, the frustrations of Louisiana's northern poor whites and redneck farmers became more acute. From 1900 to 1924, the Ring backed virtually every successful gubernatorial candidate—whose first obligation on taking office, of course, was to the Ring and its city. Only twice was the Ring set back during that period—once in 1912, again in 1920, when Ring-backed candidates for governor lost. But these were temporary setbacks that were overcome in the subsequent elections. Meanwhile the Ring, supported by its bloc-voting lawmakers, continued to dominate the Legislature. For Louisiana's rural elements it was an almost hopeless political situation.

In the hill country, rednecked farmers hammered away at the unyielding soil and pondered their disenfranchisement. Who was there to plead their cause—for roads that could be traveled in rainy weather; for hospitals and schools for the sick and untutored; for bridges free of tolls or for meager pensions to tide them over in the last years of a hard life? There was no one. "Government by gentlemen" merged with Ring rule. Candidates for office promised little and ignored the realities of the day. While the farmers and other rural elements cried for bread, the politicians evoked images of the glorious Confederacy—of cavalry charges up the hill and the unbroken spirit of the Southland. As they went through the meaningless exercise of politicking by extolling archaic Confederate chauvinism, the dispossessed listened and watched with a mounting bitterness that bordered on explosive resentment. Allan P. Sindler observed: ". . . there had developed in nineteenth-century Louisiana increasingly well-defined class antagonisms which, if the appropriately charismatic leader appeared, could stimulate another attempt at protest politics by lower-class whites. Huey Long . . . must be understood in the context of the origins of class conflict in Louisiana. The persistent appeal of Longism . . . owes as much, if not more, to repressed class bitterness as it does to the makeshift liberal policies of the Longs." [2]

Huey Long's father once put it more fervently, as he summed up the bitter resentments of the politically forgotten:

"There wants to be a revolution, I tell you. I seen this domination of capital, seen it for seventy years. What do those rich folks care for the poor man? They care nothing—not for his pain, nor his sickness, nor his death." He added: "Maybe you're surprised to hear talk like that. Well, it was just such talk that my boy was raised under, and that I was raised under." [3]

By the time Huey Long was born, plantationism had flourished for more than a century. Into backward Louisiana stepped the industrial interests to take up where the planters had left off, and the New Orleans Ring had not yet been born. On the surface, Louisiana experienced a deceptive political peace. It was soon to end. And when that happened, Louisiana would never be the same again.

[2] Allan P. Sindler, *Huey Long's Louisiana,* The Johns Hopkins Press, Baltimore, 1956.

[3] James Rorty, in *The Forum,* August, 1935, and *Where Life Is Better,* John Day, 1936.

PART I:

Birth

I

Enter the Kingfish

ON the heels of a century of planter politicians, on the eve of big-city bossism, amidst the Populist-Socialist-Wobblie agitation, Huey Pierce Long, Jr., was born on August 30, 1893, at Winnfield, Winn Parish, in north-central Louisiana.

Like the other come-latelies in Winn Parish (Father Long had lived briefly in Pennsylvania, Ohio, Indiana and Mississippi before settling permanently in Louisiana) the Longs had "poor white" stamped all over them. Huey Sr. was able to scrape together the money for a substandard 320 acres after he came to Winn, but a growing family, the vagaries of weather and the crop markets, the naturally unyielding soil, all conspired to keep daily subsistence a constant concern.

Huey Jr. was the eighth of nine children, the first to be born in the log cabin the Long family occupied. Campaigning later, he was to allude time and again to the "log cabin" as though it were a Tobacco Road caricature. In fact, the cabin, although a log structure, was a comfortable, if crowded, four rooms—a cut or two above the standard dwellings inhabited by most of Winn's poorer whites. Still later, Huey himself was to describe the Long home as a ". . . comfortable, well-built, four-room log house." (Consistency never was one of the future politico's virtues.)

Winn Parish was a depressing place, an austere, red-hilled, pine-dotted land populated by strait-laced Protestants, mainly Baptists. God-fearing, hard-working, these were the rednecks, who spent their days in the field enduring the blistering sun, their nights at Bible meetings or tending to household chores. They had little time and less inclination for fun or pursuits they considered frivolous. They battled the unyielding soil, developed a clannish suspicion of outsiders and came to be experts in the art of hacking out substandard livings. They had no truck with the easygoing, slyly immoral Catholics to the south, nor with the big-city or planter politicians who kept them economically backward. When Louisiana seceded to join the Confederacy, it was over the protests of a Winn delegation instructed to vote against leaving the Union. When the Civil War began, many of Winn's sons left home for hide-outs to avoid Confederate service. Others traveled north to join the Union Army. In appearance, inclination and deed, Winn differed radically from the romantic image of the Confederate South.

From the beginning, Huey developed in the grim, depressing mold of the strait-laced farming community. The Longs were Baptists of the old hard-shelled school and Father and Mother Long made certain that the children knew their Scriptures "from cover to cover." Huey, like the others, spent the Sabbath at Sunday school and church in the morning, at a young people's church meeting in the afternoon, at more church services Sunday evening. Wednesday nights, there were the inevitable prayer meetings. Community life centered around the church, neighbors and relatives. Said Huey, "We went to every funeral within ten miles."

While the others stolidly went about their farm chores Huey took every excuse to skip his. He was to confess later: "From my earliest recollection I hated the farm work. In the field the rows were long; the sun was hot; there was little companionship. Rising before the sun, we toiled until dark, after which we did nothing except eat supper, listen to the whippoorwills, and go to bed."

Even as he worked on the hated farm, however, there was early evidence that Huey's trigger-quick mind probed, then took advantage of the angles as he saw them. When he wasn't working for his father, Huey hired out to chop cotton for neighboring farmers, who paid him the going rate per hundred pounds picked. His first experience as an incentive wage earner ended abruptly; his employer discovered that Huey had become adept at slipping watermelons into the cotton, thus dramatically increasing the bale's weight. Huey wasn't fired, but thereafter he was paid by the day, not the pound.

At home Huey was quick to flash the temper-and-tantrum behavior that went with the rust-colored hair, the impish, upswept nose, the bright, darting eyes. An older brother described his early domestic conduct briefly: "As a child, he was always disagreeable among his sisters and his brothers." [1] Later, interrogating his politician brother, Earl, Huey clucked mournfully at an answer he didn't relish. "It's a sin to lie," he remonstrated gently with Earl, who casually snapped back: "You must have committed a million sins in your lifetime." [2] Later, the older brother, Julius, was to write scathing articles denouncing his brother as a thief and a liar; Earl was to join in the attack and a sister was to taunt Huey publicly by delivering a campaign speech against him. Clearly, Huey was not much loved by his family, in his youth as well as at various times in later life. And the feeling, from all accounts, was pretty well mutual. Huey grew particularly bitter when his father, after selling some land to the incoming Arkansas Southern Railroad, could send six of the children to college before the money ran out. It ran out when Huey's turn came. When he ran away from home, then returned, a sister greeted him with a sarcastic toss of the head. "Come in, tramp," she quipped, as the future Kingfish shuffled dejectedly through the door.

Running away did little to soften Huey's attitude toward farming and the grim community life about him. A year later, he tried to slip off again, managed to get less than fifty miles away before the family caught up with him.

At thirteen, casting about for some way to earn money, Huey landed a job in a print shop. But when a traveling peddler gave him and a schoolmate a supply of books on credit, the two hitched horse to buggy, took off for the backwoods, cajoled, wheedled and outtalked the farmers into buying the lot. By nightfall, recalled Huey, "we had only a banjo and a pair of scissors left in the wagon. We sold them, too." Homeward bound, in high spirits as they fingered their profits, the two wrecked the wagon. "Bang went the profits," said Huey.

The book-selling experience evoked a natural propensity in the youth who would later talk his way to political immortality.

[1] *Real America,* September, 1933, "What I Know About My Brother, Senator Huey P. Long," by Julius T. Long.

[2] U. S. Senate, Hearings of the Special Committee on Investigation of Campaign Expenditures, 72nd Congress, 1932–33.

He found an excitement in the romantic figures he read about (he was to fall back on Ridpath's *History of the World* in his later political harangues), especially statesmen or generals. He discovered, too, that with his mouth open he was someone, because people had to listen. With his mouth closed, no one noticed him.

"I can't remember back to a time," he was to say later, "when my mouth wasn't open whenever there was a chance to make a speech." Understandably enough, long after Huey was dead and Brother Earl ruled Louisiana, Earl would justify his own ineptness or offensive outbursts by proclaiming: "The only chance I can get before the people is with this big mouth of mine. If it ever closes up, God help Ole Earl. God help him."

Sometimes, Huey's talk got him in trouble. Always ready to start or jump into an argument, he had no stomach for fighting. Once, Brother Earl hove in sight as a group of boys pelted Huey, who was trying to break away. Grabbing a broom handle, Earl waded in. Soon he was getting his lumps, too. Looking around for Huey, he spotted the latter high-tailing it up the roadway. Later, when the brothers met as lawyer and witness, Huey accused Earl of once challenging him to a fist fight. Replied Earl casually, "I may have, but I knew you were not going to meet me; I never heard of you meeting anybody." The "physical coward" tag was to plague Huey through most of his political life. Opponents gleefully retold stories of how he had fled from an aged ex-governor, of how he ran from a one-legged voter during a campaign, of how an elderly Shreveport attorney had rapped him several times with an umbrella at the height of a political fight. Huey himself did nothing to ease the stigma of these charges. After he came to power, he was seldom seen without a brace of burly bodyguards.

By the time he was fourteen, Huey was acquiring some practical experience in politics. Hearing of a candidate for the local tick inspector's post, Huey beat a path to the man's door to strike up a quick deal. For five dollars—$2.50 in advance, the other half on delivery—he could guarantee the man's election. The candidate paid. Huey put his printing experience to work, distributed circulars on behalf of his candidate, unleashed his rhetoric when he found more than two people idling about. The Long candidate won by fourteen votes, a veritable landslide. Huey had a taste of politics and he liked it. He rarely missed a chance to mix in political wars thereafter, whether he had a personal stake or not.

Between politicking and running away, Huey left home—this time legitimately—to take up the drummer's trail in the backwoods. First he sold soap products and patent medicines, later a shortening compound called Cottolene. Bumping over the back roads in a horse and buggy, Huey came upon his first comprehensive sampling of rural discontent. Appalled at what he saw in areas so remote that politicians rarely included them on stumping tours, Huey's amazingly retentive memory stored up facts and impressions. He would evoke them later.

The drummer's life was pretty tame for Huey, but he liked the salary (he made up to $100 per month on the road) and the expense account. "For the first time in my life," he wrote, "I felt that I had hit a bed of ease. I was permitted to stop at the best hotels. . . . I had arrived." His arrival almost coincided with his departure. He was fired for padding his expense accounts.

Huey returned briefly to high school at Winn, then trooped off to Shreveport to a "four-year" high school where he thought opportunities were greater. His initial appearance was dramatic. He simply walked into a classroom and announced: "Class, I'm Huey P. Long and I'm here to stay." When a chemistry instructor asked the class to define a compound, Huey rose instantly: "Cottolene is a compound . . ." and he was off on what amounted to a sales pitch, a condition that, for Huey, was becoming chronic.

Leaving high school at Shreveport, Huey tried a succession of jobs—all in sales—at Houston, Memphis, Kansas City, Oklahoma City. He attended the Oklahoma State University Law School briefly, where his stay was notable only for his political agitation. Sneering at a student-organized Wilson-for-President Club, Huey announced for Champ Clark, staged a walkout when the original club held its meeting. Huey's group unanimously endorsed Clark. His dictum, as a result of this experience: "In a political fight, when you've got nothing in favor of your side, start a row in the opposition." It was a technique he employed later with devastating results—and for higher stakes.

Tiring of law school, Huey once again hit the drummer's trail, this time with the experience of his previous meanderings.

In back-country hill towns he faced the "unwashed" and beguiled them with stories of his travels and political plans. At one town, he staged a cake-baking contest (to promote Cottolene, of course) and awarded the blue ribbon to a Shreveport belle named Rose McConnell. Miss McConnell didn't know it at the time, but she really hit the jackpot. In short order, Huey proposed and the two were married. At nineteen, Huey had responsibilities—and a new goal. He decided to get "an education."

A bride on his arm, a valise in his hand, Huey arrived in New Orleans in October of 1914. There, with a few hundred dollars he had saved from his salesmanship (and $400 loaned by Julius), Huey enrolled at Tulane University Law School. In eight memorable months, following a "special law course" carefully prescribed for him by Brother Julius (who had taken the same course himself), Huey hit the books and the classrooms for as much as eighteen hours a day.

In their airless two-room apartment, Huey studied while Rose transcribed notes he had dictated. His weight dropped to 112 pounds but his energy and disposition stayed on an even keel. Later, he would astound political opponents—particularly older ones, who required big doses of sleep—by seemingly working around the clock, making long-distance telephone calls, cementing deals, salting away votes, while the opposition slept.

By May the money was gone. Huey had to make his move. Into the offices of State Supreme Court Chief Justice Frank A. Monroe he strode, hat in hand, to tell the jurist that he was broke, that he couldn't wait until June to take his bar exams, that he needed emergency help. The judge nodded, responded sympathetically to the ambitious youngster on the make and arranged for the special examinations. Said Huey: ". . . Justice Monroe assembled a majority of the court, gave the necessary examination, and on the 15th day of May, 1915, at the age of twenty-one, I was sworn in and declared a full-fledged lawyer in the State of Louisiana." The Kingfish had his education and his opportunity. Now he had to put them to use. "I came out of that courtroom running for office," said Huey. But it took four years of running to land the first office.

Most of the running was done in his northern home-town parish of Winn, but at first it was more like a walk. Back in

Winnfield, Huey rented a four-dollar-a-month, one-room office (he bought a typewriter on credit, almost lost it when he fell behind on payments) and hung out a tin shingle that said simply: HUEY P. LONG, LAWYER. But clients were hard to come by. The first month Huey had to write a worthless check for the office rent. Slowly, however, the clients drifted in and Huey soon had going what he liked to call a "chip and whetstone practice"—marginal cases.

Most of the cases came straight from the railroad yards—workmen's compensation, injury suits and the like. But Huey's first big-time political contact came when a widow asked him to sue a bank for money she thought the bank owed her. Huey took the case, but neither he nor the widow had the money for the required legal bond. With characteristic cheek, Huey went to the bank, met one of the directors, State Senator John Harper, and talked the senator into loaning him the bond money so he could sue the bank. While he chatted with the banker, Huey for once was more impressed with what he heard than with what he said.

Senator Harper was Winn Parish's leading dissident, a man who saw most of the country's troubles in terms of a lopsided accumulation of wealth. He wrote a flaming protest against what he called the possession of 72 per cent of the country's wealth in the hands of 2 per cent of the citizens. America was on the eve of war. Harper asked that money, in addition to men, be conscripted. For his radicalism he was later indicted by a federal grand jury, which charged him with violation of the Espionage Act. Huey helped get him acquitted.

Harper's bright-eyed, pie-in-the-sky propaganda registered with his new follower, the fledgling reformer. Two years later, in March of 1918, in a letter to the New Orleans *Item,* Huey outlined for the first time in public, his views on the concentration of wealth and its evils:

> A conservative estimate is that about sixty-five or seventy per cent of the entire wealth of the United States is owned by two per cent of the people. Sixty-eight per cent of the whole people living in the United States own but two per cent of the wealth. From the year 1890 to 1910, the wealth of this nation trebled, yet the masses owned less in 1910 than they did in 1890, and a greater per cent of the people lived in mortgaged and rented

> homes in 1900 than in 1890, and more lived in rented and mortgaged homes in 1910 than did in 1900. . . . But the greatest cause of industrial unrest is that of education. Authorities on education tell us that eighty out of every one hundred people in the United States never enter high school; only fourteen out of every thousand get a college education; 690 out of every thousand never finish the fourth grade in school. Does such a condition give the ordinary man his proper return of the nation's prosperity?
>
> This is a condition, north, east, south and west; with wealth concentrating, classes becoming defined, there is not the opportunity for Christian uplift and education and cannot be until there is more economic reform. This is the problem that the good people of this country must consider.[3]

At twenty-four, Huey had his political pony. Without serious modification, but with sophisticated enlargements, the Kingfish's later "Every Man a King" and "Share Our Wealth" creeds were to be rough approximations of his "concentration of wealth" letter to the editor.

In May of 1916, after criticizing the state's laughable workmen's compensation laws, Huey—at Harper's behest—wrote an amendment to the law and accompanied Harper to Baton Rouge to appeal to the Legislature for its enactment. It was his first visit to the legislative halls he would later dominate. He later wrote: "It was my first time to have seen a legislature in session. The formalities, mannerisms, kow-towing and easily discernible insincerities surrounding all of the affairs of the session were, to my mind, disgusting."

Disregarding the legislative committee's useless and pointed efforts to keep him from speaking, Huey spoke his two cents' worth anyway. For lawmakers accustomed to "government by gentlemen," politics by the book, it was a rare experience.

Adopting the hand-flailing tactics that were to become so recognizable on the political stump, Huey ripped into the group:

"For twenty years has the Louisiana Legislature been dominated by the henchmen and the attorneys of the interests. Those seeking reforms have . . . bowed their heads in regret and shame when witnessing the victories of these corrupting influences at

[3] New Orleans *Item,* March 1, 1918.

this capitol. But, gentlemen, with all this, not until 1914 did they possess the brazen audacity to command the General Assembly of Louisiana to pass unanimously a law by which a laborer's family should not receive over an average sum of $300 for a life upon whom they depend for education and support. . . . What a subterfuge . . ."

The committee turned down Huey's bid, but it listened until he finished. Huey's words made the newspapers and people around the state began to take their first serious notice of him.

War came to America, but Huey, with his natural dexterity, avoided the draft by claiming a family and status as a public official. His title was grounds enough; he was a duly registered notary public. Since he stayed at home, Huey did the next best thing; he participated in Liberty Bond drives. Justifying his deferment, Huey said later, "I wasn't mad at nobody."

Tramping his neighborhood in the bond drives, Huey cast about for a public office. He was only twenty-four and every major state office was closed to him. He studied the state constitution and found what he was looking for; the Railroad Commission (now known as the Public Service Commission), the board charged with regulating utilities, carried no minimum age as a requirement for office. Besides, as a watchdog of big business—oil, telephone companies, electric combines—it offered the perfect opportunity for the young radical to practice what he had been preaching. Huey announced his candidacy for railroad commissioner of the North District of Louisiana. Four others, including the popular incumbent, Burk A. Bridges, opposed him.

The campaign Huey waged was a revelation to the people of the district. Accustomed to platitudes, long-winded speeches and empty promises (in some cases, the farmers rarely saw a candidate), the rednecks met a man who blasted the commission as a tool of corporate interests. Huey stumped the backwoods from dawn till late at night. He was to recall later: "Nothing in my campaigning seemed to please the farmers more, or cause them to recollect me so favorably, as to call them from their beds at night." The farmers, awed at the spectacle of a candidate actually burning to reach them, listened, called their neighbors to listen, and spread the word.

Huey didn't play down to the rednecks; he urged them to

fight for what they wanted—whether they deserved it or not. Instead of aping the country boy by wearing baggy clothes and driving a horse and buggy, the candidate rolled into town wearing a smart business suit and driving a secondhand car.

While Huey stumped, Rose mailed out campaign literature and Brothers Julius and Earl loped around the countryside tacking up campaign posters and nailing down votes. Once, when Huey ran out of campaign money, he borrowed it from Oscar K. (O.K.) Allen, a boyhood friend from Winnfield, who himself had to borrow it from a bank. In the primary, Huey got additional backing from another significant source—Alexandria attorney John H. Overton, who was running for a United States Senate seat. Huey never forgot the favors he received from both Allen and Overton and they, in turn, never regretted giving them.

Huey's campaigning paid off. Three of the candidates were swamped. Huey came in second to the popular Bridges, thus forcing him into a runoff election. By applying more of the same pressure in the second campaign, Huey whipped Bridges by 635 votes. At twenty-four, he became a member of the powerful Railroad Commission.

The six-year-long, state-wide office was exactly what the ambitious Huey needed and wanted to get himself solidly into the public eye. He moved his home and offices to Shreveport, opened a law office there with Brother Julius. He bombarded the newspapers and friends with his circulars which detailed injustices in the state's handling of corporate interests. He became more of a peacock than ever, once remarking that he thought he and the other railroad commissioners would wear gold badges ". . . so that the people will know us and give us the respect we're due." The young demagogue wanted attention. Soon, he was getting it from all sides.

In his days as a Winnfield lawyer, Huey had represented some oil friends and corporate interests. He had been paid in oil stock, then had invested some of his own money in independent oil ventures. Suddenly, he saw his personal investments threatened. The giant Standard Oil Company of New Jersey, the dominant vested interest in Louisiana at the time, summarily moved to put the independent oil interests out of business by denying them the use of the Standard-owned oil pipelines necessary to carry their oil from the fields to the refineries. Here was an octopus flexing its tentacles, threatening to crush the economic life out of the competition. Here was an arrogant, power-mad combine bent on wrecking the fortunes of a struggling lawyer who had plaintively hoped that "I might some day be mentioned among the millionaires" (at which time, presumably, he would share his wealth). It was a combination too good to pass up. Huey set up his soapbox and never got off again.

"This octopus," cried the new commissioner, "is among the world's greatest criminals. It was thrown out of Texas following its raid on Spindletop; it was ousted from Kansas; it was forced to terms in Oklahoma. . . ." Huey blasted the corporations that squeezed the pennies out of the little man, their cigar-chewing lawyers and the officials who let them get away with it. This was high piracy of the lowest order.

The newspapers and the people of Louisiana chuckled at such unrestrained bile. Standard Oil and its lawyers laughed too. Everybody—except, perhaps, the small oil companies—stopped laughing as soon as Huey played his trump. After cajoling and browbeating the Railroad Commission chairman for weeks in an attempt to have the pipelines declared common carriers (and thus subject to commission regulation) Huey looked out the window of the commission office overlooking the Mississippi River at Baton Rouge one day. Turning to the chairman, he said, "Look at that . . . there now is a ship coming up the river loaded with Mexican crude [oil] to go in the tanks where they will not let us put our oil." The chairman signed the order. Now Huey's will was the commission's official expression. Only the Legislature was needed to make that expression law.

It was political harvest time in Louisiana again in 1920. Up for grabs between John M. Parker and Frank Stubbs was the gubernatorial seat to be vacated by R. G. Pleasant. Although Redneck Huey and Bull Moose Gentleman-Farmer Parker had little in common, the two got together. From Parker, Huey got a guarantee. If elected, Parker would back legislation designed to put the pipelines under commission supervision. Parker also pledged to end Ring rule in New Orleans. Huey, in turn, promised to back Parker in the section Parker needed most to carry —the hill country of North Louisiana.

Huey hit the campaign trail for more than two months, the corporations—especially Standard—and big-city rule his prime targets. Parker carried North Louisiana by 761 votes, enough to carry him into the Governor's Mansion. Huey now had a toehold at the top, a powerful ally at the heart of government. Or so he thought.

While the old administration died and Parker waited to take office, Huey turned his attention elsewhere. In his absence, the commission generously raised the rates of the Cumberland Telephone and Telegraph Co. by 20 per cent. Huey hurried back, outraged. Reopening the case, he had the order rescinded. When the company appealed, Huey traveled to Washington and won his case before the U. S. Supreme Court. Back to telephone subscribers went more than $450,000 they had paid in overcharges and Huey announced that the lower rates would mean savings of "more than a million dollars a year."

The newspapers applauded the new giant killer. "Mr. Long has put action into the Commission. He would have it really regulate public service corporations. . . . A rebate from the telephone company is like manna from Heaven," exulted the New Orleans *Item*.

"He is entitled to the gratitude of the people for the fine fight he has made in this case . . . the public could not have got as much but for Mr. Long's persistent efforts in their behalf," intoned the New Orleans *Daily States*. Said the Baton Rouge *State Times*: ". . . The credit for a reduction . . . belongs to Huey P. Long. We do not enroll ourselves as a champion of Mr. Long, but we always want to be fair."

Huey worked a reduction in the rates charged by intrastate railroads, then bludgeoned Shreveport's streetcar lines into lowering the fare from six cents to a nickel. The Southwestern Gas and Electric Company came in for its share of attention too, as Huey maneuvered the commission into lowering its utilities rates, thus continuing his growing reputation as a "friend of the people."

Now friendly John Parker took office. Comeuppance for the Standard octopus was at hand. Huey hurried to Baton Rouge for the Constitutional Convention and to be in on the kill.

Governor Parker had labeled himself a reformer and a conservative, with the emphasis on the latter. Now, he lived up to the name. Forgetting his deal with Huey, Parker and the convention entered into a "gentlemen's agreement" with Standard: the Legislature would impose no more than a 2½ per cent severance tax on Standard's oil if Standard's attorneys would agree not to contest the legality of the measure. Both sides shook hands on the deal. Later, the Legislature reneged and upped the severance tax to 3 per cent. Standard protested, but lost. When the issue of common carrier regulation came before the Legislature, however, Parker's efforts far from satisfied Huey.

Double cross! charged Huey, labeling Parker's inaction and the gentlemen's agreement a fake and a fraud. "You have seen," he told the Legislature, "an administration trade in offices which belong to the people and barter them away in a manner unbecoming an ancient ruler of a Turkish domain. Better to have taken the gold hoarded in the Standard Oil vaults at 26 Broadway and deliberately purchased the votes with which the administration has ruled this state . . . than to have browbeaten, bulldozed and intimidated the Legislature for the benefit of the corporate interests through the free use of the people's patronage. Bold and amazing is the Governor's cry that he has no bill to submit to you, for the reason that it is at 26 Broadway for its final polish. Are you lawmakers of Louisiana to return to your people as fallen chattels . . . ?"

The barbs hit home. Shame, cried Standard. Foul, cried Parker. "Their sins have found them," retorted Huey. Called before Parker to justify his invective, Huey reiterated that the governor had welshed. Parker had him arrested for libel and Huey went to court with Brother Julius and John Overton to defend him. The court upheld the charges, found Huey guilty on two counts and sentenced him to thirty days in jail (suspended) and a fine of one dollar or one hour in jail. Strutting to the bench, Huey milked the incident for its last drop of publicity value. "Judge," he said defiantly, "I am not going to pay that dollar." Sighing, the judge produced a fifty-cent piece, asked lawyers for both sides to chip in a quarter each. Huey grinned in triumph and walked out of the courtroom to continue the war.

In the first years of the twenties, Louisiana headed toward a political climax. From top to bottom, a wave of reaction and protest arose against the established order. The protest had little depth or direction at the time. There was only a gnawing, creeping discontent, a feeling that "something has to be done."

Parker, during his campaign for governor, had promised to end New Orleans Ring rule once and for all. No longer would three-fourths of Louisiana have to come to the Legislature, hat in hand, to curry favor with the big-city delegation. Moreover, Parker had told New Orleans voters themselves, they would share in the blessings. With the end of Ring rule, vice and corruption would go and the decent citizen would get his say. Moreover, said Parker, he would do "all in my power" to bring cheaper, natural gas to New Orleans.

Parker had been swept into office as a reform governor, while roly-poly Mayor Martin Behrman, the Ring's perennial City Hall overseer, had lost his re-election bid. The Ring had been challenged and beaten. New Orleans and the rest of Louisiana were going to see a new day. Or so it seemed.

By the end of 1921 the bubbles of Parker's promises were bursting all over the state. Behrman was out of his New Orleans office, but the Ring continued to rule the city and the vice parlors. Moreover, there wasn't a whiff of natural gas in sight.

Until 1921, parish and local governments had been directly responsible for the building and upkeep of roads. Only the wealthy parishes like Orleans (New Orleans), Caddo (Shreveport) and East Baton Rouge could foot the bills. The rest of the state had a mish-mash of inadequate roadways that impeded commerce and stifled farmers. Now, the Constitutional Convention agreed that more state aid was needed to give Louisiana a modern highway system. Where would the money come from? From gasoline and license fees, ruled the convention. And how would the roads be financed? By the "pay-as-you-go" plan backed by former Governor Jared Y. Sanders' group. In other words, no immediate financing action at the state level to get the program into high gear. The dirt roads would be with Louisiana for some time to come. Meanwhile, Parker failed on another score. In the gas fields of North Louisiana, the corporations siphoned off the carbon black in the natural gas and let the rest go to waste. Disgraceful, cried conservationists, and called on Parker to make good on his promises. The conservative governor directed the attorney general to "investigate," but nothing came of it.

One of Parker's former supporters, O. C. Dawkins, summed up the growing disillusionment of the governor's casual approach to these problems. "You," wrote Dawkins, ". . . were on record against the smut makers, these wasters and stealers of natural gas . . . you have become silent and inactive while the carbonites have run roughshod over you, your Constitutional Convention, your Legislature, and your conservation law that has nothing in it but soft teeth . . . you have apparently gone to sleep at the switch and there is very little time left for you to wake up and prevent the awful wreck and destruction of one of Louisiana's greatest natural resources. You should do something for the people of Louisiana by conserving this rich gas field [in North Louisiana] from pillage by foreign corporations that don't give a damn for you, your conservation laws or the people of Louisiana." [4] To New Orleans letter writers who protested the continued absence of cheaper, natural gas, Parker could only reply lamely that cheap gas for New Orleans "was not practical, profitably or financially." In the north, the rednecks who failed to reach a market every time the rains gullied the roads, shook their heads. Things, after all, were the same

Parker's regime was a mild disaster for the hopes of thousands of Louisiana voters. In New Orleans, the disaster was climaxed when Ring Mayor Behrman rode back into power in the city election of 1923, thus emphasizing the complete collapse of the Parker "reform" movement. But if Parker's program left Louisiana wanting, it was a godsend to Huey Long. On his thirtieth birthday—the minimum age for a governor—two days before the official filing period for state office ended, he announced that he would be a candidate for governor in the 1924 election.

Huey rampaged into the campaign of 1923–24 without any recognizable machine support, but with a king-sized reputation for being a champion of the "little man." His two principal opponents, Parker's lieutenant governor, Hewitt Bouanchaud, a New Roads Catholic attorney, and Henry Fuqua, a Baton Rouge hardware store owner turned manager of the Angola State Penitentiary, boasted solid bloc supporters. Bouanchaud, as a Catholic, could lay claim to most of South Louisiana. Moreover, he had the support of Colonel John Sullivan's New

[4] Letter from O. C. Dawkins to Governor John Parker, April 4, 1924, Governor's correspondence, Department of Archives, Louisiana State University.

Orleans "New Regulars," a dissident group that had broken away from the "Old Regulars," or New Orleans Ring, over local policy. Fuqua could count on some Protestant support, in addition to the political group headed by ex-Governor Jared Sanders and the New Orleans Ring.

The country boy on the stump was a compelling spectacle. Standing there in the early autumn heat, perspiration rolling down his cheeks, Huey introduced a give-'em-hell, firebrand note into Louisiana politics that had never been seen before. Windmilling his arms high above his head in gestures that became famous, he blasted the corporations and the "rotten" state administration. In North Louisiana, he advocated free hunting and fishing the year round and promised to rid the state of that "coon chasin', possum watchin' brigade," the State Conservation Commission. Declared Huey, "I'll cut the tail off the Conservation Commission right up behind the ears."

For the rednecks and the small-towners Huey had a wagonload of promises. Miles of black-topped and paved roads and more money to the state's hospitals and mental asylums to free the inmates "from their chains." Education? Yes, but not just aid to education. Huey would see to it that the state's children got free textbooks and better schools, that tuition was lowered at the state university so that every child could go to college. And where would the money come from? Why, from the fat-cat corporations who milked the state of its natural wealth and gave nothing in return. To get back some of what the corporations took from Louisiana, promised Huey, he would impose a five-cent "occupational tax" on oil refining, and that included the Standard octopus. Huey told how he had been suckered out of his meager stockholdings. "As a country yap, I put $1,050 in oil stock. . . . Standard Oil . . . issued notices that they would take no more oil from independent producers and my oil stock wasn't worth forty cents. . . . Do you think I can forget that? Do you blame me for fighting the Standard Oil?"

While Bouanchaud and Fuqua campaigned in the traditional, restrained manner, Huey blasted his opponents and their supporters with all the invective he could command. Both candidates, roared Huey, were bad eggs from the same rotten basket. "One of them has been put in the incubator of the New

Orleans Ring, and the other has been put in the nest of the Sullivan Ring. Both . . . eggs are to hatch" with nothing more than the "cackle, cluck and strut as you had during the last four years."

Huey stayed away from the big towns and hit the backroads. His car loaded with pamphlets and posters, the sides dotted with his pictures, he hit the farms and rural crossroads to talk about hogs and "horspitals" for the needy. Slowly, the crowds grew, and as the show got better the embryo Kingfish heard shouts of encouragement. "Give 'em hell, big boy," and "Go to it, Huey," shouted the delighted rednecks. From time to time, Huey stepped into the crowd to pass the hat.

At times he had to tread gingerly. One of the main accomplishments of the Parker administration had been an anti-masking law aimed at destroying the Ku Klux Klan. Feeling against the Klan ran high in Catholic South Louisiana, but there were a lot of Klansmen in the northern part of the state. Bouanchaud came out against the Klan; Fuqua had the support of the administration in power. Huey straddled the issue. Some grumbled about Huey playing both sides against the middle, about his being pro-Klan in the north, anti in the south. Huey kept mum.

The newspapers denounced the swaggering peacock. "Huey P. Long," ranted the New Orleans *Times-Picayune,* "by his irresponsible and violent utterances, his proved perversions of recorded fact, his vicious tirades against decent men whom the commonwealth has honored . . . has proved himself unfit for the post of governor." They laughed at the attendance at Huey's stump stops. "To hell with the lyin' newspapers," roared Huey as he looked out over several thousand faces. "The New Orleans *Times-Picayune* will report in the morning that there was a crowd of about three hundred." The crowd roared. On January 14, election eve, Huey closed out a giant rally at Alexandria and left for New Orleans for another. That night, he delivered his first speech over that new medium, radio, an instrument that later was to become a prime propaganda outlet for him.

Huey knew he had a big slice of the country vote in his pocket. He had no illusions about South Louisiana or the New

Orleans vote—they were lost. What he worried about now was the weather. If it rained, the rednecks would be mud-bound, unable to get to the polls. He waited.

The first weather reports that night were inconclusive. Later, they hinted of rain. By election morning Louisiana was swamped by downpours. Huey hovered over the first country box as election officials opened it. "Sixty-one votes cast there and you got sixty," said a friend. "I'm beat," mourned Huey. "There should have been a hundred for me and one against me. Forty per cent of my country vote is lost." Fuqua beat Bouanchaud in the runoff, but Huey had no illusions about what had beaten him. It was a combination of rain and religion—two Protestants running against a single South Louisiana Catholic. Huey knew then that if he tried again and kept his country vote, he had to pick up a slice of the southern vote, too. His next four years were devoted to planting a toe in the door at New Orleans.

Back he went to being a public service commissioner (the Railroad Commission got a new name from the 1921 Constitutional Convention) and a lawyer. He built a $40,000 home in Shreveport, developed his law practice, and cast a hungry eye toward New Orleans.

His chance to win converts in the south came when he backed U. S. Senator Edwin Broussard, a South Louisiana Catholic who was up for re-election in 1926. Opposing him was Huey's old enemy, former Governor Sanders, an East Louisiana Protestant. Huey pitched in north and south to help Broussard. The rednecks needed nothing more than Huey's appeal for good ole Ed Broussard, but they got it anyway. Sanders, charged Huey, was the same evil genius who advocated toll bridges and opposed free river crossings. Broussard won and Huey claimed credit for the victory.

Next, Huey marched into the offices of Colonel Robert S. Ewing, publisher of the New Orleans *Daily States* and the Shreveport *Times,* to ask for his support. Huey needed a newspaper ally badly. Colonel Ewing had a condition. Ewing was fighting the New Orleans Ring. He was supporting John Sullivan's New Regulars. Said Huey, "To get Ewing, we would have to take Sullivan first." Huey took them both. Huey's campaign manager quit, charging that Sullivan was as bad as a Ring boss.

Huey didn't care. He needed the colonel's papers. Meantime, Huey took as a running mate and candidate for lieutenant governor a South Louisiana Creole, Dr. Paul N. Cyr.

Now New Orleans began to get a brighter picture of the crude country boy. Word swept through the New Regular ranks—Huey was the man to support. He tossed his hat into the ring in 1928. With his came the hats of two others—Governor O. H. Simpson, who became governor when Governor Fuqua died in mid-term, and Congressman Riley J. Wilson, himself a Winn Parish product. Huey took them both to the cleaners.

For Simpson he had outright anger, charging his administration with corruption, graft, and ineptitude. For Wilson he had mild contempt. "So they seek to re-elect the gentleman because of his flood record?" he asked. "What is that flood record? Why, he has been in Congress for fourteen years and this year the water went fourteen feet higher than ever before, giving him a flood record of one foot of high water to the year."

But in the end Huey returned to the story the rough backwoodsmen wanted to hear—and he poured it on. Louisiana was a cesspool of corruption with the old political hogs trying to get back to the patronage trough. There were few schools for the children, few hospitals for the sick, no free bridges or passable roads for the bilked taxpayer. Huey roared out his solemn promise to change it all and to return a share of the wealth to the people. "Every man a king, but no man wears a crown," bellowed Huey, borrowing from William Jennings Bryan's "Cross of Gold" speech. The "unwashed," so long the political underdogs and have-nots, could hardly believe their ears. But there it was—"Every Man a King." The meek could and would, by crackey, inherit the earth—if only Huey got in. When he rolled south for the crusade in the lower parishes, Huey had North Louisiana stuffed tightly in his hip pocket.

In South Louisiana, where the Acadians had settled after fleeing from Canada, Huey delivered perhaps his most memorable political speech. It brought tears to the eyes of some of the moody, emotional French.

"And it is here under this oak where Evangeline waited for her lover, Gabriel, who never came. This oak is an immortal spot, made so by Longfellow's poem, but Evangeline is not the only one who has waited here in disappointment.

"Where are the schools that you have waited for your children to have, that have never come? Where are the roads and the highways that you send your money to build, that are no nearer now than ever before? Where are the institutions to care for the sick and disabled? Evangeline wept bitter tears in her disappointment, but it lasted through only one lifetime. Your tears in this country, around this oak, have lasted for generations. Give me the chance to dry the eyes of those who still weep here!" [5]

The opposition wilted under the flood of oratory, invective and emotion. Election day dawned bright, clear, with no hint of rain, and the "unwashed" poured out to cast their ballots. It was almost a walkaway for Huey. He got forty thousand more votes than Wilson, who led Simpson by slightly more than a thousand. In all, Huey got 43.9 per cent of the vote.[6]

Ordinarily, there would have been a runoff between Long and Wilson to decide the election. It never took place. The New Orleans *Times-Picayune,* supporting Simpson but opposing Wilson more, called for Wilson to withdraw. Simpson announced his support of Huey. In the face of the announcement Wilson withdrew, leaving Huey as the Democratic nominee, a sure winner in all-Democratic Louisiana. In turn, Simpson became a $5,000-a-year attorney in Huey's administration, but no one talked swap or deal at the time; the victory was too impressive. The country boy had made it into the hallowed Governor's Mansion—the first of his unpolished, untutored, rednecked, backwoods kind to turn the trick.

In his hotel room at New Orleans, an exultant Huey crowed to the sky. "That's showin' 'em, by Gawd. We're in the saddle now. Look out, I'm gonna be President some day." He lost no time in taking over the office. Before his inauguration, even before his victory had been certified, Huey called on Governor Simpson to begin operating free ferries parallel to the toll bridges that spanned the state's rivers. Simpson hastily complied, in a gesture symbolic of official Louisiana from that moment on.

5 *American Mercury,* "Huey Long: American Dictator," by Hodding Carter.
6 The vote: Huey, 126,842; Wilson, 81,747; Simpson, 80,326.

2

Dynamite

HUEY'S victory at the polls had been impressive, but it was purely personal—the accumulated fruit of ten years of vocal protest against the smug complacency of the *status quo*. He had maneuvered endlessly, compromising, making deals and, above all, spelling out the promise of a brighter tomorrow for the have-nots. He had identified himself with the untutored, gallused, red-necked hill folk, and inauguration day saw fifteen thousand people from all sections of the state stream into Baton Rouge. Some arrived on foot, others on horseback, in trains and buses. Some of Huey's enthusiasts from the marshy south even made the trip in pirogues. But they all came for the same reason—to see Huey take office. The brighter life was at hand.

Now Huey had to face realities. His campaign had been anything but negative. He had denounced the absence of good roads, the indifference to better schools and the lack of improved hospital facilities. But he had not stopped there. He had promised that his followers would have all these things, and more. The time had come to implement the program, fulfill the promises; in short, to deliver. It was, at the least, a formidable undertaking, and Huey had to establish a new order before he could redeem his pledges.

In taking over the governor's office, Huey had some concrete advantages on his side. As governor, he held the single most powerful state office, with all the appointive and patronage power the post traditionally implied. He was in tune with the political times; he had cried for change and the voters, by their ballots, had agreed that change was necessary. And Huey had swept into office with him two important members of his ticket, his lieutenant governor, Paul N. Cyr, and State Treasurer H. B. Conner. Moreover, Huey had youth, boundless energy and a solid background of public service.

On the opposite side of the ledger, however, he had some marked deficits to overcome. There was, in the first place, the size of the plurality that had elected him—43 per cent. He had not convinced the majority of the voters that he was the best man for the governor's job. Only after Huey had demoralized the opposition into withdrawing and supporting him had he been able to take office without engaging in a bitter second-primary election. In effect, the voters of Louisiana never got a chance to show that they would have cast a majority of their votes for Huey instead of another candidate. For that reason, as he took office, Huey still had a lot of convincing to do. But this time he would have to gain support through deeds, not words.

New Orleans was a problem for the ambitious Huey. The city had turned its back on Huey in 1924 by giving him a paltry 18 per cent of its total vote. Four years of feverish activity on Huey's part had done little to soften the city's attitude. In the 1928 election, despite the support of Publisher Ewing and John Sullivan of the New Regulars, Huey was able to increase his percentage of the total New Orleans vote by only three points. Only some seventeen thousand of the seventy-eight thousand Orleans voters who cast ballots chose Huey.

At the official level, Huey had few illusions about his prestige or popularity. He admitted that he faced a "very queer and difficult situation" in his first legislative session because only twenty-seven of the 139 legislators (eighteen representatives and nine senators) had supported his candidacy. "To pass any legislation," Huey reflected, "I had to recruit my support among legislators who had not favored me for governor." Clearly, the people had voted for Long. Longism, as it was to evolve, was yet to be perfected and tested.

In the beginning, too, Huey was rather widely regarded as something of a political flash in the pan, at best an irritating—but not dangerous—buffoon. Polite New Orleans and Baton Rouge society shunned him, as did the big business interests, which never forgot his anti-Standard tirades as a public service commissioner. Indeed, a majority of the Public Service Commission itself opposed him. (He was later to gain his revenge for this.) And in the Legislature, the opposition leaders, confident that they possessed a majority of the legislative vote, early threatened to block his programs unless he allowed them to share the patronage pie. Characteristic of the national reaction to Huey's election was the airy nonchalance with which *The New York Times* greeted his victory: "Mr. Long has always been good copy. Let Senator [Tom] Heflin [of Alabama] and Governor [Theodore] Bilbo [of Mississippi] note the appearance of a worthy competitor in the field of light political farce."

What Louisiana got from Huey was highly political, but it was far from light and farcical. There were laughs, of course; Huey was a master showman who knew a laugh often meant a vote. But there was nothing funny about the way he bludgeoned his political opposition into submission. Behind the laughs and the public clowning (leading the LSU band, or signing a bill into law while wearing a nightshirt), Huey played the political game with an expert's finesse, a puppeteer's concentration. He made mistakes, miscalculated opposition strength, floated trial balloons that his enemies promptly shot down. He was, in short, far from infallible. But he was more often right than wrong, quick than slow, adroit than clumsy. The thesis needs no further support than the final score of the game Huey played. When he finished, he had Louisiana in his hip pocket, lock, stock, parish and Legislature, New Orleans notwithstanding. His first step was to take over control of the state's party machinery.

Traditionally, Louisiana's delegates to the Democratic National Convention, which was to meet in 1928 in Houston, were selected at a state convention on the strength of the legislative blocs. The New Orleans Ring, of course, had a hefty bloc and, as he admitted, Huey could be sure of only minor support there. Just as he dug into the state constitution to find that he was old enough to run for railroad commissioner, Huey looked up the law, discovered that as far as his purposes required, the state convention was mere window dressing. The constitution didn't actually call for a convention. The New Orleans faction, in a courteous tip of the hat to the new governor, had offered to deal squarely in the matter of selecting delegates. But Huey would have none of this implied collaboration with his political enemies. Calling the friendly and amenable State Democratic Central Committee into session, he persuaded them to forget the state convention and name the delegates themselves. The Ring, furious, cried betrayal, denounced Huey, who calmly pointed out that he had broken no law, had merely shifted the selection of delegates to a broader base. Not until 1932, at the Democratic National Convention in Chicago, could Huey exclaim, "The Democratic Party in Louisiana? I am the Democratic Party in Louisiana." But he nevertheless had virtual control of the 1928 delegation.

Huey's highhandedness in circumventing the state convention should have warned the legislators who came to Baton Rouge for the session of May, 1928. But many of them succumbed to a combination of promise, compromise or threat. Huey's office became the capital's focal point and when he couldn't be found there he could be reached in his favorite suite in the Heidelberg Hotel. For all who came to talk to him, Huey had something to give—but also something to take. Lacking a majority in the Legislature, Huey first wanted leadership of both houses. His official campaigning paid off handsomely. When the Legislature organized, Huey's candidate, John B. Fournet, was elected speaker and his ally, Philip H. Gilbert, was elected the Senate's president pro tempore. With this legislative lever, Huey went to work in earnest.

To establish a political organization that owed him its complete allegiance (and to reward campaign supporters), Huey swept out of office every major and minor employee whose job he controlled. Into their places went Huey's people, avowed supporters, vocal allies. He made no effort to disguise his intention of using the state's patronage for his own purposes. An opposition legislator asked him if there would be patronage for his people. Huey answered, "You lost that as the spoils of war."

While he cleaned out appointive officeholders, Huey moved also on the state's powerful boards and commissions—the Highway Commission, the State Board of Health, the Orleans Parish Levee Board. Where he could fire the old members and appoint his choices, he wasted no time in doing so. Where he couldn't fire the incumbents, he tried any device that might work. Thus, in the case of the Levee Board, he employed a stratagem that was to become a powerful weapon for him. By explaining to friendly board members that he wanted their resignations temporarily in order to get—and enforce—the resignations of opposition members, Huey sometimes tricked an official into unwittingly resigning his post. He used this political sleight of hand to get rid of two Levee Board members and to appoint staunch supporters in their places.

He wanted the president of the State Board of Health out so he could appoint a Long supporter to the job. But the president's term would not expire until 1932. Huey denounced the board as a time and money waster, explained that he had to have control of the board if his program for revitalizing the state's medical institutions was to be realized. When he had a bill introduced in the Legislature to cut the president's term short, the Legislature went along with Huey. Out went the old president; Huey's man went in.

Early in the session, Huey learned a lesson in parliamentary tactics that was to stand him in good stead. The lesson: Don't waste time fighting the opposition's bills in the Legislature; concentrate on getting your own passed; then veto the opposition. The obvious advantage of the system was in speeding up the legislative procedure. There was another advantage. If the opposition saw its own bills getting through, it was less likely to bottle up Huey's bills. Said Huey to his friendly legislators, "You can clear the calendar in a day in that way. I will veto every bill after it is passed that I don't want." Later, he admitted that he "vetoed the objectionable bills by the score."

Huey seemed to be everywhere at once during that first session. Former Governor John Parker had treated the Legislature as an equal, believing that the legislative and executive branches had their separate roles to play. Huey treated the Legislature as an extension of his office. He called in his friendly representatives and senators daily to tell them what bills he wanted passed, then went to work on the opposition to see that the bills became law.

He was rarely content to stay in his office, as Parker had been, to await the results of a vote. Instead, Huey charged along capitol hallways to buttonhole opposition members, followed them into the House or Senate, where he paced up and down, inside the bar, in violation of the legislative rules. He appeared before legislative committees, frequently interrupting the proceedings to campaign for his bills.

Huey had promised New Orleans its first natural gas. Other

governors had talked around the subject, promising evasively that they would try to get it for New Orleans, or that they would do their best for the city. Huey had promised unequivocally—natural gas for New Orleans if he got in, not the high-priced artificial gas the city had been forced to accept. There was heated opposition in the Legislature; the company supplying the artificial gas threw its lobbying resources into the fight to keep the *status quo*. Huey outmaneuvered the opponents, compromised with the company by allowing it to charge a higher than expected rate for the natural gas. The Legislature passed his bill and New Orleans got its natural gas. It has had it ever since.

Other matters claimed Huey's attention. He had promised to eliminate the job of attorney for the inheritance tax collector of Orleans Parish. The post, said Huey, was unnecessary, while the thirteen to fifteen thousand dollars the appointee drew annually could be diverted to the building of a new hospital for tuberculars on Lake Pontchartrain. Huey promptly forgot the promise. Instead he named his brother Earl to the post. His elder brother, Julius, later privately denounced him for the move. In a story that failed to reach print, Julius argued that Huey's appointment of Earl had been a callous gesture of convenience. At the time of the appointment, said Julius, he and Earl were contributing to the support of a tubercular sister and had tried, vainly, to get Huey to chip in with weekly contributions. When Earl offered to assume Huey's share of the sister's upkeep if he got the then lucrative state job, Julius recounted, Huey readily agreed. Earl got the job and a New Orleans newspaper parodied the appointment by showing Earl's picture. The caption beneath the picture of Earl read: *New Lakefront TB Hospital.*

Huey had promised free schoolbooks to the state's children. Now he had to find the money to pay for them. Like a salesman who offers an article at an inflated price so he can bargain, Huey proposed stiff increases in the oil and gas taxes, and carbon and sulphur taxes as well. The opposition balked at the price tag, but Huey smoothly assured them he was ready to compromise. He had proposed a four-cent-a-pound tax on the manufacture of carbon black; he settled for a quarter of a cent and went along with smaller levies on other minerals.

Opposition to the schoolbook plan developed in other quarters. Louisiana had a law that said no state funds could be spent on sectarian or private schools. The state's Catholics grumbled that they would be discriminated against if only the public schools got the books. Huey, with an eye on the sizable Catholic vote, slipped around that stumbling block. By passing a bill that said specifically the books would go to the children—not the schools—Huey could announce with a showmanlike flourish that, as promised, all the children would benefit from his plan.

Oil companies, who would pay most of the free schoolbook bill, took the proposal to court, calling it unconstitutional. It was far from settled by the time the state's children prepared for the new school term in the fall of 1928. As long as the case was held up in the courts, Huey could not get the money to pay for the books. He wrote later: "The matter could not be longer delayed."

Huey called the state's Board of Liquidation to a meeting. When he walked out, the board had authorized a half-million-dollar loan to buy the books, to be repaid when the legal questions were resolved. Huey went to the state's bank at New Orleans to ask for the loan, but was told that the bank's attorneys considered such a loan illegal. Momentarily stumped, he played his ace.

Didn't the bankers know, asked Huey, that the Board of Liquidation already owed the bank $935,000? Oh, yes, replied the bankers, but the last Legislature had already ordered that paid back. Well, snorted Huey, it hadn't been paid and "it ain't going to be paid. Your attorneys ruled those loans illegal, and if it's illegal to make them, it's illegal to pay them. We'll keep the $935,000 and buy the books and have $435,000 to spare." Glumly, Huey returned to his hotel where he ordered a "thin sandwich." As he waited for it, a banker arrived to tell him the bank had reconsidered and that Huey could have his loan immediately. Said Huey as the waiter approached, "Take back the sandwich. Fry me a steak."

Now Huey had the money to pay for the books. To his surprise, however, he found someone who didn't want them. From Shreveport, an old antagonist, Mayor L. E. Thomas, airily announced that Shreveport's school children didn't need any free schoolbooks. As in the past, Thomas announced, Shreveport would take care of its own.

Huey and Thomas had locked horns on a number of occasions in the past. During Huey's Public Service Commission days, and later in his gubernatorial campaigns, each had sought to ridicule the other. Mayor Thomas had told a story about a man who passed through hell. Seeing a box, the man started to open it, only to be stopped by the devil, who cautioned, "That's Huey Long in there. We can't let him out. He'd take charge of hell if we did." Huey had retorted with the story of a "Chinaman, a Fiji Islander and Thomas" going, in turn, into a polecat's cage to see which of the three could stay locked up with the animal the longest. As Huey told the story, the Chinaman came out in ten minutes, the Fiji Islander in fifteen. But after five minutes with Thomas the polecat stalked out. Thomas tried to have Huey arrested for slander, but a faulty bill of information resulted in the dismissal of the charges. Now Thomas was getting his revenge. Huey bided his time until the time was ripe. Then he struck hard. From Shreveport, a delegation called on Huey to ask for support for a project that would be important to Shreveport's economy. The federal government, expanding its military air facilities, wanted to build an airfield for its Third Attack Wing adjacent to the city. All that was needed was an eighty-acre plot, which the state controlled. It would be a paper transaction for the state to deed the land to the city so the requirements for the airfield could be met.

No trouble at all, Huey told the delegation—provided Shreveport took its free schoolbooks. But what, asked the delegation, if Shreveport thought it was wealthy enough to supply its own books? Growled Huey: "People so well off don't need an airport." Shreveport got the message, and the schoolbooks. It also got the airport.

Not all the decisions went in Huey's favor, and few came as dramatically as the bank loan or the Shreveport schoolbooks. In many cases Huey had to compromise or promise his way through, or wait for months before the stage was properly set for his move.

Huey had hoped, for example, to kick out the incumbent, Dr. Val K. Irion, as chairman of the "coon-chasin' " Conservation Commission, against which Huey had railed during his campaigning. Irion refused to be replaced and Huey had to put that problem aside for a time.

With the Legislature in session, Huey tried his version of a court-packing plan long before Roosevelt took office. There were nine members of the powerful State Court of Appeals. Huey asked the Legislature to increase the membership to fifteen, but the proposal was rejected. Similarly, the Legislature rebuffed Long when he sought legislation that would have given him control of the governing board of the New Orleans Charity Hospital (Huey was to get it later anyway) and the Orleans Courthouse Commission. But for a first legislative session in which he lacked a majority of the membership on his side, Huey was doing remarkably well.

He never forgot a friend—or an enemy. The state highway department would soon have a thirty-million-dollar bonanza in the form of the public bonds. To supervise the expenditure of this jackpot, Huey appointed as his new highway commissioner his old Winnfield friend O. K. Allen. When a state supreme court justice who had upheld the free schoolbook law came up for re-election, Huey successfully campaigned for his re-election. The superintendent of the New Orleans Charity Hospital was the son of a Standard Oil attorney. Huey dismissed him and named a country doctor in his place. He took to keeping a little black book in which he jotted down the names of enemies, opponents, and incidents in which he had suffered real or imagined slights. Louisianians came to know the book well; they called it "Huey's sonofabitch book." When the truculent Public Service Commission asked for an extra appropriation and the Legislature passed it, Huey promptly vetoed it.

His power and prestige increased with each move he made. His New Orleans natural gas and state-wide free books were flashy testimonials to his political techniques, and the boards and commissions and state house offices that began to fill with Long people were visible reminders of his burgeoning organization. Now he had to show the country folk that he hadn't forgotten them, or the good roads and free bridges he had promised. He asked the Legislature to approve a constitutional amendment, to be sumitted to the voters, for a thirty-million-dollar bond issue to pay for the improvements. The issue, Huey told the Legislature, could be financed by a two-cent increase in the state's gasoline tax. The proposal passed the Legislature easily and awaited only the approval of the voters, who would decide the following November.

Meantime, Huey tidied up his home grounds. Having looked over the archaic nineteenth-century gubernatorial mansion, he decided it wasn't a fit home for the governor of Louisiana. He called in the Baton Rouge building inspector, who agreed. With this ammunition Huey talked the Board of Liquidation into authorizing $150,000 for the construction of a new mansion, subject to legislative approval. But Huey didn't wait for anybody's approval. As soon as the board authorized the money, he ordered the old mansion torn down. When the Legislature finally got to the appropriation, it had little choice but to approve it; the old mansion was already being torn down and a new one had been planned. While he waited for the new mansion, Huey took up quarters in the Heidelberg. His wife, Rose, returned to Shreveport with the Longs' three children.

The legislative session ended in general triumph for Huey. He had been able to obtain most of the important laws he had sought. He had been handed several defeats but, for the most part, they were minor. The major exception was his request for an occupational license tax on the oil industry, which would have been used to pay for improvements in the state's hospitals and mental wards. In November, the people would approve the thirty-million-dollar bond issue and the administration would have money available for road and bridge construction. Huey's family was in Shreveport. In Baton Rouge, for the first time since he took office, he found himself with time on his hands. Soon he had Louisiana astir again; this time, however, Huey's performance was as bungling as his handling of the Legislature had been adept.

To the south, adjoining Orleans Parish, lay the Mecca of Louisiana vice and gambling, Jefferson and St. Bernard's parishes. Traditionally, they had gone their merry way, operating under the noses of corrupt local police and indulgent newspapers. No one bothered them and they apparently bothered no one. True, a delegation from the New Orleans Association of Commerce had once called on Huey to protest that the gamblers in the neighboring parishes were hurting city business. Huey had dismissed them by noting that New Orleans was far from free of vice. Besides, the sheriff of St. Bernard's was a political ally.

But by August, Huey had changed his mind about interfering. Warning that he would "call out the militia" to put an end to the evil that was hurting the city's business, Huey declared that vice and gambling must stop. When his edict went unheeded, Huey peremptorily ordered out the National Guard.

Into the gambling halls, rifles at the ready, trooped the militia. They broke tables and chairs, ripped out roulette wheels and slot machines, searched private citizens and confiscated a reported $25,000.

The newspapers denounced Huey, and the state attorney general declared that the raid had been illegal. Snorted Huey, "No one asked him for his opinion." In New Orleans, Publisher Ewing, who, despite his opposition to the administration's schoolbook program, had continued to support Huey, now broke with the governor. Ewing's ally, John Sullivan of the New Regulars, took the hint and broke with Huey too. Huey fired off a charge to counteract the Ewing-Sullivan defections. The real reason for the break, he wrote, was that he could no longer stomach Sullivan's "business as a gambler." Moreover, Huey added, the support of Ewing and Sullivan hadn't meant much to him in New Orleans. He had done as well without them.

There were three possible motives for Huey's raids on the gambling parishes. The raids would sit well with his predominately Baptist, hill-country following; they would be a reprisal against a section that was largely anti-Long; the gamblers were laggard in contributing to the expanding Long machine. Whatever the case, Huey had, on the face of it, little to gain from the raids. He had deliberately alienated the last of his influential New Orleans support, had unnecessarily stirred up opposition in the lower parishes and had contributed to the growing belief that he was a dangerous political ne'er-do-well.

Huey seemed impervious to the consequences. The following February, he ordered the troops into the gambling parishes again, but this time the move boomeranged as Huey became involved in an embarrassing incident.

The second raids were set for February 13, 1929. Huey rode to New Orleans to be on hand when the results of the forays came in. As he whiled away the time in his Roosevelt Hotel suite, he was invited to a party at the French Quarter home of wealthy bachelor Alfred Danziger. Huey accepted.

Later testimony revealed that the party had been a red-hot affair. A party girl named Helen Clifford revealed that she had danced a seminude hula, and once had perched on the governor's lap. The governor, she testified, had "plenty" to drink. The New Orleans *Daily States* published affidavits from cabaret girls who said they had been hired to entertain Danziger's guests. The paper poured it on, calling Huey a "boon companion of indicted criminals, a chronic distorter of facts, a habitual double-crosser, a traducer of character, a beneficiary of funds contributed by gamblers, a tyrant suffering from delusions of grandeur." Worse still, Huey had spilled the beans about the impending raid while at the Danziger party that night. One of the cabaret girls had telephoned a club owner as soon as she had heard about the raid. The club owner in turn spread the word. When Huey's troopers stormed into the clubs, there was no gambling in sight.

Meanwhile, having alienated Colonel Ewing and John Sullivan, Huey now did the same with his lieutenant governor, Paul Cyr. Louisiana was shuddering at one of its most sensational murder cases—the so-called Dreher-LeBoeuf case. Dr. T. E. Dreher and Mrs. Ada LeBoeuf had been accused of killing her husband and throwing the body into a lake. It was a vicious crime, and the state asked for the death penalty. The two were convicted, sentenced to hang. Thus, Mrs. LeBoeuf would become the first white woman in the history of the state to go to the gallows. Ewing's *Daily States* and other newspapers suggested clemency, a commuted sentence. Dr. Cyr, who had been a practicing dentist in a parish neighboring the one in which the two murderers lived, also thought Huey should commute her sentence to life. "Never," declared Huey, "had a more conscienceless murder been known." He refused to commute the sentence. "How long," roared Cyr, "have I been humiliated by having to deal with this man?" Cyr's name promptly went into Huey's black book. Later, like many others before him, he felt Huey's vengeful wrath.

The net effect of Huey's maneuvering can scarcely be measured. Certainly he had succeeded in alienating friends that he could well have used. Where he had not been able to buy off or persuade legislators to support his programs, he had created a sullen discontent among them. In the House, vocal and articulate enemies like Representatives Lavinius Williams and J. Y. Sanders, Jr., the son of Huey's perennial political enemy, needed little more than the mention of Huey's name to denounce him. Whether true or not, stories of Huey's flippant contempt for individual legislators began to make the rounds. Of one legislator Huey is supposed to have said, "We bought him like a sack of potatoes." Of the Legislature in general, Huey is supposed to have sneered that he "shuffled 'em like a deck of cards."

By December, after the voters had approved the thirty-million-dollar bond issue the previous month, Huey called the Legislature into special session (always an irritant to legislators, who try to avoid lost time on their principal jobs at home) to ratify the highway program. With the sentiment of the voters clearly expressed, the Legislature could do little but stamp the highway program for approval, despite the opposition of members of the New Orleans Ring. Legislators might be sullen, the newspapers antagonistic, Huey's political friends in various stages of revolt. But there was as yet no direction or dimension to the dissatisfaction. It took Huey to provide these.

With the spectacle of Huey's military raids on the gamblers still fresh in their minds, having finished a special session of the Legislature a scant two months before, the state's lawmakers were jolted by a call for another special session. This time, Huey directed the Legislature to convene on March 18 for a six-day session.

In the regular session, ten months before, Huey had introduced his "occupational license" tax of five cents a barrel on oil but had withdrawn it in the face of obvious opposition. The money from the tax, Huey had explained, would be used to improve the state's hospitals and mental wards, the schools, the tuberculosis sanitariums and for the indigents in general. Now, in his call for a special session, Huey demanded the same five-cent tax. In addition, he included in his call a bill that would have eased the tick eradication laws, a popular measure with farmers and ranchers all over the state.

There was little doubt that the state's indigents and public institutions would have benefited from the proposal. But there was equally little doubt that at least part of Huey's motive lay in penalizing the Standard Oil Company, the "Octopus" against which Huey had never ceased to rail. That Standard itself felt it was being singled out as a target never was in question. Standard President D. R. Weller, hearing about the special session, immediately came to Baton Rouge, established headquarters in the Heidelberg and stayed for the whole session.

Huey's successes in the December special session and in the previous regular session had perhaps swelled his ego. His call for another special session, limited this time to six days, was in itself evidence that he expected little difficulty in getting what he wanted. But even before the session began, Huey was in trouble.

Rabbi Walter Piser, offering a prayer to open the session, refused to call down "the blessings of God on such a governor." A few minutes later, Huey's floor leaders failed in their attempt to have the legislative rules suspended in order to allow the occupational tax bill to go to a committee. Huey himself, striding up and down the legislative aisles, became the target of an embarrassing rebuff. Spotting him, Representative Lavinius Williams called for enforcement of the House rule that forbade "visitors" on the floor without the express invitation of the House. Told indirectly to get out of the House, Huey made it just ahead of a sergeant at arms who advanced on him to enforce the rule.

Two days later, his occupational tax no nearer introduction or discussion than it had been the first day, Huey asked the Legislature to adjourn the session, then promptly called a new one—this time for a more realistic fifteen days. The new call was the same as the first, except that this time Huey dropped the olive branch he had extended in the form of the tick eradication bill.

But now there were angry eruptions over the state. In New Orleans, Colonel Ewing's *Daily States* published the names of legislators on the state payroll, or doing business with the state. A salesman admitted that he had supplied $20,000 worth of refrigeration equipment to the state's prison farm without having bid on the sale. How had he sold the equipment, when state law specifically required bids on purchases exceeding one thousand dollars? Simple, said the salesman. The purchase had been broken up into separate parcels, all less than a thousand dollars. The owner of the firm selling the equipment, the newspapers noted, was a friend of Huey's and a campaign contributor.

But these were shadowy attacks—one aimed at the legislators instead of Huey, the other a broadside charge against his administration, not Huey personally. Suddenly, new and more explosive fuel was added to the growing fire.

THIS, GENTLEMEN, IS THE WAY YOUR GOVERNOR FIGHTS, went the headline of the signed message in the March 21st issue of the Baton Rouge *State-Times*. Then, in a restrained, carefully worded message, Editor Charles Manship charged that Huey had ordered him to "lay off of me" or he would publish the names of his opponents' relatives in state mental institutions. Editor Manship carefully noted that his own brother had been confined to one of the state's mental hospitals.

"I might say, however," added Manship, "that my brother Douglas . . . is about the same age as the Governor. He was in France in 1918, wearing the uniform of a United States soldier, while Governor Long was campaigning for office."

The Manship charge—that Huey had resorted to a gutter-low tactic in trying to intimidate the opposition—was bad enough. Now Lieutenant Governor Cyr followed with another. The governor, charged Cyr, had signed over more than a million and a half dollars of oil-bearing leases to a favored Texas oil company. In return, charged Cyr, Huey had received $214,000 and a one-eighth royalty. "From today on," cried Cyr, "I promise to keep as close an eye on the governor as one man ever kept on another." Finally, a member of the Board of Supervisors of Louisiana State University, Dr. Roy O. Young, confided to newspapers how Huey had arrogantly vowed to replace the then LSU president with his own choice. As Dr. Young described the interview, Huey had roared, "I get control of any board I want and I want and I do as I please." Meanwhile, Huey charged, Standard and the other oil companies were buying legislators with cash and cushy jobs, the newspapers with fat advertisements. "In the Capitol City," he wrote, "the apparent free use of money exceeded anything I had ever seen."

Suddenly, impeachment talk was heard in the capitol corridors. The Shreveport *Journal,* in an editorial entitled "Time to End Tyranny," called for an investigation of all the charges, with a view toward impeaching Huey. In Oklahoma, by coincidence, the Legislature was winding up successful impeachment proceedings against Governor Henry S. Johnston. Said the New Orleans *Morning Tribune,* in comparing the cases, "Johnston is the more unfortunate; of the two states, Louisiana." In the face of the mounting storm, Huey lost some of his cocksure swagger. He recalled: "My ground had begun to slip from under me. Rats began to leave the apparently sinking ship."

The night of March 25, 1929, when the Legislature reconvened in answer to Huey's new call, has come to be known as "Bloody Monday." That night, an air of electric tension hung over Baton Rouge. Long before the legislators met, people from all parts of the city hurried to the capitol to take up stations in the spectators' gallery. The legislators who stalked to their desks were serious, grim-faced.

Hardly had the session come to order when Representative Cecil Morgan of Caddo Parish (Shreveport) jumped up with a plea to speak on a point of personal privilege. On the rostrum Huey's House speaker, John Fournet, ignored the request.

Morgan leaped away from his desk, his hand waving a document. "I am speaking, and I will not yield the floor," he yelled above the rush of voices. "I have in my hand an affidavit . . . that the governor has tried to procure the assassination of a member of this House."

Fournet tried to gavel Morgan into silence. He directed the sergeant at arms to "seat the gentleman." As the sergeant advanced on Morgan a score of legislators formed a human wall around him. The sergeant stood blinking as Morgan slammed home his accusation: "This is a dastardly outrage. You shall not vote me down until I have had my say. It is charged in this affidavit that the governor of this state planned the assassination of J. Y. Sanders, Jr." Morgan elaborated. The affidavit, he charged, had been signed by Huey's former bodyguard, "Battling" Bozeman, who had described how Huey had ordered him to kill Sanders and "leave him in a ditch." Huey had added, according to the document: "I'm the Governor of this State and if you're caught I'll give you a full pardon and pay you well."

Even as Morgan spoke, Fournet lifted and dropped his gavel. A motion to adjourn the session, made by a Long legislator, had been recognized. The House would vote.

Consternation reigned in the House, punctuated by wild yelling and stamping of feet, as the representatives rushed to their desks to vote no on the proposed adjournment. Lights flashed on the voting machine—green for no, red for yes. The machine showed a blaze of red, a sprinkling of green. The speaker banked his gavel; the House was adjourned.

Stunned legislators slumped to their seats, rubbing their heads, shouting "But I voted no and my light shows yes." Several of the legislators started toward the speaker's rostrum. There were shouts of "You damned crook," and "The machine's fixed." One member slumped to his desk, tears streaming down his face, mumbling "Oh, God, do something, we must do something. . . ."

One legislator, leaping across desks and press tables, reached the rostrum, jerked the gavel from Fournet's hand, and tried to pound the meeting into silence. Another legislator fell. As he started up again, something whipped through the air, catching him on the head, laying open the skin. Legislators and spectators alike pulled off their coats, ready for an all-out battle.

Speaker Fournet slipped out a side door during the confusion. The House clerk followed. Representative Harney Bogan, who had taken the gavel from Fournet, had left the rostrum to help the injured lawmaker to his feet. The gavel lay idle until another legislator, Representative Mason Spencer, grabbed it and yelled the House into silence. The members voted a temporary speaker to take the place of the departed Fournet. The confusion subsided; cooler heads took over, asked for an adjournment until the following day. "Bloody Monday" ended the wildest free-for-all in a Louisiana legislative hall since the days of Reconstruction. The anti-Huey forces charged that he had deliberately rigged the voting machine, that the whole procedure had been planned in advance to prevent the lawmakers from taking impeachment steps against him. Huey retorted with a reasoned and restrained argument. The voting machine itself must have been at fault, he said, and he pointed out that the nephew of a political enemy had been in charge of the machine at the time the buttons were pressed. Most observers, including the New Orleans *Times-Picayune,* agreed with this version. But the next morning, when Speaker Fournet appeared again to apologize for the faulty voting machine, he was greeted with silence by the angry members. The House, including some of the members who might normally have sided with Huey but who believed he had tampered with the machine, was clearly impeachment-minded.

The state's—and some of the nation's—press reacted in predictable fashion. The New Orleans *Times-Picayune* came out strongly for impeachment in its March 27 columns, declaring that Huey was "temperamentally and otherwise unfit to hold the office. His tactics and methods reveal him to be a cruel political tyrant, willing to resort to almost any expediency to carry out his own wishes." The staid *New York Times* called "Bloody Monday" "as stormy and violent as a fight in a frontier saloon." The Memphis *Commercial Appeal,* reviewing the charges against Huey, could find little in their broadside content for Huey to worry about. Said the paper, ". . . It may be that some legislator will discover that Governor Long has been guilty . . . of having at one time played the saxophone."

The charges against Huey might just as well have included the saxophone indictment. By the time the impeachment list arrived at legislators' desks, it included every charge under which a Louisiana governor could be impeached, with one exception—"habitual drunkenness." Some of the legislators thought that should be included too.

The charges, nineteen of them, accused Huey of every conceivable defection, from bribing and attempting to bribe legislators to attempting to intimidate the press in the Manship affair. Some of them had little or no substance (for example, Huey effectively countered the charge that he habitually carried concealed weapons by pointing out that he was the state's chief peace officer), but others were seriously damaging. Huey holed up in his suite at the Heidelberg to plot his strategy. Legislators friendly to him reported that on one occasion he had been found stretched out on a bed, face down, sobbing. It was a precarious time.

The Senate that met to hear the charges could not have acted less effectively. The prosecution took up the charges in buckshot order, hopping from one to another. Helen Clifford, the party girl who had danced a seminude hula at the New Orleans party, was startled, then resentful, when questioning legislators insisted that she supply them with her telephone number. Eventually she gave it. Seymour Weiss, assistant manager of the Roosevelt Hotel at New Orleans and a staunch Huey supporter, unwittingly threw the hearing into a mild uproar when he testified about a party Huey had tossed at his hotel for executives attending a national governors' convention. The legislators wanted to know how the $6,000 advanced to Huey for entertainment had been spent. Weiss could account for all but $2,000 of the expense fund, then added that it had been spent on a "party of such a nature that I would hesitate to give details until I had the permission of certain others." Governors from around the country bombarded the Legislature with telegrams, each protesting that all parties he had attended had been proper. One legislator deplored the use of state money "to raise hell in brothels and everywhere else."

Legislators testified that Huey had bribed or tried to bribe them. One testified that Huey had offered him a pick of state jobs if he would support the occupational license tax. Moreover, said the lawmaker, Huey had assured him he needn't worry about bank loans to conduct his business in the future. "Do you feel that your conversation with the governor in his office . . . was in the nature of a bribe?" he was asked. "Yes, sir," he replied, "I do." Another legislator testified that Huey had given a colleague a one-hundred-and-fifty-dollar-a-month job (which he accepted) and expenses if he would "get right" on voting. The lawmaker "got right," his colleague testified. "Battling" Bozeman was called. He corroborated the statement made in his affidavit—that the governor had tried to persuade him to murder Representative J. Y. Sanders, Jr. A Highway Commission telephone operator testified that the governor had ordered her fired when she failed to connect him quickly enough with his highway commissioner, O. K. Allen. The governor, said the lady, had used "profane and obscene" language over the telephone "on many occasions."

There were highlights which bordered on the ridiculous. Brother Earl, campaigning hard in the capitol corridors, spotted Huey's friend, Bob Maestri, talking to an unfriendly official. "What are you talkin' to him for?" demanded Earl. Before the two could reply, Earl leaped on the man, sinking his teeth into the official's cheek. He had to be pried loose. One pro-Huey legislator sought to compare Huey with Christ. "Nineteen hundred years ago," warned the lawmaker, "there was a cross of wood erected and a Divine Creature" was nailed to it. "Sacrilege," shouted one lawmaker, as the body shouted down Huey's man. "Take my life," gasped the apologist, "but spare me my privilege," as he fainted, to be subsequently revived with cold water.

One legislator tried to halt the impeachment proceedings on the grounds that they were illegal: The governor had not included impeachment in his official call. Did the representative think for a moment, said one Long opponent, that Huey would call for his own impeachment? One of Huey's mainstays in the House, Representative Allen Ellender, seriously proposed that when Huey had accosted Editor Manship with a threat, he was not acting in "his official capacity." Perhaps, suggested Ellender (now the senior U. S. Senator from Louisiana), Editor Manship could legally prosecute for blackmail; but the charge had nothing to do with Huey as governor. A legislator snorted down the appeal. "What a weak defense that is," he chortled. At times, the spectators' gallery, so crowded that building inspectors ordered those standing to leave, shook with laughter, particularly when another witness described how Huey had taken over the bandstand in a New Orleans hot spot to lead the band and croon popular tunes. The witness testified that following Huey's appearance, the governor had come to be known in the saloon as "the Singing Fool." The newspapers gleefully picked up the tag.

Huey, meantime, was far from idle. For his defense, he had selected nine attorneys, who flanked him at the defendant's table during the hearings. One of the attorneys was John Overton, Huey's friend of old, who solemnly declared that in his fight to vindicate the governor he would be "found either standing by his side or lying by his side." Huey never let such loyalty pass unrewarded. Three years later, he practically handed Overton a seat in the United States Senate.

Huey counterattacked with a speed and vigor that unbalanced his enemies. The word went out to political friends, state job holders, those doing business with the state: Huey needed money to take his fight to the people. "Voluntary" contributions began to pour in. Huey estimated these at $7,000. But more than five times that amount would be needed, he said. His good friend, Bob Maestri of New Orleans, came to his rescue. How fast did Huey need the money? Right away, said Huey. "I will take care of that," replied Maestri.

Some of Huey's attorneys advised him to concentrate his fire in the Senate, where the charges were being heard. His friend O. K. Allen advised Huey to forget the Senate and take his case to the people. "Fight fire with fire," advised Allen. "Get up a mass meeting."

Huey got up the meeting. He put out a call for his friends to come to Baton Rouge to let the Legislature know how they stood. As before, when they came to see him inaugurated, Huey's people streamed in from the four corners of Louisiana, some still in their working clothes, others carrying babies, tugging children.

The night Huey's folks swarmed into Baton Rouge he talked for two hours. He told country jokes, quoted the Bible, railed at his enemies and the old "Octopus," Standard Oil. He charged that "immense" amounts of money were being used to insure his impeachment, that the "old gang," failing in its purpose at the polls, was now trying to take over the state by unseating him. ". . . The man who dares to undertake the destruction of these entrenched forces and the taxation of the powerful interests of this state faces an impeachment," roared Huey. As on other occasions, Huey whipped the crowd into frenzy, then belted home what had become his favorite bromide, "Invictus." "My head," quavered Huey, "is bloody, but unbowed." Thirty years later, Brother Earl was to evoke "Invictus" to fortify himself in his own political struggles.

Now Huey developed a special propaganda technique that was to serve as the model for his later political battles. Out over the state went thousands of vitriolic circulars, some in the mails, others delivered by state troopers who raced along on motorcycles, dropping the bundles like pony express saddlebags. The circulars, whipped out in a constant stream, gave Huey a bigger ready-made audience than he had hitherto commanded. They pounded home a persistent theme: The "Octopus" and its subservient press had combined to destroy him, and with him the hopes of the plain people of Louisiana.

THE SAME FIGHT AGAIN, shrieked one. THE STANDARD OIL COMPANY VS. HUEY P. LONG. Said the text, "I had rather go down to a thousand impeachments than to admit that I am the

Governor of the State that does not dare to call the Standard Oil Company to account so that we can educate our children and care for the destitute, sick and afflicted." Another described the "Standard Oil Regulars—The Paid-off Newspapers; Paid Henchmen of the Oil Trust . . . the New Orleans Ring—the Whole Gang That Is Out to Scuttle the State." Everybody, in short, who opposed Huey.

Huey followed the circulars with personal forays into the districts of unfriendly legislators. In Shreveport he laughed at the "concealed weapons" charge. The Legislature itself, said Huey, had passed a law empowering the governor to act as a police officer, but "the damned jackasses don't know yet that they passed the law."

He poked fun at the accusation that he had tried to intimidate Editor Manship by revealing his brother's confinement. "I don't have to do anything but look at Manship to wonder if his brother hasn't got more sense than he has," said Huey.

In Abbeville he told his growing audiences the real reason for the impeachment: "I fought the Standard Oil Company and put them pie-eating members of the gang out of office." In Vermilion he described the difficult time he'd had kicking out the "old gang of pie-eaters." Said Huey, "I used a crowbar to pry some of 'em out and I'm using a corkscrew now to take the rest out piece by piece. But because I made good my campaign pledge, they think to throw me out." And in Vermilion, too, he touched off titters by reducing the most serious charge—that he had tried to get J. Y. Sanders, Jr., killed—to an absurdity. Scoffed Huey: "They say I tried to get that numbskull, J. Y. Sanders, Jr., killed. Why, if J. Y. Sanders, Jr., lives twenty more years I may be President of the United States. A Sanders is what I need to assure my political future." Everywhere he went Huey slipped in sly hints that constituents should recall certain legislators ("I'd rather you'd recall him, but I want you to watch him"), that the "filthy" newspapers "would not dare face an election tomorrow."

When he wasn't bombarding the state with circulars or making personal appearances, Huey worked deftly behind the scenes. There were thirty-nine senators. Two-thirds of them would be needed to impeach him. He needed one more than a third of them to win.

Huey pulled out every stop in nailing down his quota. Some of the senators were called in quietly, told they could name their jobs if they voted against impeachment. Others were given the iron fist with the silk glove off. They were reminded about the frequent difficulty of doing business with certain banks, of relatives on the state payrolls, of past favors received.

Huey worked into the night, while the legislators slept. Once he waited for a weekend when "every member of the Senate had gone to his home." Suddenly, sleepy senators—fifteen of them—picked up telephones almost simultaneously. At that moment, they were told, Huey had a car waiting outside each of their doors; he wanted to see them in Baton Rouge immediately. They came and Huey asked them to sign a "Round Robin" statement calling for an end to the "illegal" impeachment session, a statement in which each would say that he could not "conscientiously . . . approve the impeachment proceedings and charges preferred against the Governor." In short, those who signed the "Round Robin" would not vote to impeach.

Huey got his fifteen signatures. Some of the fifteen, reported Huey, "signed without a quibble." Others he found trying to evade him in locked hotel rooms, at out-of-the-way places. Once at a Monroe, Louisiana, hotel where he delivered a speech, Huey took the elevator to his room, turned out the lights, slipped out a side door and drove all night to Baton Rouge to surprise a senator in his hotel room. The legislator signed.

In the Senate, the prosecutors quibbled over technicalities. They cut a charge here, strengthened another there. Finally they reduced the list of nineteen charges to eight. There was talk that the seemingly impossible would happen, that with the pruned list, the Senate would vote to impeach. "With one Senator absent," reported the Shreveport *Times,* "the anti-administrationists were Monday night within three Senators of a sufficient number to impeach."

Huey saved his big surprise for Sunday, May 16. Casually, methodically, his Senate leader, Philip Gilbert, filed the famous "Round Robin" petition with the clerk. Fifteen senators, said the document, believed that the remaining charges against Huey were unconstitutional and invalid. They would "not vote to convict thereon," said the "Robin." Moreover, it added, further impeachment proceedings would be "ineffectual, vain and will incur a useless cost and expense to the State of Louisiana." The fifteen moved for adjournment.

The grand attempt collapsed. Two months of sensational tugging and pushing had not lifted the impeachment balloon off the ground. Huey had broken the Legislature's back coldly, ruthlessly, expertly. The Legislature scattered and Huey ordered carpenters into the Senate Chamber to tear down the platform that had been built for the trial—the one he said reminded him of a "pre-Revolution French hanging." In high glee, his supporters crowding around him, he passed out autographs reading, *Huey P. Long, Governor of Louisiana, by grace of the people.* When the newspapers howled at the "Robineers," as the signers of the "Round Robin" came to be dubbed, Huey laughed and agreed with the papers that "theirs is the earth and the fulness thereof." When he stopped laughing, Huey's voice had a more menacing ring to it: "I used to try to get things done by saying 'please.' That didn't work and now I am a dynamiter. I dynamite 'em out of my path." [1]

[1] Forrest Davis, *Huey Long, A Candid Biography,* Dodge Publishing Company, New York, 1935.

3

The People's Choice

THE impeachment fiasco produced an immediate, but lasting result; it accelerated Huey's sustained bid for political dictatorship. But the road to dictatorship in Louisiana proved to be a tricky one. Sometimes Huey advanced a mile, then fell back two. At times he was forced into wide detours. Huey had promised to become a "dynamiter." In the end he became one. For at least another year, however, he found it expedient to say an occasional "please."

There is a popular notion that the end of the impeachment hearings marked the end of organized political resistance to Huey. This is far from accurate. Huey's position remained precarious for months, but his opponents never again succeeded in seriously threatening his political existence.

Part of Huey's uncertainty in official affairs stemmed from the disposition of the charges against him. The charges were not dropped when the Legislature adjourned. Instead, they were merely shelved. Conceivably (although it was unlikely) they could have been revived at a later session. In any event, Huey was uneasy about their presence until much later, when he finally had them swept away for good.

Huey's position, immediately following the impeachment attempt, was further weakened by the composition—and the temper—of the Legislature. He had succeeded in saving his skin, but not, as he intimated, "by the grace of the people." It had been, instead, by a blatant display of patronage. He had, in short, bought his way out of trouble. The "Famous Fifteen" could save Huey's neck again, if need be. But they couldn't hope to implement his expansion programs. And without these expansion schemes—roads, bridges, buildings, charity, all the tangible evidence of the welfare director—Huey's political stock could drop swiftly. No one knew this better than the legislators who had tried to remove him but who had succeeded only in embarrassing themselves in the attempt. They were, for a while at least, largely dedicated to the proposition that anything that made Huey look bad was good.

Some Louisianians were disposed to believe the worst of Huey anyway. In his ramblings around the state during his impeachment defense, Huey had pressed his case before a good many people. He had succeeded in convincing many of them—chiefly his staunch country supporters—that he was being railroaded by a power-mad Standard-Press-Ring combine. But he failed to convince everybody. Some of the charges against him, some believed, might well have been substantiated in an impeachment trial. Henceforth, for a certain segment of the population —white-collar workers, professionals, small businessmen—Huey was stamped as a demagogue who regularly and completely perverted the truth.

The first evidence of this continued antipathy toward Huey came, as might be expected, from New Orleans. There former Governor John Parker announced the formation of the Constitutional League, a group of citizens banded together to restore "constitutional government in the State." The league was aiming straight at Huey when, in its opening announcement, it declared that its chief purpose was "to prevent Governor Huey P. Long from treating the organic law of the State as a scrap of paper." In addition, the league said, it would "stand by members of the Legislature threatened with a recall by the Governor." The league struck tellingly by publishing a list of Longs on the state payroll—twenty-three in all. It showed that Brother Earl had taken up his duties in the inheritance tax collector's office; that a sister had been placed on the faculty of a state school; that two brothers-in-law had good jobs in the Bureau of Criminal Identification and in the state charity hospital at Shreveport. In addition, a cousin had been appointed president of a state college at a salary of $7,200 yearly, second only to the $7,500 Huey drew as governor. The New Orleans *Times-Picayune* heartily endorsed the league. "This newspaper long ago avowed its belief that Governor Long by his own acts had revealed his unfitness for the office he holds."

Huey, ever the swaggering peacock, gave the citizens' group the back of his hand. He called it the "Constipational League," proclaimed that "the backbone of the organization, as usual, was the Standard Oil Company and the old New Orleans regular organization." He laughed, too, at the published list of Longs drawing state salaries. Considering the number of cousins he had all over Louisiana, he explained, the percentage of relatives working for the state was pretty low. As usual, however, Huey didn't stop at ridicule. General Campbell Hodges had been named the president of Louisiana State University, but hadn't formally taken the office. General Hodges' brother, said Huey, had been "prominent in the formation of the Constitutional League." Huey sent word to the general: Don't bother to come to LSU. Instead, Huey announced, LSU's new president would be a "person of the highest collegiate standing." There was immediate indignation; howls of protest came from the league. But before the matter reached a boiling point, President Herbert Hoover appointed General Hodges to a federal post. It was an appointment the President had been considering for some time. Fortunately for Huey, it came in time to steal the league's thunder, and Huey had his way. Then he turned to more pressing matters.

The "Famous Fifteen" had acted with dispatch and determination in snatching Huey from the "pre-Revolution French" gallows. Huey acted in the same manner in doling out the rewards.

To find out who should get what, Huey took some of the "Robineers" on a weekend sailing trip to Grand Isle, a fishing and hunting retreat near New Orleans. The island was to reappear in Louisiana politics under more ominous conditions, but now it became the site of a victory celebration as Huey divided the spoils among his allies.

One of the signers became the Highway Commission's chief enforcement officer, another the chairman of the fish and oyster division of the Conservation Commission. One became a judge; two others were retained as Highway Commission attorneys. Huey remembered his friends in the House—Speaker Fournet was retained as a Highway Commission attorney (later, he became a judge) and another friendly representative became the warden at the state penitentiary. It seemed for a time, however, that Huey's largesse had outdone itself. In February of 1930, shortly after the rewards were handed out, the state Supreme Court ruled that elected officials could not legally hold state jobs. The ruling threw sixteen legislators off the state payroll. One by one, however, Huey later installed them in other, less obvious, positions of affluence and opportunity.

Just as Huey remembered his friends, he unfailingly pursued his enemies. Out into the hinterlands went Huey's agents, armed with circulars and petition forms, to persuade constituents to recall legislators who had been troublesome during the impeachment proceedings. There were two reasons for the reprisals. Huey wanted to make it plain that opposition didn't pay. Moreover, who could tell when the troublemakers would resurrect the charges against him? Better a pound of prevention than a ton of cure. But the agitation for recall fell flat in most cases. Huey succeeded in having one lawmaker removed on a technicality, but in every other instance the harassed legislator was able to rally his home folks around him to abort the attacks. Finally, two representatives from Avoyelles Parish stopped the recall movement cold by persuading a judge that legislators were not subject to recall. The ruling gave other besieged lawmakers a powerful precedent. Moreover, Huey's tactics, always blatant, were becoming scandalous. The editor of the Tangipahoa *Parish News* revealed that the State Highway Commission had employed him as a "plain clothes detective." The real reason for his employment, the editor revealed, was to support the recall movement in that parish. Having drawn his state pay check for $187.50, the editor cashed it, then promptly sent the cash back to the state's general fund. Huey's recall efforts collapsed.

The dynamiting efforts had, it now became apparent to Huey, either fizzled or flopped. The time had come to speak softly and use the big stick only in extreme situations. But a man has to be close to his target when he speaks softly. Huey, accordingly, loaded his lawbooks, some furniture and his personal belongings into a truck, then drove to New Orleans and set up a temporary executive headquarters there. Soothingly, he began to court the Ring.

The New Orleans Dock Board, a state agency, was forty million dollars in debt. Perhaps, hinted Huey, the board could use a little help. It was, after all, a state responsibility. There was a mayoralty election coming up in the city. The candidates would be T. Semmes Walmsley, the Ring choice, and his anti-Ring opponent, Francis Williams. A close contest was forecast. Ordinarily, Huey would have leaped at such an opportunity—a chance to whip the Ring on its home grounds. Would he take part in the campaign? Certainly not, said Huey. Purely a local contest. Walmsley defeated Williams by fewer than ten thousand votes. Huey probably could have swung the majority to Williams had he interfered. This, however, was the time to mend old fences, not build new ones. A delegation of the state's businessmen called on Huey to discuss the ill-fated occupational license tax (in the impeachment fireworks, the bill had been shunted aside). Louisiana, said the businessmen, was trying to attract, not discourage, industry. An occupational tax would drive it away. Would Huey promise not to press for it in the next session? Reluctantly, in his efforts to cement peace, Huey agreed.

Meantime, a new image of the would-be dictator began to emerge—the delightful country bumpkin whose unpolished mannerisms concealed an engaging charm. Huey launched a lighthearted campaign to get people to eat "potlikker" and corn pone. Not only did he recommend the combination, Huey gave out advice on how to eat it. It had been perfectly all right to crumble the corn pone into the potlikker at one time, explained Huey. But "with the progress of education, the coming of 'style,' and the change of the times . . . refinement necessitated that corn pone be dunked in the potlikker." Huey's advice met with national pro's and con's. He invited other governors to express their views on how the "delectable concoction" should be eaten. President Roosevelt (then a mere governor) sent a telegram to the Atlanta *Constitution*. The future President's verdict: Crumble, don't dunk. Said Huey, "I compromised—I compromised with all foes on the basis that it would be a commendable pursuit to eat potlikker with corn pone, whether it be done by crumbling or by dunking." It would prove to be only the first of his compromises with the man he later expected to succeed.

It was March, 1930—Mardi Gras in New Orleans. The German cruiser *Emden* steamed into port on a courtesy call. The man-of-war's captain, Lothar von Arnauld de la Perière (for a German, it wasn't a bad name to have at Carnival time), accompanied by Consul Rolf L. Jaeger, marched briskly into the Roosevelt Hotel to present their compliments to His Excellency. Huey greeted the pair in green pajamas and a colorful robe—a horrendous breach of protocol. The Germans departed, miffed. Only a properly executed courtesy visit by Huey would mend the situation. But protocol, so delicate a requirement after the pajama *faux pas,* required the full-dress treatment—striped trousers, spats, cutaway, silk hat. Huey put out a call for help. Seymour Weiss of the Roosevelt, the tactful party giver, scoured the hotel. Bell boys raced along corridors. The costume became a crisis of state.

Finally Huey had his rig, except for the silk hat. Strangely, a silk hat was unavailable. The word went out again. Alfred Danziger, in whose Vieux Carré apartment Huey had relaxed to a Hula dance, promised to deliver the hat on time. It would be the one he had worn when he and a group of lawyers from the American Bar Association called at Buckingham Palace the year before. The time for Huey's departure arrived, and so did Danziger. He had no hat—only an apology. The hat could not be found.

Huey decided to brazen it out. Clutching a gray fedora, he strode up the ship's ladder while the cruiser boomed a 21-gun salute. The hat went unnoticed and the visit took place without incident. The city relaxed as the *Times-Picayune* breathed: REX WILL REIGN TODAY IN PEACE.

It was about this time, too, that Huey took on the name that would indelibly identify him in United States political history—the Kingfish. There are several versions of how he took the tag. Huey's own explanation had him attending a Highway Commission meeting at which some of the commission's bonds were to be sold. A prospective buyer, objecting to Huey's interruptions, pointed out that the commission, not the governor, was in charge of the bidding. Huey waved aside the objection: "I am participating here anyway, gentlemen. For the present you can just call me the Kingfish." The other version had Huey borrowing the name from the chief character of one of the popular radio programs of the day, Amos and Andy. Whatever its origin the name stuck, as first Louisiana, then the nation, came to recognize it immediately. Huey himself encouraged the title. Inevitably, a call from him would begin, "This is the Kingfish." And in a judicial hearing, when the opposing attorney implied once that Huey was Louisiana's political boss, Huey snapped, "Kingfish of the Lodge."

The time for Huey's return to Baton Rouge neared. His peace mission to New Orleans, although not a total failure, had been far from a success. Green pajamas and the nickname had given the state (and the country) a few laughs, but they had produced no tangible political benefits. The Ring was still on one side, Huey on the other; the impeachment charges still hung heavy on an uneasy neck.

But Huey could not be contained indefinitely. He had lost ground in the Legislature. Now he tried to recoup some of it in another quarter. Months before, he had appointed his New Orleans friend Bob Maestri as chairman of the powerful Conservation Commission. The incumbent, Dr. Irion, had refused to give up the post. Although Huey recognized Maestri as his commission chairman, Irion continued to occupy the office. When Huey applied pressure to oust him, Irion resorted to the courts. His petition reached the state Supreme Court, which refused to allow it to go to the U. S. Supreme Court, as Irion had hoped. He found himself suspended, without benefit of legal ruling.

Huey now became the law. Ordering the Louisiana National Guard mobilized, Huey declared that Irion would be evicted at bayonet point if need be. The state Supreme Court's decision had reached Huey first. Irion had received no official word of it. When Huey's agent appeared to order his eviction, Irion asked for time to get confirmation of the ruling. One telephone call did the trick. Irion resigned immediately. A short time later a Long legislator appeared in the office. Gathering the employees about him, the man identified himself as an agent of the new commissioner. The news he brought was short but far from sweet: "You're all fired—now."

Back to Baton Rouge rode Huey, to prepare for the regular session of the Legislature. There would be work for him there. Across the state, Allen's Highway Commission set up a mighty cloud of dust as graders smoothed out roadways, trucks poured asphalt or concrete. But there was an uneven rhythm to the road building. Rarely was a major highway improved, or a minor one completed. Instead, road crews laid down erratic stretches of road—five miles here, then stop; another stretch twenty miles away. The system had two immediate advantages. There was visible evidence of road construction in more sections of the state than there would have been if a single road had been built, and voters—especiallly country folk who rarely saw good roads—would get a taste, but just a taste, of what a stretch of good highway felt like. They would be inclined to want more and pay for more, and Huey would give it to them.

As the spring session of the 1930 Legislature neared, Huey grew more restless. The number of bodyguards around him multiplied and he seldom appeared without them. The technique of mass appeal via circulars which Huey had developed during his impeachment fight had proved adequate then. With decisive political battles plainly in sight, with every major newspaper in the state working against him, Huey decided to perfect the technique by publishing his own newspaper. On March 27, 1930, the first issue of the *Louisiana Progress* appeared. It was a journal that would, from that moment, be Huey's official, highly vocal and thoroughly inflammatory editorial mouthpiece.

To get the *Progress* rolling, Huey hired New Orleans newspapermen and a well-known Louisiana cartoonist (whose salary he more than doubled), then set up the paper's plant just across the state line in Mississippi (to make libel proceedings more difficult). The paper served a double purpose. It would saturate the public with glorified accounts of Huey's progress in public works construction; it would also magnify his opponents' shortcomings, ridicule their achievements and, where possible, drench them with a continuing stream of adverse personal publicity. Huey was pictured as the benign and kindly messiah of Louisiana's downtrodden, his enemies as power-mad, perverted political leeches.

From the standpoint of circulation and financial stability, the paper was an immediate success. It could hardly have been otherwise. Virtually every state employee suddenly became a "voluntary" subscriber; firms doing business with the state found it expedient—and profitable—to advertise in its pages. Getting the paper to its readers never amounted to much of a problem although the *Progress* never had much of a circulation department. State troopers had delivered the anti-impeachment circulars. Now squads of them, assisted by the ubiquitous highway crews, gave the paper the most unique circulation organization in history. It was freewheeling journalism with a captive and singularly loyal readership. The frequency of its appearance was almost a barometer of Huey's political fortunes. The *Progress* began as a weekly. For a time it appeared irregularly. By the time Huey was master of Louisiana, the *Progress* had slowed to a monthly.

The Kingfish had a heady program ready for the Legislature when it convened in May of 1930. The thirty million dollars in highway money had been a teaser, a drop in the bucket. Huey wanted another sixty-eight million dollars to complete his highway system. He had already ordered his new executive mansion. Now, he wanted five million dollars to build a new state capitol building. He threw a hook in the direction of New Orleans—enough money to reduce the forty-million-dollar indebtedness of the Dock Board, thus improving the Port's rating. The gesture wasn't entirely magnanimous; the revitalized Port would create a slew of state jobs. Moreover, Huey confessed, he didn't want to be held responsible, later, for the bond indebtedness of other governors. His enemies, he explained, might attribute the debt to "the orgy of extravagance of Huey P. Long." In all, the price tag on the package Huey presented to the Legislature came to one hundred million dollars.

But the huge highway money outlay would have to come from bonds. These would have to be approved by constitutional amendment, which would require a two-thirds vote. When the House, in an attempt to remove Huey's speaker, John Fournet, tried to reorganize itself, forty-three of the original sixty-one impeachment-minded representatives voted for the change. Huey had succeeded in winning over seventeen of the hostile band (one had been replaced) but the total number of votes he commanded, although enough to sustain Fournet, fell short of the required two-thirds. Huey's program stalled before it started. For the moment, his entire welfare system threatened to collapse around him.

He reacted predictably—at times adroitly, then clumsily. Tick eradication was anathema to farmers and ranchers, who found it annoying and unprofitable to have to round up herds for dipping, or build fences to keep them enclosed. But the Legislature wanted a tick eradication program. Huey offered no resistance. When the bill passed, he vetoed the appropriation to enforce it. He had wooed the Legislature, but had played politically safe with agriculture.

The Ring, Huey knew, had used its bloc vote in the House to stifle his new program. His peace mission to New Orleans had accomplished nothing. Now Huey used the bludgeon again and New Orleans was thrown into near panic. The state bank examiner, Huey told the people, had just finished looking over the records of some New Orleans banks and had discovered that millions of dollars the banks had lent the city appeared to be "illegal and unjustified." Through his banking department, Huey ordered the banks to hold up further loans and call in others where they could.

New Orleans operated on money borrowed from the banks for the first six months of the year. Tax collections were made in June and July. Now, in addition to the banking edict, Huey ordered the city's assessment rolls delayed in Baton Rouge. Without the revised assessment lists, the city's collections would be impeded. Pressed long enough and hard enough, the city's fiscal foundations could crumble.

New Orleans refused to submit to the tyrant. Wealthy private citizens underwrote loans, which the city made from out-of-state banks. Business went on as usual. Huey had swung the big stick and missed. Reluctantly, he lifted the blockade. The sullen Legislature adjourned, leaving Huey without a single new revenue-raising device, his program a worthless stack of paper at the bottom of the legislative hopper.

Now he played his trump. The people, said the Kingfish, should decide whether they wanted all the improvements he had outlined. Huey would give them the chance by running for the United States Senate in the following September primary elections. He put his political reputation on the line. He would interpret a victory as a popular endorsement of his proposals. If he lost, Huey said, he would know the people had no confidence in him. If that happened, he promised, he would resign as governor. Said Huey after making the announcement, "For once the public press was united—all against me." Huey attached a rider to his candidacy. If he won, he declared, he would not go to Washington immediately, but would finish his two years as governor to "complete the work" he had begun. His staying, moreover, would prevent his archenemy, Lieutenant Governor Cyr, from stepping up to governor. There were hurried protests about the possibility of leaving one of the state's Senate seats vacant for so long. Huey brushed the objections aside by saying that wouldn't be anything new. The seat was vacant now and had been since Joseph Ransdell, the incumbent, had taken it.

Huey hit the campaign trail with more impact and organization than either Louisiana or the country had ever seen. His *Louisiana Progress* rolled out its biggest type and blackest ink. Senator Ransdell, a goateed, seventy-year-old campaigner who was rounding out his thirty-second year in Congress, was pictured as a cadaverous bungler asleep at the switch, as a charter member of the "old gang" of sapsuckers who milked the state and gave nothing in return, as a groveling tool of the bloated Ring. Huey poked fun at his opponent's goatee; henceforth, Ransdell became known as "Feather Duster" and "Old Trashy Mouth."

The Kingfish introduced a new campaign technique. He invested in a fleet of sound trucks, which roared across the state blaring their pro-Huey spiels. The sound truck became, in Huey's words, "the first portable appliance . . . ever used in a political campaign." Splashed with huge lettering, plastered with posters, the trucks gave Huey the loudest and most mobile campaign device in existence.

Huey waited until almost August to whip his campaign into gear. Ransdell had preceded him, moving from one town to another, conducting his campaign in the courtly, restrained manner of traditional southern politics. Huey let him have his say, then roared in behind him like an express train after a tricycle. His campaign was superbly financed, too. Huey had seen to that. In August, the word went out to the thousands of

Highway Commission employees. The loyal ones should make "voluntary" contributions to the Kingfish's campaign—10 per cent of one month's salary. Brother Earl supported the levies by declaring in New Orleans that the contributions were "a legitimate and honorable way of raising funds from people who owe their jobs to the administration and who would have nothing otherwise." The commission, it turned out, was filled with "volunteers"; Huey's war chest swelled.

The campaign innovations and refinements seemed inexhaustible. Huey made wide use of a technique used only intermittently in the past, the practice of using "dummy candidates" in the race. Under this system, the Kingfish would let two or three of his supporters file for a minor elective office in each parish. Each of the candidates would then, under law, have the right to name a prescribed number of election commissioners. The list of commissioners would then be lumped together and the legal number drawn from a hat. In this way, Huey could be assured of having at least one pro-Long election commissioner at each polling place, an important safeguard in a state where ballot box stuffing and deadhead voting sometimes flourished. The dummy candidates, having performed their duties, inevitably withdrew.

Crews of highway "surveyors" suddenly began to appear in virtually every section of the state to stake out highway lanes. Having laid down a route, the highway crews tacked down gaily colored flags, dropped a few hints about a highway soon to be built, then rode off, leaving the flags as bright reminders that a "right" vote meant tangible, speedy progress. So many employees became "highway surveyors" that the Baton Rouge *State-Times* was moved to cry, "Jobs! Jobs! The Simpson-Payne regime was nothing compared to the present wholesale handout of jobs by Huey Long."

The campaign rolled along with only minor obstacles. Early in September, when a Kingfish rally in New Orleans threatened to clog traffic, city police resented the "outside" interference of the state police directing traffic. They raced in to protect their prerogative. Soon the air was thick with fists, clubs, boots and blackjacks, as blue-shirted city police and gray-clad state troopers slugged it out. A state police sergeant landed in jail. Huey seized on the incident to spotlight the low character of the Ring and its paid henchmen. He vowed to march on the city jail to save the trooper.

There is an old political campaign maxim to which most politicians adhere: When things are going too well, find out what the trouble is. For Huey, the campaign went exceedingly well, but he didn't have to look for the hitch. The trouble found him.

One of the most enigmatic figures in the official family that surrounded the Kingfish was comely, but cool, Alice Lee Grosjean, an intensely ambitious office girl who hitched her wagon to Huey's political meteor. Miss Grosjean had been Huey's secretary at Shreveport. When he became governor, she moved into the executive offices. As Huey's political stock shot up, Alice Lee's fortunes rose too. She became, in succession, a supervisor of accounts, collector of revenue and secretary of state. Once, with other officials out of the state, she served as acting governor for a day. She was the image of executive efficiency and political savvy.

Alice Lee's uncle was named Sam Irby. She introduced him to the Kingfish, who promptly put him on the state payroll as an assistant maintenance engineer in, as usual, the Highway Commission. In this job, Sam saw the machine in action, from the inside out. He was friendly with his niece; for a time she lived in the same house with Irby and his wife.

Miss Grosjean had been married before, to a man named James Terrell. After three years, the two divorced. Terrell went his way, while Alice Jean stayed with politics.

At some point in 1930, Uncle Sam Irby and his niece fell out. He claimed later that he asked her to leave his home. But her leaving apparently failed to sooth Sam Irby's feelings. He began to drop embarrassing innuendoes about the Highway Commission and the Long administration. When the state's attorney general launched an investigation into the commission's affairs, Irby volunteered to tell what he knew. Subsequently he and Alice Lee's former husband, Terrell, were seen together frequently.

Suddenly Irby announced to newsmen that he and Terrell would fly to Shreveport to file suit against the Kingfish. Irby said he would charge Huey with "slander." Terrell chimed in with a vague promise to file his own suit—against "the person responsible for breaking up my home." The announcements could not have come at a worse time for Huey. It was September 3, six days before the election.

Irby and Terrell arrived in Shreveport that night, checked into a hotel and retired. Shortly after midnight, they were awakened by knocks. When the callers identified themselves as State Bureau of Identification agents, the two refused to admit them. Instead, they called local police. The city police, confronted by the state troopers, knew what to do. They paid their respects—then left. The agents took Irby and Terrell into custody for "questioning."

The next day Irby and Terrell were gone, missing. Lousiana seemed to have swallowed them up. A Shreveport attorney who announced that he was representing the two demanded to know their whereabouts. The newspapers broke out in big type and feverish editorials, while Louisiana's citizens indulged in an orgy of speculation. The rumors covered every conceivable contingency—murder, kidnaping, bribery, intimidation. The fact that one of the state agents had been a cousin of the Kingfish, Wade Long, added just the mysterious spice the affair demanded.

At first Huey maintained an external calm. But, as the clamor increased, he issued vague or conflicting statements. He took to radio to explain the disappearance; the two, he said, were safely locked up in the Jefferson Parish jail, booked there for investigation by the parish district attorney. To prove it, Huey read off telegrams from the men saying they were "where they wanted to be." Reporters went to the jail to investigate. The two could not be found.

The case began to take on an ugly hue. If it was a campaign prank, it had been stretched too thin. Two men were missing, perhaps murdered. The people looked to Huey for an explanation.

He responded, on radio again, by reading off more telegrams; one allegedly from Terrell to his mother in Arkansas. With this, the Kingfish stumbled badly. Investigating newsmen found that Terrell's mother had remarried. Her name was now Hasselroth. The telegram Huey read had been addressed to a "Mrs. Norman," a clumsy error her son could not have committed.

Huey ducked behind evasions: "Now, with all I have to do

running the state as governor, and my campaign, and building roads and taking care of these lawsuits, I had to get out and hustle this afternoon and find out where in the hell these two men were to keep from being called a kidnaper." It wasn't good enough. The public demanded Irby and Terrell. Kidnaping charges were filed against Huey and the agents who conducted the raid. The Kingfish was hailed into federal court in New Orleans to explain the disappearance. He offered little to clear up the mystery. The hearing stumbled, then recessed.

Three days before the September 9th election, Huey reduced the episode to absurdity. In a radio talk from his Roosevelt Hotel room, he dramatically produced "Sam Irby," who haltingly told his radio audience that all this talk of kidnaping was foolishness, that he was a Huey Long friend and admirer, that the whole commotion was a synthetic brew. Two reporters were allowed to see Irby. They caught a glimpse of him being hustled down a service elevator between guards.

Irby's "appearance" completely changed the complexion of the case. A day earlier it had smacked of official intrigue, foul play, vicious criminality. The essence or accuracy of the facts was no longer disputed; the tone had simply been altered. The ominous overtones dissipated themselves. The disappearance-appearance-disappearance became a kind of high-level Keystone Kops routine. Louisiana, which had sucked in its breath, now exhaled heavily and laughed. It was, as usual, high jinks and low comedy, politics with a Kingfish flavor. Besides, what were a couple of would-be troublemakers compared with all those good roads, schools, bridges and public buildings? The people forgot Irby and Terrell and went to the polls.

Huey steamrollered Ransdell in every section of the state. Fifty-three of the sixty-four parishes gave him top-heavy majorities. In New Orleans, the heart of his bitterest opposition, he trailed by only forty-six hundred votes. State-wide, his machine swept two pro-Long congressmen into office. Huey's margin over Ransdell was more than 38,000 votes.

Peace doves, an almost extinct species, appeared over Louisiana. The day after the election, the Constitutional League issued a terse announcement: It had disbanded. New Orleans Mayor Walmsley, the Ring's standard-bearer, appeared in Huey's Roosevelt Hotel rooms with a delegation of civic leaders to congratulate the Kingfish. The group came bearing olive branches. A short time later, the Ring's elite turned out for a New Orleans banquet for Huey. Walmsley struck the keynote: "After the election, a friend of the Governor, and a friend of mine, called upon me and said we should rise to the occasion and forget our petty differences for the good of the state and the city. I said I was willing." Overwhelmed by the spirit of the occasion, the mayor added: "Even in the hour of our defeat, we feel that he has stretched to us the hand of friendship for the good of the state."

To these and other tributes Huey replied with a mocking good humor. He told of the husband who had died, and of the widow who wept while the preacher delivered a stirring eulogy. Each time the widow wept, the mother-in-law, "who probably knew his faults and virtues better than the community at large," walked to the side of the casket, then sat down without a word. Finally she said, "I just want to stand here . . . to be sure that the man you are talking about was my son-in-law." Added Huey pointedly: "I am still hoping it's me here tonight with all these former opponents as well as my friends."

Sam Irby and James Terrell reappeared. They told stories of kidnaping, of being spirited to Grand Isle and tied to a tree, of torture at the hands of certain henchmen. Irby later wrote a lurid account of the episode in the pamphlet entitled "Kidnaped by the Kingfish." But now no one listened. The Kingfish was speaking.

4

Completing the Work

TWO days after Huey's triumph, placards suddenly appeared in every section of the state. Dotting houses, barns, trees and telephone poles, they proclaimed an intriguing message: LONG FOR PRESIDENT. At the approaches to New Orleans, whose days as the principal anti-Long bastion were numbered, a great canvas flapped in the September breeze: HUEY P. LONG, PRESIDENT OF THE UNITED STATES IN 1936. In the city itself, Huey's personal conservation commissioner, Bob Maestri, pinpointed the prospect in even more optimistic tones: "Governor Long is an outstanding leader in the South. It is certain that the Democrats will walk to victory with Huey P. Long. He is your next President."

The display was too pat; there was too much of the flavor of rigged spontaneity about it. The placards had been on hand too quickly, in too many sections of the state, to deny the organization that produced them. Indeed, no one took pains to explain them. They were there and they said all that needed saying. People were beginning to know Huey too well to laugh them off automatically, as laugh they might have a couple of years back.

Huey encouraged the possibility. To newsmen he coyly hinted that he might "consider" the job "if the opportunity presented itself." His country followers had heard more definite promises from the stump on many occasions before. Huey had told them in the hill country and along the marshes that there was no doubt that he was headed for the White House. His subsequent statements, taken from his later writings, leave no doubt that at one time or another, he actually did believe he would live in the White House.

Former President Coolidge and his wife stopped in New Orleans on their way west. Huey rode with them in an open car, chatting amiably, pointing out the sights.

"What part of Louisiana are you from, Governor?" asked Silent Cal.

"I'm a hillbilly like yourself," retorted the Kingfish. His features lit with a thought. "Are the Hoovers good housekeepers?"

"I guess they are," said Cal, cautiously.

Huey frowned. "Well, when I was elected I found the Governor's Mansion in such rotten shape I had to tear it down and rebuild. It started a hell of a row. When I'm elected President I don't want to have to rebuild the White House." The Coolidges said nothing, but the Kingfish turned to a photographer who had just snapped a picture. "You've just taken a picture of an ex-President of the United States and a future one." The Oracle sat back, vastly pleased with himself. For the moment, he was content with two titles. Autograph seekers and recipients of his official correspondence noticed that the signature sported still another embellishment. Now it read: *Huey P. Long, Governor of Louisiana and United States Senator-elect.*

Huey had outlined a program to the last Legislature, but the lawmakers had rebuffed him. The Kingfish, in turn, had turned to the people, staking his political future in an election. The people had sustained Huey, who took the endorsement as a popular mandate for his program. Now, with a call for a special session, Huey summoned the legislators back for an accounting. It was the beginning of a pattern they were destined to learn by rote. Later, as an unchallenged dictator, he would call them to whip through any legislation his whim demanded. He was to do it seven times in a single year, each time to tighten his hold on his subjects.

Within a week of the election, the Legislature was passing Huey's bills: a constitutional amendment, to be voted on by the people in November, for $75,000,000 in new highway bonds; $5,000,000 for a new skyscraper state capitol building; money to bolster the Port of New Orleans' sagging credit; $7,000,000 (out of the 75) for a free bridge across the Mississippi at New Orleans; annual appropriations for the repair of New Orleans' streets.

The new alliance—the Kingfish and the New Orleans Ring—

worked smoothly, decisively. A scant few months before, the Ring's bloc had voted as a unit to stymie the Kingfish. Now the Legislature had a sense of mission, accomplishment, camaraderie.

The bonds would be financed by a one-cent increase in the tax on gasoline. In a burst of good will, Huey allowed the Legislature to set aside a generous chunk—45 per cent—of the new gasoline tax collections to be applied to the Port's debt. The Ring, surveying the initial results of the entente, exuded comfort and confidence. It had entered into high-level collective bargaining with a tough negotiator; it had come out with a package that should keep the municipal rank and file happy for a good while to come.

But Huey exacted his tribute on a lavish scale, too. His program had been accepted, if not welcomed, to the last detail. The road bond issue would provide a magnificent stream of public improvements, an impressive set of monuments, all testifying to Huey's concern for public welfare. His new capitol might not last the thousand years Hitler had predicted for his Reich, but it would be around for at least a hundred, like its predecessor. Moreover, all that treasure—the road bond money, the capitol fund—would serve to add new and impressive numbers to the already burgeoning political machinery being fashioned by the Kingfish.

Huey lost nothing by being generous with New Orleans and its Ring. State help meant state control, the degree of the latter depending on the amount of the former. The city was to learn that later, the hard way, after Huey had reduced it to the status of a colony. For now, however, the alliance was expedient.

Huey had two other principal demands, one born of fear, the other of revenge. He demanded, as the price of co-operation, the removal of the impeachment charges that had hung over him like a shadow for eighteen months. And he had an old score to settle. That traitor, John Sullivan, who had returned to the Old Regular ranks after his split with Huey, must be disciplined. The Kingfish's demands received instant attention. The impeachment charges were abolished once and for all; Sullivan, who by this time had fallen to ward leader, was stripped of Ring machine office. Another potential troublemaker faded into obscurity.

To be sure, there were minor irritations as the Huey-Ring combine eased through its agenda. For one thing, Brother Earl opposed the construction of a new capitol as a waste of money. When the special session convened, he went to Huey's office to demand that the Kingfish give it up. The state, argued Earl, didn't need a new "silo." Huey was adamant; the "silo" would go up. He bade Earl to mind his own business.

The day for the vote on the new capitol arrived and Huey was present in the House to see the "silo" approved. He knew exactly how the voting would go. But suddenly everything went wrong; legislators who had promised to vote for the new capitol pushed the wrong buttons. Only Huey's House speaker, Fournet, saved the day by refusing to call a vote, while Huey rushed among the desks to find out what the trouble was. He found out in a hurry that it all boiled down to Brother Earl. He wrote: ". . . My enemies, using my brother . . . had told the legislators that I wished the proposition voted down; that I would make a public display at the eleventh hour in order to appear sincere; but that friends of mine, wishing to serve my wishes, should vote to defeat it, and that my brother was simply serving my real desire." A few hurried conferences between Huey and legislators, and another vote was taken. The capitol vote passed easily.

Not everyone in the House forgot the bitter impeachment fight. Judge Gilbert Dupré of Opelousas, a venerable pillar of integrity, a gentleman of the old, florid school of political debate, would not go along with the Kingfish's program. On September 6, 1930, he outlined his stand in a memorable dissent. Said Dupré, "A man's conscience should govern him, provided it is not corrupted. . . . The election just held was for a senatorship. No amount of cant can resolve otherwise. . . . He [Huey] won the senatorship. Now I am requested to recant, to surrender, apologize and eat up what I have spoken, what I have written. Others may do this. I will not. . . . On the contrary, I adhere to all I have written and spoken. . . . The Legislature may ratify what they propose, the people confirm it, but I am not going to be included in the bargain. I am going to vote NO, even if I am the only member of the house to do this." [1]

[1] Baton Rouge *State Times,* September 17, 1930.

Judge Dupré's rhetoric was a voice in the wilderness. Huey's friends laughed and told the story of how an enraged Dupré had demanded that the governor fix a leaky capitol roof. Huey had asked him, the story went, if he would support a new capitol building, to which Judge Dupré had rasped, "Hell, no." Huey then had Dupré's chair moved under the leak, came to him and whispered, "Die then, damn it, in the faith."

The special session, with Huey's program intact, was over. Now he took time to tidy up some fringe matters. In October, James Bailey, the secretary of state, died, leaving almost three years of his tenure to be finished. Even before the public heard of his death, Huey had clamped a lid on the office and demonstrated once again that loyalty paid off. Into the spot went Huey's twenty-four-year-old Girl Friday, Alice Lee Grosjean.

The new mansion was finished and Huey moved in. During his dark days, he had often boasted that anybody could see the governor at any time. Now Huey made the arrangement a bit more businesslike. He established rigid "office hours"—1 P.M. to 2:30 P.M., Mondays, Tuesdays and Wednesdays. And no interviews except for those who had advance appointments.

He had his subordinates drop hints in the right places—Huey would like to be honored by the state's foremost academic institution, his legal alma mater, Tulane. Tulane thought about it and rejected the idea. Huey was furious. He was the Kingfish, but a snub was a snub. Later, the snub cost Tulane dearly. Huey got his honorary degree anyway—from Loyola University. In conferring the Doctor of Laws on him, Loyola called him a "true representative of American ideals." Thereafter, Huey wore his cap and gown to all important academic functions.

He had been, as he called it, a "prisoner" in his own state since his breakup with Lieutenant Governor Cyr. Once or twice, he had been able to sneak out of the state unnoticed and Cyr had been none the wiser. But once Cyr had got wind of Huey's departure, he sped to the capitol to take over the governor's duties. Huey beat him back to the office after getting a tip that Cyr was on his way.

Cyr had been having trouble collecting an expense account he claimed the state owed him. Huey had held up the payments each time Cyr had tried to collect. Now Cyr made his play. Marching into a notary public's office, Cyr took the oath as governor. Huey, said Cyr, had lost title to the governor's office when he accepted his election to the United States Senate. Cyr advanced on the capitol to present his papers to the secretary of state, Miss Grosjean.

Huey galvanized his forces into motion. State troopers planted themselves at Alice Lee's doors and refused to allow anybody in or out. Police ringed the capitol. Huey called out the National Guard, which deployed around the city. He took up his position in the governor's office.

Cyr arrived, but couldn't pierce the cordons. Everywhere he went he met guards, locked doors, officials who were out, in conference, too busy to see him. He gave up the frontal assault and went to the courts.

But the move was just what Huey had hoped for. Well now, announced the Kingfish, Cyr had taken the oath as governor, had he? That meant he was no longer lieutenant governor. And since he wasn't governor, either, that didn't leave him anything. Huey had his friendly Senate president pro tempore, Alvin King, sworn in as lieutenant governor and duly ensconced in the office, as poor Cyr watched from the side lines. Cartoonists showed Cyr dangling between two offices. In towns across the state, people with the price of the swearing-in fee suddenly began to visit notary publics to be sworn in as "governor." The state and the country laughed at the Louisiana Kingfish's shenanigans, but Huey had his way. A later court ruling upheld him. Now he could turn his back without worrying about someone flopping into his chair. The Kingfish had settled an old, long overdue account.

Huey turned his attention to LSU, the state university to which he had come as a teen-age debater, but which a reverse in the family fortunes had prevented him from attending. Now he set out to take it over like, in his words, "any other damned department."

Tulane, in New Orleans, had one of the finest medical schools in the South. Traditionally, its students had enjoyed a working rapport with the Charity Hospital in that city, using it as a laboratory while they completed their training. But Tulane's blood was a bit too blue to suit Huey. The school had snubbed him and he had vowed to get even. Now Huey ordered a new medical school for New Orleans, this one to be called the LSU

Medical School. It would be built on the Charity Hospital grounds where it, too, could receive preferential treatment in using the hospital facilities. As medical dean, Huey named the same man he had appointed to head Charity Hospital, Dr. Arthur Vidrine of Villa Platte. Tulane fumed and fussed, but Huey ordered the new medical school construction to go ahead anyway. Louisiana needed doctors, said Huey, and too many students who wanted to be doctors couldn't gain admission to Tulane because "of lack of that institution's facilities."

The president of LSU became sick, had to retire. Huey chose his next president with care. He didn't want a big name, a blue-nosed educator, a man with too many ideas of his own. For the job he selected an obscure country educator named James Monroe Smith. Asked once what Smith's qualifications were, Huey replied that he had a "hide as thick as an elephant's." Moreover, he knew who the boss was. He was just the man for the job. Huey told him to get started with some new buildings. Where would the money come from to build them? Said Huey, "That will be my part of the job."

LSU had no money for construction, but that didn't faze the Kingfish. Over at the Highway Commission, they were rolling in money—$68,000,000. And the state capitol fund had $5,000,000 to work with.

During the administration of Governor John Parker, LSU had moved. It still owned the land at the old site. Huey ordered part of the old grounds bought for the new capitol building and saw to it that the state paid LSU $350,000 for it. That was enough to get those new buildings started.

But more was needed. Huey called the Highway Commission. They were going to be spending millions on roads, weren't they? Well, they needed some permanent buildings of their own. And they could use a "maintenance school," where commission engineers could learn the finer points of highway building, maintenance and beautifying. Why build their own building when they could just buy one or two at LSU's old site? The Highway Commission got the point. They bought the land and buildings for $1,800,000, although court records put the valuation at $600,000. Huey's enemies howled about the unconstitutionality of the whole arrangement, that state highway funds were being diverted illegally to build up LSU.

Huey ignored the howling. He told his president to keep building and forget the uproar. "You have got to dare a bit if you build this school," he said.

LSU became an extension of the governor's office. Huey passed the word—anybody who wanted to enroll at LSU was to be let in. Louisiana's youngsters, and many from outside the state, gravitated toward the campus. Housing them all became a problem, but still they came. When Huey began the expansion, the school had 1,600 students. It ranked eighty-eighth in size among American universities. Ten years later, bursting at the seams, it had 8,500 students, ranked in the top twenty in size in the United States, among the top ten in state universities.

Huey's regime saw a big new women's dormitory go up, a Fine Arts Building with a complete theatre, a Huey P. Long Field House with clubrooms for students, eating quarters for athletes. Huey ordered a swimming pool built. Midway through its construction, he visited to see how the work was getting along. Was it the biggest in the country? he inquired. No, there was one on a West Coast campus about ten feet longer. Huey ordered the LSU pool lengthened to beat its competitor.

Huey imported football players from other states, housing them for a time in the executive mansion, then later at new quarters on the campus. He increased the size of the band, at times called the band director in to jot down, in musical notes, the tunes he hummed. He composed the school's marching song, "Every Man a King"—a cry that was to make him a national force.

He promoted the school. At football games he led the band, marching up and down the field, or through the streets in the pregame festivities. During the game he sat on the bench or paced up and down in front of it, cheering his team on. When it won, he was exultant. When it lost, he was a study in dejection. He gave the team half-time pep talks, flavored with the salty countryisms that colored his appearances on the political stump. Carleton Beals tells of perhaps his most famous half-time talk, when he gave the team this morsel of practical philosophy to chew on: "What the hell do you care if they break your legs while you're breaking their necks?"

He saw to it that as many students as wanted attended out-of-town games. LSU was scheduled to play Vanderbilt, but many of the students couldn't go. Why not? Huey demanded. No money for train fare, came the reply. Don't worry, said the Kingfish. He was on the telephone to the railroad in a wink. A little talk about railroad property assessments, and the matter was settled. The railroad showed the proper, home-town, get-behind-the-Tigers spirit. The fare to the game would be a low seven dollars. Huey put out the word: Any student who didn't have the seven bucks could go anyway. Just come in to the office and sign an IOU. The students trooped in, got their fives and twos, signed the IOU's and trooped out again. More than 4,000 students went to the game.

Huey's antics were the talk of the nation's sports pages. The antics served a purpose. There were thousands, indeed millions of sports-loving Americans, voters all, who never got beyond the sports pages of their newspapers. Many of these might never have heard of Huey. To them, as to the more serious-minded, he was a living legend, a master showman and—a sportsman.

Huey could crack the whip, too. He brooked no interference with the shows his school, his band, his football team and he put on.

Rice Institute was coming to Baton Rouge to play LSU. There was to be a big parade downtown that afternoon. But there was a conflict. On the same day a circus was scheduled to ride into town, perform the traditional afternoon circus parade, then open that night. Huey was furious. He called the circus management, still in Texas, and asked them to delay the parade until that evening, after the football festivities were out of the way. The circus management protested, insisted on keeping to the original schedule. Huey lowered the boom. They were ready, of course, to dip their animals—tigers, lions, elephants, the works, weren't they? Dip? asked the management—what the hell did Huey mean, dip?

Well, Huey explained, Louisiana had strict animal health protection laws. If they were to be observed rigidly, every animal in that circus that hadn't been dipped would have to be dipped at the state line, before they were allowed into Lousiana. It was only natural that the governor should want to protect the health of the people of Louisiana against possible infection. The management got the idea. There was no dipping, but there wasn't a circus parade that afternoon, either.

LSU's student body was finding it increasingly difficult to find living room. Huey solved the problem. The stadium, like any other in the country, had those empty spaces between where the seats sloped down and where they met the various landings. Unused triangles of space, said Huey. He had carpenters put in wooden sidings. The space was cut up into cubicles, rooms where double-decker bunks were placed, room enough for two students to live, wash and study. One observer called it the stadium that seated 45,000 and slept 2,500.

At times Huey's "baby," as he called the school, appeared to be more trouble than it was worth. And it displayed a disconcerting brand of ingratitude, too. The editor of the campus paper printed a stinging letter criticizing Huey. Huey had the editor fired, appointed a newspaperwoman as a "censor," at one point suspended twenty-six journalism students to break up a spreading revolt. The dictator had a practical point: "This is my university, and I ain't paying anybody to criticize me." It was disclosed later, that a high percentage of the student body was on the state payroll, in one way or another, with part-time and full-time jobs. Huey liked to boast that under his administration both the main school at Baton Rouge and the LSU Medical School at New Orleans received A ratings from both the Association of American Universities and the American Medical Association. Within five years of the Kingfish's passing the school was to be rated in a different way—as probably the most corrupt academic institution America had ever known. It was to become the focus of scandals that would convulse the state and end—temporarily—the gaudy Longism that had begun a decade earlier.

On June 5 of 1931, Huey's old friend, later his enemy, died. Publisher Bob Ewing had been a power in Louisiana politics, with newspapers in operation in both New Orleans and Shreveport. He had also been Democratic National Committeeman. Ewing's death created a vacancy and the Kingfish lost no time in filling it. Now, in addition to his two elective titles, he had a voice in the party's highest councils. The new post gave him, moreover, a tighter grasp on Louisiana's political fortunes. He was expanding his influence swiftly, solidly, impressively.

By late June of 1931, the Kingfish enjoyed a security he had never experienced during his political life. Public improvements —roads, bridges, buildings, schoolhouses—were springing up all over the state. A new university was replacing the old one, and the state's chief hospitals were functioning under a centralized bureaucracy responsible to the chief—Huey. The impeachment charges were history, as an increasingly docile Legislature, whose members needed their share of the patronage dollars to survive elections back home, became less and less of a problem. The line of emergency succession—lieutenant governor, Senate president, secretary of state and House speaker—to the governor's office was studded with Huey's followers, while the chief political opposition of the past—the New Orleans Ring—was neatly in the fold, at least for the time being.

Huey's men headed the important boards and commissions: the Conservation Commission and the Dock Board, the Board of Liquidation and the State Board of Health. A majority in the Highway Commission, the dispenser of all road funds, was firmly under the Kingfish's thumb; his leadership of both legislative houses had been an accomplished fact for some time. In addition, Huey himself held three powerful titles—Governor, United States Senator, National Democratic Committeeman. Deliberately, casually, he let the people of Louisiana in on a secret—the identity of their next governor.

To "complete the work" that had been launched under his administration, Huey announced, he wanted men who were loyal to the principles he had laid down. He named his slate: for governor, his old Winnfield friend and highway boss, Oscar Kelly (O.K.) Allen; for lieutenant governor, House Speaker John Fournet of "Bloody Monday" fame, the Kingfish's unswervingly loyal legislative chief. In addition, Huey named candidates for secretary of state, attorney general, registrar of state lands, superintendent of education and commissioner of agriculture. Huey would stick around Louisiana to run things until the slate was elected, he announced, but then he would leave for Washington to take the Senate seat he had won the year before. Meantime, with the state humming along, the Kingfish waited for an excuse to extend his influence beyond the borders of Louisiana. His chance came late that summer.

The depression had hit Louisiana and the nation. In the

North, factories, offices and banks shut down; bread lines formed and people cried for work. In the South, the bottom dropped out of the cotton market. Cotton went from twenty to five and four cents a pound, and even at those prices piled up on docks in New Orleans, Mobile and Galveston. In Washington, the Hoover administration waited for the economy to take the expected upturn; anxious farmers awaited government action.

Into the crisis stepped the Kingfish, with a message for not only Louisiana, but the South as well. Moses, cried Huey, had the right idea when he counseled that the earth should go untilled and unplanted every seven years. Only by embracing Mosaic Law could the South's farmers hope to save themselves. Huey called on the southern governors, United States Senators and Representatives to meet in New Orleans on August 21, 1931, to discuss Dixie-wide legislation that would prohibit the raising of "a single bale of cotton in all cotton-growing states during the year 1932." If the people adopted his plan, Huey cried, the South would see twenty-cent cotton "in three weeks," general prosperity a short time later. "Hold your cotton," Huey urged the South's farmers, "and my cotton holiday plan will boost the price so you won't lose any money and won't have to make a crop in 1932." He appealed partly on religious grounds: "The Lord told us to lay off raising these crops one year out of seven to let the people have time to consume them. ... Louisiana will pass this law if other states will join us."

The New Orleans meeting listened, the delegates nodding approvingly. Huey announced that the representatives from Mississippi, Alabama, South Carolina, North Carolina and Arkansas had been particularly impressed and had promised to whip up legislative support for the "drop-a-crop" proposal as soon as they returned to their states. But there was no definite word from Texas, the biggest cotton producer of all. Huey appealed to Governor Ross Sterling directly.

"I am prepared to call the Legislature together within a few hours," he announced, "...and within four days secure the enactment of legislation prohibiting the planting of cotton in the year 1932.... We are only waiting on Texas... the other states are responding all right."

In Texas, however, Governor Sterling pointed out that the

Legislature was already considering a law that would limit cotton acreage to one-third of the usual total. He sent word back to Louisiana: "It's Governor Long's baby; let him wash it first."

The invitation was all Huey needed. Calling his Legislature into special session on the night of August 25th, Huey, resplendent in a white cotton suit, took the rostrum personally to beat home his plan. Two days later, the Louisiana House passed the Kingfish's bill without opposition; the Senate followed the next day.

Huey had ordered the cotton bill rushed to him for signature as soon as both Houses passed it. He got it, sitting in bed in a cotton nightshirt. He signed it on the spot, then jerked the nightshirt off, crying, "Now I can take this damned thing off." He explained later that it itched.

Huey announced that he couldn't go to Texas to lay the new law before Governor Sterling, but that he would do "the next best thing—I'm sending the next governor of Louisiana."

Governor-to-be O. K. Allen arrived in Austin, only to learn that Governor Sterling was at his home in Houston. Arriving there, Allen cheerfully handed the law to the Texas governor, explaining, "Here is Governor Long's baby, all washed, powdered and wrapped up in a cotton dress. I'm instructed to lay it before you in person, and you'll hear it cry: 'Daddy, take me up.' "

The special session of the Texas Legislature that met in September took up the baby, fondled it for a moment, then gently dropped it. Huey's "drop-a-crop" had come a cropper, and with it his first genuine excursion into national politics.

Reacting predictably, he accused the Texas Legislature of being "blandished with wine, women and money. Cash money, that's all there is to it," he roared.

The Texans replied in kind, calling Huey an "arrogant jackass . . . ignoramus, buffoon, meddler and liar, who has the impudence and arrogance to dictate to the people of Texas." [2] One legislator characterized him as a political mule—"without pride of ancestry or hope of posterity." For a time, there was more interstate name calling, then "drop-a-crop" dropped into obscurity.

[2] Forrest Davis, *op. cit.*

Although the whole episode ended on a sour note, its issues largely obscured by Louisiana-Texas animosity, its significance nevertheless lies in the ease with which Huey almost succeeded in propelling himself into the national spotlight as a political champion. The next Democratic National Convention was less than a year off, and the country was disintegrating into economic chaos. At this point, no single, clear voice was being heard, no acceptable formula for restoring prosperity had yet been advanced. Had he pushed through his "drop-a-crop" plan, and had it met with even a modest success, the Kingfish could have rolled into Chicago, that summer of 1932, as the unchallenged economic savior of the South. He would have been the glamor boy of the convention at a time when the country sorely needed a bright, sure light to lead it out of the drabness of economic depression. The Kingfish, with his propensity for making political capital, might have ridden the tide to a Democratic nomination. As it was, he became, without the success of the cotton program, one of the convention's dominant personalities, a key figure in the push and tug that resulted in Roosevelt's nomination. With a demonstrably successful farm program behind him, the Kingfish might well have been unstoppable.

Bloody, but far from bowed, the Kingfish turned to the political wars at home. The gubernatorial primary was to be held in January, 1932, and the Kingfish had a ticket to elect. Suddenly he was in the midst of a family fight, a wrangling, querulous episode that dragged on during most of Huey's later political life. The feud was to crop up more dramatically later, in a bitter, intrafamily cross fire that would reveal to the people of Louisiana, perhaps better than anything else, the fundamentally mercurial temperament of the Kingfish and his family. Now, it boiled over briefly during the campaign.

The two relatives who had been closest to Huey's earlier political development were his brother Julius, fourteen years Huey's senior, and Brother Earl, three years his junior. Brother Julius had been a sort of family subpatriarch, second in command only to Huey's father. It was Julius who had made it possible for the younger Huey to attend Tulane (Julius, it will be remembered, had lent Huey half the money for his stay there), who had organized his early campaigns, and who had rushed to his brother's defense during the dark days of impeachment. It was also Julius with whom Huey quarreled after the two established a law practice at Shreveport, and whom Huey summarily turned out of the office the two jointly shared. A shrewd, cunning attorney with a deeply ingrained instinct for Louisiana politics, Julius was the early organizer, the money raiser, the political horse trader and detail man without whom no political organization flourishes.

Earl was cut from different cloth. Where Huey was of medium height, tending to paunch, Earl was tall, lean, graceful. Huey had a fleshy face, punctuated with a bulb of a nose, a tumbling lock of hair that flopped wildly to one side. Earl's face was finely chiseled, his hair a disciplined, curly, dark brown. Huey was the devil-may-care talker, the effusive sprite who bounced up to sell Cottolene to a housewife, or himself to a political convention. Earl was shy, introverted, a stable influence balancing his brother's impulsive nature. Huey was the gifted, voluble orator; Earl the quiet, restrained infighter. On the surface, the only thing they shared in common was their ancestry.

But Earl had political ambition, too. Through the years, when he had campaigned tirelessly as Huey ran first for the Public Service Commission, then for governor, Earl had stayed in the background, content to let his brother monopolize the political spotlight. He had tasted generously of Huey's liberal patronage. The appointment as attorney for the inheritance tax collector was one of the best-salaried state jobs. Now, he wanted advancement, public promotion, an office of his own. He told Huey he wanted to run for lieutenant governor in the coming election.

Huey's answer was a flat no. He pointed out to Earl that he had already committed himself to Allen and Fournet, that any reversal on his part would throw the ticket into confusion. Moreover, he explained later, "It would be disastrous for a brother to . . . have a brother succeed him in office or have him elected as lieutenant governor. It was already being charged that I was a dictator and that I had allowed many relatives to be placed on the State payroll. To have added a family name to the head of the ticket either for Governor or lieutenant governor would have been disastrous to the whole ticket." Huey told Earl that he was "irrevocably" committed to Allen and Fournet.

Earl decided to run anyway, announcing for lieutenant governor on the ticket headed by George Seth Guion, one of six gubernatorial candidates in the race. But he let Julius map the campaign strategy, which immediately resolved itself into a blistering attack on Huey and his slate of candidates.

"Huey Long and Oscar Allen went by my poor father's house a few weeks ago," Julius thundered at a political meeting on November 30, ". . . and tried to browbeat that poor old man to fight the candidacy of Earl K. Long for lieutenant governor. Huey begged his father to fight his own son. It was the first time that Huey Long visited our honorable old father since he has been governor."

Julius told political rallies around the state that Huey had called him to say that "unless I took Earl out of that race he would destroy Earl."

"I have let Huey Long lie long enough, and if it is the last thing I do on earth, I am not going to let him ruin the Long family name," Julius cried.

The family was solidly behind Earl. In addition to Julius, Sister Lucille campaigned for Earl and against Huey, charging that the Kingfish had double-crossed his younger brother. Huey described the political assault as a "general family barrage," but refused to answer it directly or in detail. Instead, he relied on the old war cry—that only through him were the state's poor to come into their own. "You may criticize my methods, but I do what the people want," Huey shouted from the stump. "I try to do it by begging; I try to do it by praying. I'm a Baptist and I try to do it the Baptist way . . . [they] say I stole one million eight hundred thousand dollars of the state's money in purchasing land from the University for the Highway Commission, so the University could have the money to build that medical school. I deny it. If I did steal it, you got the figure wrong. I stole $2,150,000."

The family attacks amounted to little more than a harassing action against Huey and his slate. But for the first time since he jumped into the political limelight, the Kingfish found himself in some peculiar positions for an avowed reformer. For the first time, too, Huey had to deal with the racial issue, a problem he had not faced since he successfully skirted the Klan issue in his first bid for gubernatorial office.

The Guion-Earl Long ticket attacked Huey and his slate for succumbing to the "power trust" by combining their forces with the New Orleans Ring. Huey replied that there had been no "amalgamation" between himself and the Ring. When New Orleans Mayor Walmsley burst into print by confirming the fact that there had been, indeed, a meeting of the minds between Huey and the Ring, the Kingfish fell silent on this issue.

But it was in defending the attacks on him from another quarter that the Kingfish displayed a remarkable brand of inconsistency. One of the candidates for governor was a South Louisiana Catholic named Dudley LeBlanc, a public service commissioner who later became nationally famous by colorfully promoting a patented medicine named Hadacol. In attempting to outdo the Long-Allen platform of promises, Candidate LeBlanc adopted as a plank in his platform the old age pension. He promised to work for legislation that would give every Louisianian over the age of sixty a $30-a-month pension.

Since there is today a popular notion that it was Huey who first pushed for an old age pension program in Louisiana, it is interesting to note that he attacked LeBlanc's program by pointing out that the pension, as proposed, would cost more than sixty million dollars yearly. Moreover, the Kingfish pointed out, a third of this amount would go to Negroes. It was Huey's first attack, direct or indirect, on either an expanded welfare system or on a racial group, but he did it in his typical, wide-open fashion.

LeBlanc headed a mutual aid association named the Thibodeaux Benevolent Association. The association was a burial lodge, or society, operated for poor whites and Negroes. Huey directed his attack at LeBlanc's part in it.

"Then that other candidate, LeBlanc," he commented in a speech at Colfax, in Grant Parish, "he operates a nigger burial lodge and shroud and coffin club. He charges for a coffin and he charges seven dollars and fifty cents for a shroud. I am informed that the nigger is laid out, and after the mourners have left, LeBlanc takes the body into the back room, takes off the shroud, nails them up into a pine box and buries them at a total cost of three dollars and sixty-seven and one-half cents." Huey's

Louisiana Progress knew the party line. Practically every issue of it showed LeBlanc, together with Negro officers of the burial association. LeBlanc, knowing he couldn't draw much support by capitalizing on the Negro vote, replied in kind, charging that Huey and Allen were "nigger lovers" who consistently gave Negro requests precedence over those of Louisiana's whites. It was, in all, a gutter-low, unsavory political performance on both sides.

But the Kingfish's burgeoning public works program, his double title, his alliance with the New Orleans Regulars, his whirlwind campaign techniques, and his promise that the Allen-Fournet slate were pledged to "complete the work of the Huey P. Long administration"—all these proved to be too much for the opposition. In the January, 1932, first primary election, Huey swept his ticket into office with a majority over the five other tickets combined. Allen, who was to be Huey's puppet governor, polled 56.5 per cent of the vote, far ahead of LeBlanc, who could muster only 29 per cent. The Guion-Earl Long ticket ran a poor third, getting only 14 per cent of the total vote cast. It was, in every respect, a one-sided victory, a smashing endorsement of the Kingfish's program. Moreover, he had a new and important weapon at his disposal. For in the lesser races, most of the legislators who had run as Long candidates had been swept into office. His position in the Legislature was now more powerful than it ever had been, even after his peace truce with the Ring.

Huey lost no more time in Louisiana. Four days after the election, his men safely certified to office, Huey announced that he would leave for Washington to take up the United States Senate seat that he had captured the year before. Even then, however, he made sure the state was in safe—i.e., Long—hands. Before leaving, Huey announced to Louisiana that his newly appointed lieutenant governor, Alvin King, would act as governor while he was out of the state. King dutifully echoed the boss's words. The day he took office, he announced: "I'm lieutenant governor, and in the governor's absence I'll be acting governor just as if Governor Long had gone over to the Gulf Coast to play golf."

5

Kingfish of the Lodge

WASHINGTON was expecting Huey Long when he arrived on January 25, 1932. But not even Washington was prepared for the man from the red hills of Winn Parish. The legend—green pajamas, potlikker, windmill orator, political tyrant, soak the rich and help the poor—had preceded the man, and the Kingfish took pains to perpetuate it. He succeeded by adopting the same flamboyant technique that had worked so well back home; he took the rule book and tossed it into the first convenient repository.

The sophisticated capital press learned early that there was no real difference between the man and the legend. On his first morning in Washington, Huey greeted reporters in a facsimile of the green pajamas that had earned him national headlines two years earlier. Nor did the press find him the shy, wall-flower prototype of the freshman senator arriving for his first session. He seemed to be everywhere at once, with inquiries, suggestions, vague but emphatic-sounding statements about inequities in the nation's wealth.

Precedent called for the Kingfish to be introduced to the Senate by his Louisiana colleague, Ed Broussard. Would he ask Senator Broussard to do the honors? "Don't hold your breath until I do," was Huey's reply. Minority Leader Joe Robinson of Arkansas agreed to do the job, but he probably regretted it later. The day Huey was seated proved to be a memorable one for both Broussard and Robinson.

The Senate had its time-honored rules—no smoking, no undignified conduct, no ungentlemanly references to other members. In short, the rules were designed to permit the conduct of "government by gentlemen." Louisiana had had "government by gentlemen," but Huey had broken all the rules there. Now he broke them again.

Puffing on a big cigar while other members regarded him disapprovingly, the Kingfish habitually galloped about the Senate floor, glaring at one senator, backslapping another, hugging a third. He lashed out at his new colleagues with a fury that startled them. A finance committee was studying a tax amendment the Kingfish opposed. "Why . . . this finance committee would tax even the little fellow who pays ten cents for a movie ticket," he shouted in amazement. When a committeeman protested that the tax began at eleven, not ten, cents, the Kingfish snorted elaborately: "Oh, God bless the committee."

In the midst of a tax discussion, a committeeman had said, "I'll send for the Secretary of the Treasury." Now the committee hit a snag in its proceedings. Up jumped the Kingfish, mimicking the other senator's words. "I'll send for the Secretary of the Treasury," he imitated, "I'll send for the Secretary of the Treasury. He's a good man and I'll send for him. We are going to see around here in the home of the brave and the land of the free whether a committee can mess things up." A senator tried to quiet Huey. The Kingfish waved him away. "I am beginning to feel the logic of my own argument. I feel the urge to talk."

The depression was strangling America but no one seemed to have a plan to end it. "Share Our Wealth," cried Huey. That was the answer. "It is the law of God that a nation must free and refree its people of debt, and spread and respread the wealth of the land among all the people," roared Huey, leaning on the Mosaic Law outlined in Leviticus. But you didn't have to go back to the Bible to find the doctrine of Share Our Wealth, Huey reminded the senators. Jefferson, Jackson, Webster, Lincoln, Theodore Roosevelt and William Jennings Bryan—all had been apostles of wealth sharing. It was the only way America could be saved.

Share the wealth sounded good, said the critics, but how about specifics? How would he share the wealth? Huey, his answers ready, whipped out his figures. Boiled down, they looked like this:

1. Liquidate all personal fortunes in excess of $3,000,000.

(Later, he dropped this to $1,000,000.) The Treasury would thus realize $170 billion.

2. With this money, give every American family $4,000 to buy a home, an automobile and a radio. This would cost $100 billion.

3. Pensions of $30 for everybody over sixty-five. (Later, Huey changed the amount to "an adequate rate.")

4. A minimum annual salary for all workers of $2,500, resulting in a high level of purchasing power among the poor.

5. A shorter work week so laborers could enjoy the better life.

6. The government to balance farm production and consumption "according to the laws of God."

7. Immediate cash bonuses to veterans.

8. Government-paid college educations to youths of proven ability.

The Senate reacted predictably. It sounded, cautioned Minority Leader Robinson, like out-and-out confiscation of wealth. Huey wheeled on the Arkansas Democrat and senatorial courtesy, "government by gentlemen," went out the window.

What did Robinson know? Why, he was a front for the Republicans, one of the high and mighty Huey was talking about. "The Senator's law firm represents every nefarious interest on the living face of the globe.... When a man comes into the Senate without enough clients to make a corporal's guard, and winds up representing every big corporate interest, if that doesn't mean something, what does?" The Senate gasped at the uninhibited attack, the bare-fanged indictment, but Huey refused to backpedal. With a flourish that gained him another shower of national publicity, he resigned from all his committee assignments, a dramatic gesture of protest against party and government alike. Meantime, he made a significant little addition to his now expanded "sonofabitch book." Into its pages went the name of Joe Robinson of Arkansas.

But Washington was still Huey's second love at this point. Back to Baton Rouge he sped, to personally supervise the 1932 session of the Legislature. Ordinarily, a United States Senator would have no business—or authority—at the state Legislature. But Huey was different. Allen was his governor, Fournet the man who had been elected by Huey's machine. A majority of the legislators had campaigned on a promise to complete the Kingfish's program. Huey's appointees had continued to hold office under Allen. The face in the executive mansion was different, but the same machine controlled the state. And that machine was Huey's.

The problem at hand was simple. The treasury was bare again. The highways, schools, free schoolbooks, the new capitol building—all had cost a lot of money. During 1931 alone Huey's administration had spent a whopping seventy-nine million dollars—just two million dollars less than the Parker administration had spent in four years. Now, the problem was to rebuild the treasury.

Huey's solution was simple, too. More taxes, this time on tobacco, soft drinks, insurance premiums, electricity, the corporations and gasoline. For a time, the Legislature toyed with the idea of a sales tax, but finally discarded it. Huey had opposed a national sales tax, had called it a "disaster." Backing one for Louisiana would have been embarrassing.

The bills, some of them drawn by Huey himself, went before the Legislature, with the Kingfish on hand to ramrod their passage. Two years before, as governor, he had trod the legislative floors gingerly, not sure of his ground. On two occasions he had been a step ahead of an expulsion-minded sergeant at arms after angry legislators had protested his presence. Now, as senator, he had less legal authority, but he had his governor and legislators and his political machine and a ringing vote of confidence from the people in the last election. As he bounded along the legislative halls, callously ignoring all appearances, he was a power unto himself.

Striding among the desks, appearing before committees, he spoke in favor of this bill, against that. When bills came up for a vote he frequently stood while the legislators made their decision, then shouted with the rest, "Aye," or "No." There was no pretense whatever about who was boss in the governor's office. When Huey came to town, O. K. Allen at times was forced to move out of his office to make way for the Kingfish. On one occasion, before a group in the governor's office, Huey revealed completely the extent to which he had assigned Allen the puppet's role.

"Oscar," barked the Kingfish, "go get me those goddam bills."

He turned back to the people in the office. Allen, either not hearing, or squeamish about having his office boy status paraded before others, moved slowly. Huey glared fiercely. "Goddam you, Oscar," he roared, "don't you stall around with me. I made you and I can break you. Get those goddam bills and get 'em quick." Poor Oscar needed no further stimulus; he got 'em quick, and stories of how Huey harassed him publicly and privately grew by the score. One story pictured Oscar as being so conditioned to sign anything that Huey thrust before him that the response became ultra-automatic. One day, the story went, a stiff wind blew a leaf through Oscar's open window, then fell to his desk. Without a word, he picked up a pen and put his signature to the leaf.

Reaction to Huey's tax bills was unexpected and sudden. Around the state, taxpayers merged into mass meetings to protest the additional levies. Spokesmen for the groups contacted each other, planned to move on the capital to protest in person. They set the date for June 13, with the gathering point the old state capitol.

Huey, flexing his muscles, more in control of the situation than ever before, countered by calling on the New Orleans Ring to send its own delegation—a "citizens' rally" in favor of the tax program. Twenty-one railroad cars filled with state or Ring employees arrived in the capital city on the same day as the dissidents. The payroll, as they came to be known, paraded with big banners: WE CANNOT CLOSE OUR SCHOOLS. WE MUST SAVE OUR STATE. DON'T LISTEN TO THE MUGWUMPS.

Both sides poured into the Legislature to speak their pieces. "I thought the election sent Huey P. Long to Washington," appealed one rebellious taxpayer, the wife of a former governor, "but it seems he is still in Baton Rouge." She singled out Huey's former secretary, Alice Lee Grosjean, now the supervisor of accounts, as a "twenty-six-year-old girl who doesn't know the difference between single- and double-entry bookkeeping." She called on the Legislature to assert itself, to beat down the new taxes.

Huey took the floor for a half hour of impassioned oratory. Why, said the Kingfish, when he had run for governor in 1924, the opposition press had derided his remarks about reducing taxes by pointing out that only a small percentage of tax collections went into the state's general fund, while most of the taxes were assessed at the town and parish level. Now, he cried, here was the opposition again, demanding that taxes be kept at present levels. If the opposition was right in 1924, declared Huey, they were in the wrong place now. "The place for you to go to holler about taxes is the courthouse of your own parish," he roared.

The protests were so much window dressing as far as the Kingfish was concerned. With a majority of the Legislature in his hip pocket, either through his election help or through his Ring alliance, with his governor and lieutenant governor in office, Huey's Legislature needed little prodding to know which way to vote. His program went through, practically as a solid package. The rebellious tax groups disbanded and headed home. Huey once again turned his attention to the national scene. Two days after the legislative session ended, he was en route to the National Democratic Convention at Chicago.

In 1928 Huey had skirted the traditional practice of letting the Legislature name delegates to the national convention. Now he repeated the procedure by getting the State Democratic Central Committee to name them again.

There had been talk, in 1928, that if serious opposition had developed toward Huey's delegates, the opposition group would very likely have been seated at the convention instead of Huey's forces. Now anti-Longs staged their own "convention" at Shreveport, protesting the Long method of selecting delegates. Huey, ever the showman, denounced the "rump" convention. Then, in a broad attempt to parody the dissidents, he called his own "rump" convention.

Into Shreveport poured the "payroll squad," burlesquing the dissidents, carrying signs that read, WE WANT OUR SWAG, and pledging a platform that would bring back the gin fizz. For a presidential candidate the payrollers chose an obscure state senator, for the vice-presidency another Long legislative stalwart. When the time came for the Louisiana delegation to leave for Chicago, there were three groups in all: Huey's delegates, the dissidents, and the comedians, a group Huey promised would be introduced at the convention. As it turned out, Huey followed through on the promise. The third group was introduced. But there was method to the Kingfish's apparent madness. Had his own group been ousted, Huey would have had the comedians to fall back on as an authentic group objecting to the original dissidents.

But Huey was too well entrenched with both his Louisiana delegation and the national political powers to lose out in Chicago. Craftily he early pledged Louisiana's twenty delegate votes to Roosevelt, the convention's dominant figure. But it was before the convention's national committee that the Kingfish made his most telling points.

"The Democratic Party in Louisiana?" he roared. "I AM the Democratic Party in Louisiana." Pointing an accusing finger at the rump delegation, Huey windmilled himself into a lather. "Who's got a better right to pick out a delegation? Every one of this . . . bunch is a sorehead about the way he's been beaten by me. I beat them time and again. . . . They've been beat! Beat, beat, beat. Beat down there." The convention seated Huey's faction.

Huey's work on Roosevelt's behalf at the Chicago convention had one immediate and striking result. It elevated him to a new pinnacle of national prominence, made him a regional political giant to be feared, consulted, reckoned with. James Farley, in his revealing picture of inside politicking, *Behind the Ballots,*[1] admitted that Huey's efforts in Roosevelt's fight for the nomination, and Roosevelt's subsequent election, was a potent force in the Democratic victory. Edward J. Flynn, in *You're the Boss,* was even more precise about it. Said Flynn, "There is no question in my mind but that without Long's work Roosevelt might not have been nominated." [2] But neither Farley nor Roosevelt had any illusions about the primary stimulus that motivated the Kingfish. Farley believed that Huey's efforts were as much intended to "steal the national spotlight" from Roosevelt, and thus lay the groundwork for his own, later presidential aspirations, as they were in helping Roosevelt. And by 1935, with his re-election fight just around the corner, Roosevelt could tell Raymond Moley in an interview that something would probably have to be done to "steal Long's thunder" if Huey's grow-

[1] James Farley, *Behind the Ballots,* Harcourt Brace & Company, New York, 1938.

[2] Edward J. Flynn, *You're the Boss,* The Viking Press, New York, 1947.

ing national appeal was to be kept within reasonable bounds.[3] No one in the Democratic Party's higher councils, it is safe to assume, underestimated the drawing power of the Kingfish, his personal appeal, or the price the party had to pay for his support.

The six-month period from January to July of 1932 marked the beginning of a decisive phase in the stormy career of Huey Long. He had exposed himself to the national spotlight and, all things considered, he had fared well. His embryo Share Our Wealth schemes had found little official favor, but they had gone far from unnoticed. In Chicago, he had proved to be a wily and formidable political figure. He had come to Washington with something of a reputation for political buffoonery, a country-boy figure with a flare for the ridiculous. But his personal genius at commanding publicity, his demonstrated strength in controlling a delegate bloc at a national convention, and his growing intraparty strength had largely altered the original picture of Louisiana's Kingfish. Now, Huey turned to the difficult task of organizing regional political support outside Louisiana. His first target was neighboring Arkansas.

Huey had clashed early and bitterly with Senate Minority Leader Robinson of Arkansas, particularly over the issue of redistribution of the wealth. On the other hand, the junior Senator from Arkansas, Mrs. Hattie Caraway—serving out the unexpired term of her late husband—had been one of the few Senate voices behind the Kingfish. Huey saw his chance to score an impressive double victory by retaining a friendly voice in the Senate and, at the same time, by adding to his growing reputation as a potent regional force. For the first time, the Kingfish decided to step outside the boundaries of his kingdom to put the celebrated Long political bulldozer on national display. From Washington he called his State Highway Commission: "Get out the sound trucks. I'm going to Arkansas to campaign for Hattie Caraway."

Like a Panzer column in an open field, Huey's force of seven sound trucks and automobiles rolled northward from Baton Rouge. It stepped briefly in Winnfield, where Huey paid a courtesy call on his aging father (and, according to Brother Julius, slipped the elder Long fifty dollars), had himself photo-

[3] Raymond Moley, *After Seven Years,* Harper & Brothers, New York, 1939.

graphed eating watermelon on the Long farm, then roared into Arkansas.

With Hattie at his side, Huey demonstrated to Arkansas and the country the Long campaign techniques. While Huey and Hattie stopped at one town for speeches, the sound trucks were already miles up the road, drumming up advance crowds, setting up circular stations. Young campaign workers, mostly members of the Highway Commission "payroll squad," moved easily among the townsfolk, dropping literature here, passing out candy suckers for discomforted babies there. When the parents seemed to be having more trouble with a bawling baby than they appeared to be capable of resolving, the young campaign worker would volunteer to take the baby for a spell while the senator talked. Wrote Huey later, "I remember when I saw her [Mrs. Caraway] notice one of our campaigners take charge of the first baby. The child began fretting and then began to cry. One of the young men accompanying us immediately gave it a drink of water. The child quieted for a bit, and resumed a whimper, whereupon the same campaign worker handed the baby an all-day sucker, which it immediately grasped and soon fell asleep. Mrs. Caraway did not understand that it was a matter of design until it had been repeated several times."

Huey, with Hattie at his side, roared through Arkansas in exactly seven days. The Kingfish left her on election eve. En route to New Orleans the next night, radio bulletins told him what he wanted to know: Hattie had rolled up a majority of the vote, crushing the six candidates who had opposed her. The Kingfish had conquered Arkansas.

Now the campaigner moved to batten down another political hatch, this time at home. The primary elections for Edwin Broussard's U. S. Senate seat were due in a few weeks, in September of 1932. Huey wanted that seat. While Huey came by train, the sound trucks rolled south from Arkansas to demolish still another of the Kingfish's opponents.

Like Huey's governor, O. K. Allen, John Overton had been in the Kingfish's corner since the early Public Service Commission days. He had run for the United States Senate in 1918, when Huey had run for his commission seat. Overton had campaigned for Huey, had helped put the Kingfish across. But he had lost his own fight.

In 1929, it was Overton who appeared at Huey's side during the impeachment rallies, and Overton who had proclaimed that he would be found standing or lying beside the Kingfish in an impeachment fight to the finish. Huey had been instrumental in electing Overton to Congress. Now he tapped him for new honors. This time he named Overton as his candidate for the Senate seat held by Broussard.

The campaign was a typical Kingfish production with extraordinary refinements. The sound trucks, as usual, rolled through the state, attracting huge crowds which turned out mostly to hear Huey, not Overton. As usual, state employees who held their jobs by the grace of the Kingfish, got the word: 10 per cent of one month's salary for the campaign war chest. And, as usual, Huey blasted the "lying newspapers," the corporate fat cats, the "old gang" (with no references this time to the New Orleans Ring)—in short, he concentrated on his old whipping boys. But even these tactics were buttressed by a new and blatant addition to the vote-getting technique, the inflated ballot box. In St. Bernard Parish, for example, a later investigation revealed that there were 2,510 whites over the age of twenty living within the parish boundaries. In the election, St. Bernard recorded a total vote of 3,189. Overton got 3,176; Broussard got 13.

Although Huey's problem in Louisiana was infinitely more simple than the one he met and conquered in the foreign state of Arkansas, the Kingfish campaigned with all the fervor and vehemence that had become his stock in trade.

"Edwin Broussard," sneered Huey, "Edwin Broussard sits in his office about a block away from the Senate, and when it comes time to vote they punch a bell and Edwin comes over. Edwin meets a feller in the hall, and the feller says, 'Vote no this time, Edwin,' and Edwin goes in and he votes no. Then he goes back to his office. After a while the bell rings again and Edwin comes back over. The feller in the hall says, 'Vote yes this time, Edwin,' and Edwin, he votes yes, and then goes back to his office. Once in a while they punch the bell and they ain't no feller in the hall to tell Edwin how to vote. When that happens, Ed just waits and watches how I vote, and then he votes the other way."

Meanwhile, Huey lost no opportunity to solidify the structure of Longism that he had hammered together, to strengthen the image of Huey, the crusader, the friend of the poor, the champion of the oppressed. Standing on the steps of his new capitol building during the campaign, he delivered, in capsule form, his image of the framework he had patiently welded together:

"They'll tell you that what you've got to do is tear up Longism in this state. All right, my friends—get you a bomb or some dynamite and blow up that building yonder [the new capitol]. That's a good place to start.

"Then go out and tear up the concrete roads I've built. Get your spades and your shovels and scrape the gravel off of them roads we've graveled, and let a rain come on 'em. That'll put 'em back like they was before I come.

"Tear down the new buildings I've built at the University. Take the money away from the school boards that I've give 'em to run your schools.

"And when your child starts out to school tomorrow morning, call him back and snatch the free schoolbooks out of his hand that Huey Long gave him. Then you'll be rid of Longism in this state, my friend, and not till then." [4]

With this kind of emotionalism, with his Ring and legislative alliances, with his perfected campaign techniques and his personal prestige, with the payroll out en masse to vote, the result was a foregone conclusion. Overton swamped Broussard by more than 50,000 votes.[5] Huey had another senator in office.

But there was an even more important dividend in the Congressional races. In every district, the lines between candidates for the United States House had been sharply drawn—Longs vs. anti-Longs. In virtually every district, Huey's man romped home to a solid victory. At that moment, it would be reasonable to assume, the Kingfish stood astride Louisiana, an all-victorious, unchallenged political monarch. In fact, the Kingfish's activities to this point were a mere rehearsal for what was to come, a tightly welded political dictatorship without parallel in modern American history.

Back in Washington, Huey turned his attention to Roosevelt. FDR had shown no enthusiasm for Huey's Share Our Wealth

[4] Forrest Davis, *op. cit.*

[5] The count: Overton: 181,464; Broussard: 124,935.

schemes, a fact that galled the Kingfish. Moreover, some of Huey's aides, notably Seymour Weiss and New Orleans merchant Abe Shushan, reported to him that federal agents had begun preliminary inquiries into their income tax returns. Nothing Huey said or did changed that; the agents kept right on checking. Soon they were checking the Kingfish's tax returns, too. Huey began to snipe at Roosevelt in the Senate, and FDR retaliated by ordering patronage siphoned through New Orleans politicians. Huey continued to snipe at Roosevelt, but before he could declare all-out war on the President, he found himself embroiled in one embarrassing situation after another. Suddenly things began to go badly for him.

Filibustering against a banking bill introduced by Senator Carter Glass, a bill that would have tightened federal control over banks, Huey lashed out with such unbridled venom that the elderly Glass started for him on the Senate floor. Other senators intervened. Huey filibustered grandiosely: "The bill is as good as dead. Take this carcass away. I am glad to say that it has no more chance of final passage than I have of becoming Pope in Rome, and I am a Baptist. . . . What's next on the legislative program after you cart this corpse away?"

Glass retorted that Huey was far from the underdog crusader he posed at being. In fact, said Glass, Huey had visited the chairman of the board of the Chase National Bank on a recent trip to New York. Glass intimated that Huey, in reality, was fronting for the bankers in opposing the bill. The Kingfish tried to laugh the charge off, but the Senate passed the "corpse" by a healthy margin.

In Louisiana, again, the Sixth District (Baton Rouge) congressman, Bolivar Kemp, died. Huey tried to fill the vacancy by blatantly flouting the law. The law required Governor Allen to call an election to fill the seat. But Huey wanted no elections. He had O.K. hold back the call, ignored the petitions that streamed into the governor's office demanding an election. Meantime the election committee for the district, strongly pro-Huey, was meeting in New Orleans. At the Kingfish's prodding, it declared that there would be no election, that the widow of the late congressman would be appointed instead.

Sixth District citizens sent more petitions protesting the action, declaring that a "citizens' election" would be held if there was no official election called. The election was called, and Huey's candidate won, but there were cries of fraud. The citizens staged another election, this time with armed guards patrolling the polling places. Congress refused to seat either of the winners, and still another election was held. This time, Huey's opposition won, and Congress seated the winner. The Kingfish had taken it on the chin in his capital city.

Touring the East, Huey suffered humiliation at the swank Sands Point Bath Club on Long Island. One version had Huey insulting a lady. Another had him entering the men's room, then misdirecting his aim, thus dousing one of the other occupants. In any case, the wind-up of the story is the same in every version: Huey emerged from the men's room with a badly bruised eye, blood streaming down his cheek. As with the green pajama incident, the nation's press took up the story. But this time the laughs were on Huey, not for him. The word "Crawfish" began to appear alongside the title "Kingfish," in some of the livelier journals. Huey, claiming first that he had been attacked by political enemies, narrowed the assault down to a "Wall Street plot" to get him. By the time Huey fled back to Louisiana, the country-wide laugh had increased to a roar. Back in Louisiana, he found people laughing, too. They taunted him about the incident in the men's room, asked where his bodyguards had been. In Alexandria, as Huey delivered a political speech, what began as jeering ended with Huey being pelted with eggs. The local police were less than zealous in breaking up the demonstration.

But worse was yet to come. Reading the returns, particularly those from St. Bernard Parish, Huey's opposition cried that the election had been rigged and demanded a federal investigation. The year before, such charges might have been ignored. But Huey had made too many enemies in Washington. This was a good time to even the score. In the fall of 1932, and again in February of 1933, a subcommittee of the United States Senate's Special Committee on Investigation of Campaign Expenditures sat in New Orleans, hearing evidence. For the first time since he had become Louisiana's Kingfish, the federal government was openly investigating an election in his state. For the first time, too, the country at large—and the neutrals in Louisiana—could glimpse, through the thousands of words of testimony given, the machinations of the Long empire and the methods used to keep it intact. Most significantly, however, the nation got a close-up look at Huey the man, a picture painted by the people closest to him, his brothers. It was a shocking revelation of ruthless politics, of alleged brotherly betrayal, of family disharmony.

The appearances of Brothers Julius and Earl before the Senate subcommittee could have been calculated to produce only one result—the political destruction of the Kingfish. The 1932 gubernatorial elections, in which Earl, with the backing of the Long family, ran for lieutenant governor, had left a deep, bitter schism in the family. On the one side was Huey. Lined up against him were the other members of the family, particularly Julius and Earl. Julius, it will be recalled, had said during the campaign that Huey had promised to "destroy" Earl if the latter refused to withdraw from the race, a campaign in which Huey's candidate, John Fournet, was eventually successful.

The appearances of the brothers was a fascinating spectacle. Before Louisiana, indeed before the country, they heaped charge upon charge against the Kingfish—theft, political chicanery, bribe taking and giving, slander, drunkenness, perjury, character defamation, official malfeasance.

Under oath, Brother Julius read a statement in which he charged that Huey had posed as a friend of the working people in his first campaign for governor. In reality, said Julius, Huey "received his principal financial support from the Southwestern Gas & Electric Co. and their allied interests." Huey, sitting as a lawyer for the elected Overton, leaped up, eyes ablaze, but Julius was too quick for him. "Now don't be punctuating anything," he roared at Huey. "You told me that with your own mouth." Huey sat down as the "revelations" continued.

Huey, testified Julius, had told him of a "mysterious agent" of a trust who had given him "either ten or twenty one-thousand-dollar bills at one time." But that wasn't all. Julius had been in a room "a couple of times" when other agents had "handed my brother a large roll of money . . . which he tucked into one of his back pockets of his loosely fitting trousers. It looked like it would almost pull them off him," Julius exclaimed.

Julius roundly denounced Huey's personal character by recalling Huey's alleged threat to destroy Brother Earl. Julius had felt constrained to deliver a lecture on brotherly love.

"I told him how he had acted, how he had forgotten not only his own mother and daddy, but every sister and brother he had, and I want to say something along that line right here, since he wants to pretend he has some milk of human kindness in his heart for his family. I swear that I do not know of a man, any human being, that has less feeling for his family than Huey P. Long has. He has done the worst things that one could possibly think of and he did so toward his brother, who entered the campaign, as already stated."

Huey, charged Julius, had disgraced the family name in a crass grab for votes.

"I remember he said he did not have shoes, as I heard him tell it over the radio. No such travesty as that ever occurred in our family, and a more monumental outrage was never perpetrated toward a family than that. At other times articles appear in magazines that there is some Indian blood in us. I suppose if he went in a race up North, he would publish up there that there is part nigger in us in order to get the nigger vote."

When he had finished his testimony, Julius sat there, waiting for the Kingfish to take over the questioning. "Your witness," said the committee's counsel, General Samuel Tilden Ansell. Still seated, Huey did not look up. "No questions," he said.

It was different when Earl took the stand. He saw no one-thousand-dollar bills pass hands. He merely remembered one-hundred-dollar bills—crisp, new ones. In all, testified Earl, Huey had taken $10,000 from a public service company lobbyist. Had Earl seen the transaction?

EARL: No. Governor Long told me that he [the lobbyist] gave him $10,000.

HUEY (leaping to his feet) : That is a goddam lie.

ANSELL: You say you never saw any money passed from [the man] to Governor Long. Now, let us hear what Governor Long told you about any moneys [*sic*] passing from [the man] to himself.

EARL: I said he gave him one hundred $100-bills.

ANSELL: He told you that?

EARL: And I saw the bills. They were brand new. They looked like they just came off a machine.

Huey could stand it no longer. He counterattacked by asking Earl to be more specific about some of his testimony. Earl dodged about, attempted to give a lengthy answer. Huey exploded: "Now, I didn't ask this gentleman for an equivocation . . . he can explain. I asked him for a direct answer. I intend that this witness be prosecuted for perjury if he answers . . . directly. Now I want a direct answer."

They sat there, in the crowded committee room, hurling accusations at each other. Why, demanded Huey, had Earl tried to make people believe that he (Huey) was supporting him in his bid for lieutenant governor?

A lie, replied Earl. He had never claimed the support of the Long machine. "I never one time tried to make people believe you were supporting me, and I had people telling me you would . . . and I said you would not, and I knew you would not and I know why: I knew you knew you couldn't control me."

Huey's political opposition and his conduct in office were bad enough, Earl testified, but what hurt most were his venomous attacks on the family, including Earl. Huey objected to that. The two got into a verbal wrangle.

HUEY: Then you admit . . . that I made no statement against you in that campaign, that I never made a derogatory remark about you or any other member of my family during that campaign? If I did, tell me.

EARL: Yes. You made cutting remarks about all of them. You made the statement to a large number of people that you used to think Percy Saint [the former Attorney General] was the biggest liar in the state, but you decided your brother, Julius Long, was the biggest liar.

HUEY: Where did I make that statement?

EARL: You made that statement to a group of people in Farmerville.

HUEY: A group of people in Farmerville?

EARL: Yes, sir.

HUEY: That was not a public statement, that was supposed to be a private statement.

EARL: I couldn't say, and I want to say that . . . [to] the throng in your room, you tell them plenty about me.

At one point in the testimony Huey leaned close to his brother.

HUEY: You love your state better than you do your brother. Naturally, you are only here trying to help the public, are you not? You do not like to testify against your brother, but you are just telling the truth?
EARL: You just go ahead and make a speech.
HUEY: I say, that is your attitude?
EARL: You can get up here where they can see you. Come up here and take this chair.
HUEY: You are testifying only from motives of public good and have some reluctance about testifying against your brother, but you feel you owe the public the truth, do you not?
EARL: I think in a demagogic and sarcastic way to try to ball it up, that you have just about stated the absolute truth.

The subcommittee delved into the financing of Overton's campaign. Seymour Weiss of the Roosevelt Hotel, the Long machine's treasurer, testified that he had solicited money as the campaign needs dictated. He was asked about his personal bank deposits.

WEISS: That is my own business.
COMMITTEE COUNSEL ANSELL: It might be somebody else's.
HUEY: Don't answer that question, on my instructions.
ANSELL: On what ground?
HUEY: Because I said not to do so.
ANSELL: Is that sufficient?
HUEY: That is plenty. Kingfish of the lodge.
ANSELL (to Weiss): I will ask you why you did not deposit [campaign contributions] in a bank.
WEISS: Because I did not want to.
ANSELL: I ask you why you did not want to.
WEISS: That is none of your business.

The hearings passed into history with a peculiar finding by the committee. In short, the committee concluded that Overton had been elected fraudulently, but that he had no personal knowledge of the fraud. Said the New York *Sun:* "The inference is that Mr. Overton has a good title to a seat obtained through fraud, intimidation and corruption."

The end of the Senate hearings, however, failed to end the Long family turmoil. Suddenly Brother Julius blossomed into print in a series of two articles in a national magazine called *Real America.*[6]

> ... It is now my firm conviction [wrote Julius], reached after more than fifteen years of study and work to aid my brother Huey Long—years of growing disappointment in him—that he must be forced out of state and national public life, else he will do a harm to his family, state and nation so great that it can hardly be estimated.

His brother, said Julius, was a power-mad tyrant whose personal behavior would shock a philistine.

> He is never in his real element until he is fully loaded with booze, on a platform surrounded by his gunmen, slandering somebody for his own political gain. He always has trained gunmen with him, paid out of the funds of various departments of the state of Louisiana ... if I could lay bare to the world the exact amounts of graft taken from the funds of the various departments and institutions of Louisiana since my brother ... became governor I am sure that it would be so astonishingly large that even I would be astounded. Equally astounding would be an itemized statement of what has been expended for Huey's long-distance telephone messages, telegrams, booze, eating, wild parties, limousines, campaign literature, sound trucks, campaign expenses, and the like, since he became governor in May of 1928.

Back in the Senate, the Kingfish rose to defend himself.

"The attacks of my blood brothers and sisters are printed about me in every city. I cannot help it. They are my blood. I will go to my grave with my lips clear of one thing—I will never have spoken a word to try to harm one of them. I have paid a terrible price to not support a brother for governor or lieutenant governor in 1931–32. They spoke no harm of me until then."

The spectacle perhaps embarrassed the Kingfish, but it had

[6] *Real America,* September, 1933.

no lasting effect on his political stock. He had been through a bad time, both in Washington and Louisiana. Now he prepared to mend his fences. Within months, he would show Louisiana—and the country—what one-man rule could really be like, and how near to a feudal monarchy a sovereign American state could be brought. The Louisiana of 1934–35 would, under the Kingfish, go down in history as America's first authentic political dictatorship.

6

The Dictator

THE period from 1933 to 1935 completed the Kingfish's political metamorphosis. It was a time that saw him transformed from a regional contender into a national candidate, a would-be messiah with a simple, powerful and increasingly popular appeal to the country at large. It was a time when Huey commuted between Louisiana and Washington, shifting his momentum, rearranging his visions, creating a curious national organization. It was a time when democracy in Louisiana—as imperfect there as anywhere—was meticulously ground into oblivion, then replaced by a model twentieth-century dictatorship.

There were, of course, minor irritations for the Kingfish during this period. For one thing, Brother Julius blossomed forth with his nasty magazine articles, enlargements of the charges he leveled at election hearings. But Brother Earl, now newly married, had subsided into relative obscurity as a federal housing functionary (lawyer for the Home Owners Loan Corporation). During this period Huey saw little of his family. Rose and the children lived in the Long home in New Orleans, Huey in his Washington bachelor quarters. On his trips to Baton Rouge, he stayed in a wing of the executive mansion or in a Heidelberg suite. In New Orleans, he operated from the Roosevelt Hotel. He saw nothing of his father, now living his last years in Winnfield, where he occasionally received newspaper reporters bent on inquiring about his famous son. The remainder of the family was scattered about the state.

Sometimes Huey had to ignore or ward off embarrassing situations that, given a chance to develop, could have heaped ridicule on him, thereby endangering his national ambitions. One such situation arose early in 1933 when Congressman Hamilton Fish charged that one million dollars of Reconstruction Finance Corporation money, supposedly loaned to strengthen a Louisiana bonding firm, had gone instead to pay off the notes of a Louisiana bank close to Huey. The charges threatened to precipitate a mild banking panic in New Orleans. Huey nipped the panic in the bud by arranging another RFC loan, this time for the beleaguered bank, then by getting his governor, O. K. Allen, to close the banks until the loan came through. Huey's strategy was neat, transparent—and effective. He simply got Oscar to proclaim the Saturday on which the run was expected a legal holiday. When the bank opened on Monday, the RFC money was on hand and the run failed to materialize.

The Kingfish's critics sniped at him from a variety of quarters. A group of Louisiana citizens petitioned the United States Senate to oust him, charging that Huey was "personally dishonest, corrupt and immoral . . . repulsive to the respectable and law-abiding citizens of Louisiana and to the nation." A New Orleans attorney, Shirley G. Wimberly, wrote a pamphlet entitled "Unmasking the Crawfish, Huey P. Long." Wimberly distributed his pamphlet to the Senate and to the Washington press, then dared Huey to sue him. The Kingfish ignored him. In Milwaukee, addressing a Veterans of Foreign Wars convention, Huey further endeared himself to an already hostile press, this time by urging convention delegates to throw the "newspaper skunks" from the hall. "Don't be afraid to disturb me by throwing them out," he cried. "We don't stand for them down our way and you shouldn't let them get away with such things here." It appeared momentarily as if some of the delegates might actually attack the newsmen.

In New Orleans, the most serious threat to Huey's authority erupted—and from a not unexpected source—the Ring. Huey and the Ring had enjoyed a mutually beneficial truce, but never a comfortable alliance. Now the city's leaders charged that the state-appointed registrar of voters was stealthily cutting away at the Ring's ranks, dropping men from the voting lists. A judge impounded the registrar's books, which the Ring promptly hid in one of the parish jails. Stripped of vital city voter lists, Huey might yet have patched up the truce. Instead, he decided on open conflict. This was not the same Huey who had come to New Orleans looking for support in 1928, a man without organization or reputation. Now he had both. Moreover, New Orleans had benefited from his term as governor. There was the Dock Board, for example, and the street repair appropriations and the bridge across Lake Pontchartrain. Even Ring Mayor Walmsley had said publicly that Huey had "stretched out the hand of friendship" to the city. Huey decided to tackle the Ring on its home grounds.

Into the city elections he threw a slate of candidates, including one to oppose Walmsley, who was up for re-election. The Ring loosed its machine and won easily, while Huey's candidate, John Klorer, came in a poor third.

Huey returned to Washington to ponder the course of events. But during the campaign he had, as usual, casually castigated the Ring members, particularly Walmsley. Now Walmsley appeared in Washington, registered at Huey's hotel—the Mayflower—then planted himself in the lobby and waited for Huey to appear. To newsmen who rushed to the lobby to cover the meeting, he declared, "I don't intend to place myself in the position of a mayor lying in wait for a senator, but if I see Long I'm going to beat him up." In his rooms, behind doors patrolled by his bodyguards, Huey got the news, then meekly commented, "Well, here's hoping he doesn't run into me." The same day the Kingfish received another adverse newspaper blast, when a Washington *News* reporter, Ray Moulden, a slight 120-pounder, by-lined a story telling how he had sought to interview Huey, only to have the enraged senator attack him with a heavy cane and shove him into the snow. The bodyguards, Moulden wrote, stood by menacingly while Huey carried out the attack. This newest publicity prompted Broadway's Eddie Dowling to wire the Kingfish an offer to appear in a New York musical: I'LL MEET ANY TERMS WITHIN REASON AND GUARANTEE YOU PROTECTION FROM MAYOR WALMSLEY.

Then Huey counterattacked—a great offensive that lasted for more than a year, that ended in complete control of Louisiana and a spiraling headlong rush for the White House in 1936. Huey launched his attack by returning to Louisiana for the regular legislative session in the spring of 1934. Before returning, he assessed his strength at the capitol. His governor and lieutenant governor were in office, as were the heads of numerous boards and commissions. The Legislature of 1934 was far different from the hostile body that had forced his impeachment in 1929. Now, despite a combination of rural anti-Longs and the pro-Ring legislators (ten legislators formerly loyal to the Ring—six representatives and four senators—pledged their allegiance to Huey), the Kingfish had healthy majority blocs in both houses. He put them to use immediately.

To show the poor folks that their champion had not forgotten them, the Huey-Allen-dominated Legislature took care of the money legislation first. Into law went a property tax exemption act to help lower income groups. It was a constitutional amendment that raised homestead exemptions to a maximum $2,000 per year. (Actually, until 1939, the exemption stayed at between $800 and $1,000.) This system meant no taxes for hard-pressed homeowners on the first $800–$1,000 of assessed valuation on their property, and the new amendment allowed the exemptions to be deducted from state or parish taxes. But it conspicuously omitted municipalities—a side blow at New Orleans, whose residents would not be able to apply the exemptions to their municipal tax bills. For the lower income groups, also, the Legislature adopted another amendment, this one drastically lowering the license fees on cheaper automobiles and small trucks (the kind farmers might drive). And if the reduced auto license fees would cost the state $300,000 annually? No matter. The Legislature passed another law, this time repealing the $700,000 bonanza that had been allowed by an expansive, alliance-minded Huey.

Huey's Legislature piled up the "benefits" and struck out at business. The one-dollar poll tax, a prerequisite to the voting privilege, was repealed, thereby enfranchising thousands of poor whites and Negroes. A "debt moratorium" law went into effect, allowing the State Banking Department to work out easier payment plans for depression-plagued farmers.

To make up for the revenues lost on property exemptions, the Legislature added new taxes on liquor, public utilities, cotton exchanges. For the first time, the state adopted a personal income tax, a direct dig at the pocket of every adult wage earner in Louisiana. And, finally, Huey mounted a frontal assault on the newspapers. The Legislature passed a 2 per cent tax on the receipts of newspapers with circulations of more than 20,000, a blow aimed primarily at the big New Orleans dailies. The United States Supreme Court declared the newspaper tax invalid in 1936, but during those two years the Long-Allen-dominated Legislature held a powerful anti-newspaper weapon in readiness.

Meantime, Huey showed how a "right" parish could benefit by sticking with him. The political overseers of Plaquemines Parish, home of Louisiana's great sulphur deposits, had pledged allegiance to the Kingfish. Huey beat back efforts to raise the taxes on sulphur to the same levels as those on oil, then allowed the parish to take back one-third of the state revenues collected.

Taxes and revenues out of the way, Huey now moved on the one obstacle that could bring about his downfall, or—if he controlled it—his dictatorship. He reached out to grab the ballot box. By tradition and law, custody of the ballot boxes was assigned to parish sheriffs. The Legislature stripped the sheriffs of this power, handed control of the boxes to state election supervisors—that is, Long men. By law, also, candidates for political office had named their own election commissioners, the ballot box watchdogs. Now, the Legislature shifted this function to state-appointed election supervisors, giving the central government an additional and direct election role.

But couldn't a determined candidate get an anti-Long judge to impound ballot boxes if there was a suspicion of vote fraud? Huey's Legislature took care of that, too, in as flagrant a display of legislative chicanery as even Louisiana had seen. The anti-Long forces in the Legislature introduced a bill providing that no voting records could be taken from a registrar's office, except by court order. The Long-dominated legislative majority, over the protests of the anti-Long minority, simply reversed the meaning of the bill by tacking on a lengthy amendment. In finished form, the law specified that no court could impound the voting records held by a state-controlled registrar. Again, with a twist, Huey had stripped the ballot and voting records of their sanctity. Satisfied for the moment, the Kingfish allowed the legislators to adjourn and scatter across the state. But before they went, they left Huey and Allen with another statute on the books—power to name a legislative committee to investigate municipal affairs, particularly crime and official corruption. Hardly had the legislators settled in their home parishes than Allen assembled the committee for an investigation of official corruption in New Orleans.

Into New Orleans, surrounded by uniformed troops, rode Huey, Allen and the committee members to investigate the wicked, vice-ridden city. They set up shop in an office building guarded by troops, announced that the vice hearings would be public. But no segment of the public, except the mysterious witnesses, was allowed inside the "hearing" room. The progress of the hearings was carried by radio, but the bulletins were bizarre, unrealistic, at times incredible. Witnesses—an array of underworld characters, prostitutes, bums—described police payoffs, city hall shakedowns. The identities of those making the confessions were kept secret. Huey and the boys arrived daily to conduct their hearings, escorted by uniformed troopers every step of the way. Governor Allen announced that the hearings had produced unmistakable evidence of vice and corruption. The city, he said solemnly, would have to be purged.

Elections were imminent—for Congress, the Public Service Commission, a variety of local offices. Governor Allen declared "partial martial law," called in the National Guard, quartered them on the city's docks. A contingent of troops seized the registration offices, together with the voter lists, while another platoon occupied offices in a building directly across from city hall. There they set up machine-gun posts in the windows, then aimed the guns at city hall until the registration offices had been sacked.

"I warn you, Huey Long, you cringing coward," cried Ring Mayor Walmsley, "that if a life is spent in the defense of this city and its rights of self-government, you shall pay the penalty as other carpetbaggers have done before you." Huey's answer was to have Allen mobilize the remainder of the National Guard and speed them to the city. The Ring swore in extra police and armed them. The two sides stood their ground, tense, ready for immediate battle.

The September elections came and went, with Huey's candidates for Congress and the Public Service Commission swept into office. The tension eased. Then, having won his elections,

Huey had the National Guard leave the city. He had accomplished his purpose—electing candidates. The Ring was still in power, but the people had voted for the Kingfish's slate.

From August of 1934 to September of 1935, Huey ordered the Legislature into special session seven times, and each session drove a new spike into the lid on constitutional government in Louisiana. Huey demonstrated that what had happened during the summer and in the regular session had been a mere rehearsal for dictatorship. At the same time, he displayed for the country at large the slick efficiency of one-man rule, of government by ukase. When he finished, he had, as Allan P. Sindler observed, ". . . reduced the citizenry of Louisiana to political vassalage to the Kingfish and his faction." [1]

He began, as expected, with New Orleans, then methodically moved across the state. In the city, he reduced the Commission Council, the governing body, to an absurdity by transferring most of its important powers to existing state agencies. The police department went to the control of state, rather than local, authorities. The transfer of power was then effected in other municipal bodies. The state Public Service Commission took over the control of the city's utilities by legislative edict, while many of the parish offices were stripped of traditional functions (e.g., the issuing of business licenses) and placed under the supervision of state agencies.

Property values in the city had been set by a seven-man board of assessors. Two of the seven died and Huey had Allen appoint two Long men to take their places. The five original assessors refused to recognize the two state appointees. The Legislature simply surrounded the city group by appointing the two state men and five others as "deputies" to the State Tax Commission, then whipped through legislation making the State Tax Commission, formerly a mere review board, the absolute authority on property assessments. The Tax Commission, moreover, could apply the heat immediately, since the Legislature saw to it that its assessment powers were made retroactive for three years. A Huey friend could now have his assessments lowered, an enemy could cry to the wind as his were raised. The Tax Commission—and Huey through it—could raise or lower assessments at will.

[1] Allan P. Sindler, *op. cit.*

Then the state machine put the squeeze on the city. By legislative act, the minimum city appropriations for the operation of the fire and police departments and other municipal agencies were raised. At the same time, the total assessed valuation of city properties was lowered (to bring in less tax revenue). Meanwhile, the state took in the money collected from city license fees. The New Orleans Bureau of Governmental Research estimated that the city, in terms of a 1935 budget, would have to make $2.3 million in revenues meet $4.1 million in expenses. The Ring's operations, Thomas O. Harris observed, were so impaired that "the New Orleans city administration did not have enough patronage . . . to support the government of an unincorporated village." [2] New Orleans might have survived the onslaught by borrowing. But the Legislature turned the screw again, this time most of the way. To keep the city from borrowing, the Legislature set up a new state agency—a state bond and tax board, which had to approve any debt assumed by municipal, parish or district governments. In effect, no city, parish or town could borrow without the approval of the state government.

To meet the flood of bills introduced at the special sessions, the Legislature streamlined its machinery, tooling the business of lawmaking into an astonishingly precise procedure. From this point, a bill was referred to a single, pro-Huey committee —ways and means—to be heard briefly, passed along, then followed by another. Sometimes, the Kingfish was the only witness appearing before the committee considering a bill, and his explanations were a travesty and a wonder.

"Now this here," he would idly remark, flipping the pages of a proposed law, "this is intended to preserve the integrity of states rights." At that point he might look up. Whack! The gavel sounded and the bill had passed the committee, en route to full legislative action. Sometimes the Kingfish's explanations were even shorter. Raymond Gram Swing, in his *Forerunners of American Fascism,* described the Kingfish in action before the committee: "Huey stood there the entire time, the chair-

[2] Thomas O. Harris, *The Kingfish,* Pelican Publishing Company, New Orleans, 1938.

man's only function being to call for a vote, bring down his gavel, announce that the measure was approved." [3]

Two seemingly innocent bills came before the single committee; later, the Legislature itself. The first was billed as a "state civil service law," designed to protect the tenure of state employees. The other created a "state budget board," composed of the governor, the state superintendent of education and the state treasurer. Its purpose was simple—to review the finances of the state's schools. It was nice to see the administration in such a benevolent mood.

It was only after the bills had passed committee and had gone to sure election in the Long-dominated Legislature that the people of Louisiana woke to find out what the bills really were. The first gave the governor—to all intents and purposes, Huey—the power to appoint all nonelective municipal officials: police and fire chiefs, commissioners, department heads. In effect, it delivered every city, town and parish office, with the exception of elected officials, into the governor's hands, to fill as he pleased. The first use to which he put the new law was an exercise in sweet revenge for Huey. A year before, when crowds had pelted him with rotten eggs at Alexandria, the police had not allowed Huey's bodyguards to track down the egg throwers and Huey had been humiliated. Now it was his turn. The first man to feel the weight of the new law was the Alexandria police chief, who was summarily fired.

Including the fine print and the last-minute amendments, the law establishing the State Budget Board simply gave the new, Huey-dominated board absolute authority over the jobs of every teacher, school bus driver, janitor—every school worker in the state. Just as he had taken over LSU, Huey now reached out and swept Louisiana's public schools into the central fold. Not until 1936, when the law and the board were abandoned (repealed by the Legislature), could a state schoolteacher draw a free breath. Depression jobs were hard to come by—and school jobs hung by a slender thread.

Now the encirclement was all but complete, and Huey moved to close the ring. Earlier, his faction had gained a majority on the state Supreme Court. Four judges were friendly to Huey;

[3] Raymond Gram Swing, *Forerunners of American Fascism*, Julian Messner, Inc., New York, 1935.

three were not. Election time drew near, and one of the friendly judges had to face the electorate for a new term. He faced an opponent, Thomas Porter.

Unexpectedly, the Long judge died and Huey's faction was in a dilemma. Louisiana law clearly called for the remaining candidate to be named the Democratic nominee—and, therefore, the certain winner in the general election. But the Kingfish would have none of it. Ignoring precedent and law, Huey had the district committee (which recognized nominees) rule against the opponent's claim to nomination. The opponent took his case to a district court, which upheld him. The district court's ruling came before the Supreme Court. Here, the three Long judges employed legal sleight of hand. Suspending the district court ruling, the three set a date for a hearing on the merits of the application—a date twenty days beyond the general election. By that time, Huey's man might be in.

For the vacant post on the court, the machine came up with a choice candidate—John Fournet of "Bloody Monday" fame, now O.K.'s lieutenant governor. The move left the opposition candidate in a dilemma. If he ran, he would give legality to the election; if he refused to run, Fournet would be elected without opposition and would, undoubtedly, win the later court fight on the election's legality. Porter ran, but Huey's forces brought out the vote, beating him by more than 4,000 votes. The Supreme Court majority was secure.

Huey's Legislature also gave new powers to the attorney general—power to intervene and take over the prosecution of any criminal case in the state, felony or misdemeanor. In effect, the new law made figureheads of the state's district attorneys. The Legislature stripped the power of local sheriffs even further by giving the state-appointed superintendent of police the right to appoint all deputy sheriffs in unfriendly Baton Rouge, all deputies over the number of five in any other parish.

The attorney general came under fire from the state's lawyers—the Louisiana Bar Association, of which he was a member. The bar asked why he didn't prosecute flagrant vote-fraud charges in New Orleans after stepping in to supersede the Orleans Parish district attorney, Eugene Stanley. The attorney general, Gaston Porterie, a staunch Long man, hemmed and hawed, delayed action in the New Orleans cases. The bar kept after him and he offered to resign. The bar refused to accept the resignation, asked instead for action. Huey, infuriated, ordered the Legislature to form a "new bar." Out went the old Louisiana Bar Association and in went a new organization—the Louisiana State Bar Association. To remain in good standing, the state's lawyers were now required, by law, to obtain memberships and pay dues in the new organization. The honor of becoming the revitalized association's first president went to the organization's brightest legal figure: Attorney General Porterie. By legislative edict, Huey's lawyer now headed the lawyers who had sought to embarrass him.

The legislative pile driver never let up. The Huey-controlled Public Service Commission, now in charge of regulating all municipal utilities, was empowered to charge all expenses in connection with a rate case to the company being examined. Then Huey had the commission appoint him as its special attorney, a post in which he was able to exact fat legal fees. In addition, Huey had himself appointed as a roving prosecutor for the State Tax Commission. The new titles were important legal weapons under the personal control of the Kingfish. His word decided a utility rate, an assessment, a tax rebate or increase. And there was another facet to the appointments. Hearings before the Public Service Commission were long and frequent and Huey's legal fees were high. And in the case of the Tax Commission, Huey, as a special prosecutor, dug out delinquent tax accounts, then skimmed a neat 33 per cent off the top of the money turned over to the state. Questioned about his one-third fee, the Kingfish grinned and allowed as how the state was getting a bargain. "I'm the best damn lawyer in Louisiana, ain't I?" Anyway, the Legislature made the procedure legal.

Finally, legislative attention was directed to the police, the military and the judiciary of the state. First, the Legislature gave the governor the unquestioned right to call out the state militia at any time, at any place, for any purpose. Gone were the days when the militia was used as a psychological weapon in reserve, to be called out only at the insistence of local authority. Now it was a potential raider band, a personal army to be called at a whim and without fear of court interference. Secondly, the Legislature approved the governor's direct and uninhibited control over all functions of the state police. The governor, under the new act, could add to the number of state troopers at will, use them for any purpose he saw fit. Their ranks swelled and they came to be known as "Huey's Cossacks," later as "Huey's Gestapo." Third, the governor acquired the right to reprieve convicted men simply by signing his name. There was no review board, no court stay. The power was complete. And the Legislature added a significant paragraph to the act: The governor's reprieve power was effective in contempt cases, too. No longer need a machine henchman fear the courts. He might go before them, but a reprieve could be in his pocket and he could be out of the courthouse before the judge finished uttering the sentence. Moreover, a machine stalwart could casually thumb his nose at any judge. Who was there to hold him in contempt if the governor's power superseded a judge's authority? And if an occasional adamant judge proved to be particularly unco-operative, there was yet another threat the machine held up to him—the gerrymander. If he could not be controlled or cowed, he would simply be legislated out of office. Cases like this were few, but one in particular was a tinderbox, a result the single-minded legislators could not foresee. This was in the Evangeline-St. Landry judicial district, where Judge B. F. Pavy, a veteran jurist of thirty years, was assured of defeat at the polls after the Legislature redistricted his area. He was to be a central figure when the dictator fell.

Finally, the Legislature all but closed the book on democratic Louisiana by giving the governor the authority to add to the number of parish and municipal officials already in office. Huey immediately moved to settle an old score. Baton Rouge had always been unfriendly. Traditionally, the city had voted against him or his candidates. During his first term as governor, polite society had shunned him, looked on him as something of a crude upstart. The city authorities, too, were long-time Huey opponents. Of the thirteen police jurors (city commissioners) only two were friendly to the administration. Suddenly the state increased the number of commissioners from thirteen to twenty-six. In went thirteen Long men and the count in the capital city stood at fifteen pro-Huey, eleven against. Baton Rouge became a state outpost.

The first real test of Huey's seizure of absolute power arose when what appeared to be an innocuous license law came before the Legislature. It passed the House, then came to the Senate for final adoption. Before adoption, however, the Long leaders tacked on an amendment. When the full import of the newly passed bill dawned on everybody, the Legislature had already passed the five-cents-per-barrel occupation tax on oil refining. In 1929, just five years before, Huey had barely escaped being kicked out of office when he sought to impose the tax on the "Octopus," Standard Oil. Now, without warning, the tax was law. And suddenly the unexpected happened to a regime that had become singularly used to having its own way. In Baton Rouge, revolt broke out. As soon as the Legislature passed the tax against Standard and other companies, Standard retaliated by dismissing 1,000 of the 30,000 workers at the huge Baton Rouge refineries. The embittered Standard employees, without jobs in the middle of a depression, met, formed the Square Deal Association and threatened to march on the capitol.

Standard met with the administration to work out an accommodation, and both sides gave ground. Standard promised to increase its production and refining. Governor Allen, on the other hand, had the Legislature give him the power to reduce or suspend the tax at any time he saw fit. He immediately lowered it to one cent a barrel instead of the original five, and Standard moved to take back the discharged workers. The crisis appeared to be over.

Then a rumor was heard in Baton Rouge. One of the Square Deal members had been "kidnaped" by Huey's Cossacks. The Square Dealers, armed with whatever weapons they could find, assembled at the courthouse. Lacking direction, soothed by ministers' prayers, they grumbled, disbanded, then returned to their homes. But the challenge to the machine had been raised and had to be met. O.K., now the complete master of the militia, called out the National Guard.

Armed guardsmen patrolled the streets. Military notices, tacked on telephone poles and public buildings, ordered the city's residents not to hold group meetings, carry arms or create disturbances. On the outskirts of the city, reinforcements of the militia stood poised for any emergency.

Chafing at the military edicts, inflamed by the kidnap rumors, a small band of the Square Dealers—about a hundred—gathered the following day at the municipal airport in a gesture of defiance. The militia advanced on the civilians, threatening them with rifle fire, bayonets, tear gas. The Square Dealers broke and ran, but one man was shot. The revolt ended, but the Square Dealers must have pondered the irony of it all, for the "victim" of the kidnaping turned out to be a machine informer.

The *Putsch* was over. Huey had laid siege to New Orleans and that citadel of opposition was crumpling fast. His agents, from the governor on down, were everywhere ready and willing —and, in most cases, eager—to do his bidding in an instant. He controlled the state—election machinery, police, militia, judiciary, fiscal, education. No body or area lay beyond his reach. His appearances before the Legislature, in the final stages of the assault, became studies in confidence, almost nonchalance, as he watched his legislators race through bills that had his sanction.

He no longer hesitated to discuss his methods, and he conceded that they often met with public disapproval. To Raymond Daniell of *The New York Times* he confided, "They say they don't like my methods. Well, I don't like them either. I'll be frank with you. I really don't like to do things the way I do. I'd much rather get up before the Legislature and say, 'Now this is a good law; it's for the benefit of the people, and I'd like you to vote for it in the interest of public welfare.' Only I know that laws ain't made that way."

Relieved of all strain, secure in his power, he could even laugh now at the cartoons, the adverse editorials, the jokes and stories that went the rounds about him. One in particular might not have amused him, but it summed up his now undisputed status:

KING GEORGE: Who is this fellow, Huey Long? Is he a Chinaman?

PRIME MINISTER: No, Your Majesty, he is the Kingfish of Louisiana.

KING GEORGE: My word, what is a Kingfish? Is it a new title for rulers, like that of Hitler, der Fuehrer?

PRIME MINISTER: Yes, Your Majesty, it means that he is the dictator of that sovereign state.

7

Exit the Kingfish

THE Kingfish, fresh from his triumphs in Louisiana, returned to Washington to battle the Administration, to expand his national organization (Share Our Wealth clubs) and to promote his presidential candidacy in 1936.

There were many reasons for Huey's original break with Roosevelt, whom he had zealously supported in Chicago in 1932. First, Roosevelt's Congressional leaders had shown no inclination to back Huey's early pleas for wealth sharing. The Kingfish's first overt attempt to have a wealth distribution program enacted into law, for example, received only fourteen votes. Later, support grew to twenty votes, but the scheme never enjoyed any noticeable Administration support.

Income tax inquiries against prominent Louisianians, including some of Huey's closest supporters, had been launched as far back as the Hoover administration. Far from dismissing them, the Roosevelt group pressed them and eventually succeeded in obtaining a number of indictments. Huey himself came under tax scrutiny.

Roosevelt's advisers had been quick to shift federal patronage to Huey's opposition in Louisiana when Huey originally criticized the President's program. Later, Huey was to challenge the method and the amount of federal spending in Louisiana as his own ambitions clashed with those of Roosevelt. In the beginning, nevertheless, Huey was on the outside looking in, in terms of federal patronage money at his disposal.

Finally, Huey had grand ambitions of his own. He made no secret of his plan to seek the presidency—in 1936 if possible, surely by 1940. To Forrest Davis he spelled out a plan to organize the country on a kind of national precinct basis, with Long leaders in each of the "precincts." Said Huey, "I'm going to organize the country like I organized Louisiana . . . where do you think the old parties are going to get off when they find out that Huey Long has got a majority of the voters in the country organized?" [1]

If he had been intemperate with his Senate colleagues when he first came to Washington, impatient with what he considered to be Roosevelt's foot-dragging on anti-depression measures, Huey now became a veritable fire-breathing dragon. Even before he returned to the capital, he seriously proposed (in a New Orleans speech) his most drastic remedy for Louisiana—nothing less than secession from the Union.

"The only way for us to get out of this here depression," Huey told the people, "is to secede from the United States, sever all connections and make a clean start. I think we ought to have some kind of agreement with the government to let us get out altogether—a friendly agreement—or, if necessary, some other kind of agreement, so we could be independent or join up with Mexico or something. We ain't going to get any place until we get rid of all those damn bureaucrats, hobocrats, autocrats and all the other 'crats up there. The State of Louisiana is big enough for me to handle; I don't know nothin' about any other states. There's two million people in Lousiana . . . but leave us alone and we'll have forty-five million."

How long would it take forty-three million people to flock to Louisiana? "Oh," said Huey, "it'll take five or six years, reckon, but we'll set up a real Utopia in this state. But we've got to get out of the United States. We've got to run our own business and not have any of those damn folderols that's goin' on up there." Huey's secession talk, of course, was patent nonsense. But it contained an element of shrewd psychology. In effect, he told America that while the Administration offered little hope for economic recovery, Louisiana—that is, Huey—had the answer to a bright tomorrow. Earlier he had put it more succinctly. Except for being a part of the United States, Huey had said, Louisiana "would never have known a depression."

In Washington, however, Huey quickly forgot secession and

[1] Forrest Davis, *op. cit.*

turned toward discrediting the Administration, at the same time advocating wealth sharing. Distribute the country's wealth, he urged, "so we will have no more men sleeping on park benches and no more starving while our bins are filled with food. Take it away from the top: Mr. Rockefeller, Mr. Baker and Mr. Morgan." The money the millionaires lost would hurt them not at all, Huey cried—a portion of the wealth could be removed "without taking away any palaces in Switzerland or any of their hundred limousines."

Did Roosevelt know what he was doing, up there in the White House? Why, said Huey, "if he doesn't get a better understanding of conditions in this country than he has had in the last two years, it would be a fine thing if Congress made a contract with Mr. Vincent Astor and his five-million-dollar yacht, not only to take the President out in the British waters to fish for a few weeks, but to keep him there for several more months and trust to luck the country would find itself back to normalcy."

Huey ridiculed Roosevelt's official family with newly coined names. Secretary of Agriculture Wallace became "Lord Corn Wallace," the "Ignoramus of Iowa." Postmaster General James Farley became the "Prime Minister," the "Nabob of New York." Harold Ickes was described as the "Chinch Bug of Chicago." Roosevelt himself became "Prince Franklin, Knight of the Nourmahal."

Increasing the tempo of his attack each time he rose to speak in the Senate, Huey reached a peak of sorts on May 2, 1935, with a stirring denunciation that equaled in emotional impact the "Evangeline Oak" speech of 1928.

"While millions have starved and gone naked, while babies have cried and died for milk, while people have begged for meat and bread, Mr. Roosevelt's administration sails merrily along, plowing under and destroying things to eat and wear, with tear-dimmed eyes and hungry souls made to chant for this New Deal, so that even their starvation dole is not taken away, and meanwhile the food and clothes craved by their bodies and souls goes for destruction and ruin. . . . Is this government? It looks more like St. Vitus dance."

As his chief Administration target—save for the President himself—Huey chose Farley, Roosevelt's chief political organizer. Farley, Huey charged, was engaged in all sorts of shenanigans: improper influence in the granting of RFC loans, giving away expensive new stamp issues, handing out federal patronage to New Orleans men who were stockholders in a realty company that handled buildings in the "red-light district."

Federal patronage to improper persons in Louisiana? By heaven, he roared, Louisiana would "fill the jails so full of them Roosevelt henchmen you can't see the dust. They'll be diggin' ditches on relief themselves if they try to mess" down there. And, Huey added, he would never concede his principles just to get on the patronage gravy train:

"If all the burning of midnight oil that I have done to gain the little bit of learning that I have obtained, and all the political crusading that I have done have to be bent down to Jim Farley, then I don't want their patronage. I am the head of the Democratic Party in Louisiana. The voters have made me so. I have been governor. They have elected me to the Senate. I am the national committeeman, and a few days ago they made me state chairman. But if recognition must come through a league with the imps of hell, then I must retain my self-respect." The President, Huey told the Senate, had "enshrouded himself in a cabinet at least partly composed of corruptive persons," and he predicted that Farley "can't remain in the cabinet very long."

The charges and the frequency with which Huey repeated them could not be ignored. The Senate refused, by a 62–20 vote, a formal investigation, but Post Office Committee Chairman Kenneth McKellar issued a statement charging that Huey was trying to "destroy the character of a man who doesn't agree with him." It was not good enough for Huey:

"Farley has apparently been exonerated. He'll be introduced around at a few more banquets and suddenly some day or night it will be found that Mr. Farley is no longer able to sacrifice himself for the people. You say he will retire to run the Democratic campaign. Oh no, he'll never dare be put at the head of the next campaign. You have covered up the grave, but you haven't buried the corpse. We'll bury him face down so that every time he scratches he goes nearer home."

Huey's influence in the Senate dipped to a new low. He staged a fifteen-and-one-half-hour filibuster against the NRA, only to have the Senate extend its life. Into the hopper he tossed a bill to earmark one billion dollars for the college educations of needy students. The Senate brushed it aside, 75–5. He opposed in vain the confirmation of Henry Morgenthau as Secretary of the Treasury. Dr. Hiram W. Evans, Imperial Wizard of the Ku Klux Klan, denounced Huey as "un-American." Huey replied, "You tell the tooth puller he's a lying sonofabitch. That ain't secondhand information and it ain't confidential." But McKellar of Tennessee aptly summed up the Kingfish's Senate status: "I don't believe he could get the Lord's Prayer endorsed in this body."

But if his Congressional influence sagged, Huey's personal popularity expanded by leaps and bounds. His Senate speeches packed the galleries and visitors to the Senate office building peppered guides with questions about Huey—where his office was, was he speaking today, was he really as colorful as the newspapers said? His office became a beehive, clogged with filing cabinets, alive with jangling telephones, the reception room filled with visitors from all parts of the country. He appeared almost daily on the pages of the major newspapers as Huey the orator, the administration critic, the showman.

As early as January of 1934, he was urging the formation of local Share Our Wealth clubs for the whole country. He took every opportunity, used every device, to spread his gospel. The organization grew steadily.

As formal organization went, Share Our Wealth was a loosely knit phenomenon. Anybody could join, and Huey refused to entertain the idea of levying dues. The clubs, he said, should be kept a "poor man's" movement.

Members were recruited by the blanket method. Anybody who wrote to Huey for any reason got, by return mail, an application blank to fill out and return, complete with names of other local Share Our Wealth enthusiasts. Members on the mailing lists got copies of Huey's speeches, his new national newspaper, the *American Progress,* the successor to the defunct *Louisiana Progress,* together with a copy of Huey's autobiography, *Every Man a King.* Huey never explained where the money to pay for the lavish use of the mail came from. At times, however, copies of Huey's speeches, sent out under his Senatorial frank, were accompanied by Share Our Wealth circulars and application blanks.

The Administration put General Hugh Johnson, formerly of the NRA, on the radio to argue for pump priming, federal works, and to deflate some of Huey's claims. The radio networks offered Huey equal time to reply, explaining to him that he was much in demand. If that was so, Huey cagily told them, "I think I ought to get paid." The networks hesitated, then offered him an extra fifteen minutes of air time in lieu of payment, which was exactly what the Kingfish wanted. He spoke to a nationwide audience estimated to be one of the largest ever reached in America, with the possible exception of some of the President's important talks. He was too clever to use the radio time to answer Johnson's charges; instead, he devoted the major portion of the time to outlining and hammering home his favorite theme, Share Our Wealth.

His radio technique was as effective a tool as any politician had employed to that day. Before speaking, the Kingfish called on his audience to round up "half a dozen of your friends" to listen in, too. Filling the air with jokes, favorite stories or anecdotes about the latest happenings in Washington, Huey would wait until he was sure the friends had arrived before launching into his talk.

"This is Huey P. Long speaking, ladies an' ge'men. Now before I start my speech, I want each one of you who are listening in to go to the telephone and ring up a half dozen of your friends. Tell 'em Huey Long is on the air. Tell 'em to tune in, an' stay tuned in. I'll wait till you get through phoning. I'm going to tell you things them lyin' newspapers won't tell you. I'm going to tell you the God's truth, so help me."

The Kingfish took on a right-hand man in the Share Our Wealth organizing, a Shreveport preacher named Gerald L. K. Smith, a big, good-looking Bible thumper who had his picture taken with Huey, then announced that he was 100 per cent for Share Our Wealth and the Kingfish. Later, Smith was to attempt to step into shoes much too big for him. The result would be his turning away from Share Our Wealth as a rallying point, and turning to anti-Semitic haranguing as a subject for his soapbox oratory.

The Kingfish's Share Our Wealth correspondence became the largest of any member in the Senate. When he began the nationwide string of clubs, he had a staff of twenty clerks at work answering mail and sending out circulars. Soon a night shift of fourteen additional people was at work. In Huey's office, Share Our Wealth became a twenty-four-hour-a-day project as the letters poured in from every state, from Alaska, Hawaii and the Philippines. By 1935 there were even seventeen clubs operating in Ontario, Canada, and the movement was only beginning there. The membership rolls grew from three million to four, then five and six. It is generally accepted that by the beginning of 1935 there were more than 7,500,000 members on the Share Our Wealth rolls, although Huey sometimes claimed as many as nine million. And another important, but subtle, change took place in the organization. Before Huey's radio broadcasts during the first two months of 1935, 90 per cent of his mail came on rough, lined note paper, the messages in pencil. Only an estimated 5 per cent of the mail was typewritten. After the broadcasts, the typewritten mail jumped to 20 per cent of the total. General Johnson, testifying before a Congressional committee in March of 1935, all but conceded the failure of the Administration's efforts to stop the snowballing Share Our Wealth movement: "Who is going to tell any man he ought not to have $5,000 a year, if Huey can get it for him—or even why he shouldn't be a king? The fact is that nobody is answering Huey in language anybody can understand. He is getting away with it without a contest."

The finer points of the Share Our Wealth scheme never concerned Huey. Or, at any rate, he never bothered to spell them out. Up to a point, his proposals were far from startling. Division of liquid wealth (that is, cash money) was already being achieved, indirectly, by income taxes, and with time the tax structure was to be broadened and sharpened. Social security would take care of pensions (although not on the grand scale envisioned then by Huey—about $300 monthly then, perhaps equivalent to $700 per month today). World War II would bring the GI Bill of Rights, under which millions of ex-service men would receive government-paid college educations. And veterans in most states were destined to receive bonuses.

But what Huey proposed was a total division of wealth—liquid and solid. This meant sharing railroads and steamship lines, buildings and factories, real estate and the very inventories on the shelves of stores. To the all-inclusive question of "How?" Huey failed to address himself.

Nevertheless, as a mere mailing list, the Share Our Wealth clubs gave the Kingfish an impressive toehold in the national political arena. No one knew this better than the Administration, which, in a survey reported by Farley, found that "Long would be able to poll between 3,000,000 and 4,000,000 votes" on a third party ticket in 1936. Said Farley, "It was easy to conceive a situation whereby Long, by polling more than 3,000,000 votes, might have the balance of power in the 1936 election. For instance, the poll indicated that he would command upward of 100,000 votes in New York state, a pivotal state in any national election; and a vote of that size could easily mean the difference between victory or defeat for the Democratic or Republican candidate. Take that number of votes away from either major candidate, and they would come mostly from our side, and the result might spell disaster." [2] Huey himself felt supremely confident. He had the usual September elections for the United States Senate moved up to January in Louisiana. In this way, he could win re-election, then concentrate on the summer's presidential campaign. To newsmen who questioned him about his chances in 1936 he replied cockily that he already had Louisiana, Arkansas, Mississippi and Georgia, and "I'll take Alabama when I get ready." Remembering the Hattie Caraway campaign, few doubted him.

That summer of 1935 the Kingfish completed his work in Washington, but he was full of plans for the future. In the Senate, he had urged amendments to the income tax laws (designed to take more money from the biggest incomes), a stiff inheritance tax, a new program to manage farm surpluses. During his 1935 stay in Washington, he had staged five filibusters, including the fifteen-and-one-half-hour marathon talk against NRA reorganization. Now he planned a nationwide tour of his Share Our Wealth clubs (in reality, a political sampling to measure his prospects for 1936), but first there was unfinished business in Louisiana. In September he returned to Baton Rouge for the fourth special session of the Legislature to be called that year,

[2] James Farley, *op. cit.*

the seventh since August of 1934. There was no reason to suppose that this session, like the others, would be anything but a mechanical exercise, with the Kingfish pulling the strings.

But the Kingfish who returned to Baton Rouge that year had been manifestly uneasy for some time. He had shown a marked interest in his personal safety. His bodyguard contingent had been increased, and Huey himself admitted that he sometimes carried a gun. In July he charged in a Senate speech that five congressmen had met in a New Orleans hotel and that there had been talk of assassinating him, but the five denied it. A year earlier, Representative Mason Spencer, one of the few remaining anti-Long legislators, had set the grim tone for events to come. Rising on the House floor to protest state control of election commissioners, the Delta lawmaker intoned, "When this ugly thing is boiled down in its own juices, it disenfranchises the white people of Louisiana. I am not gifted with second sight. Nor did I see a spot of blood on the moon last night. But I can see blood on the polished floor of this Capitol. For if you ride this thing through, you will travel with the white horse of death. White men have ever made poor slaves."

At one point, Huey had his attorney general, Porterie, actually conduct a hearing into a reported "murder plot" that had been hatched against him after the Square Deal "Battle of the Airport." And in a political speech at Meridian, Mississippi (home of the *American Progress),* Theodore Bilbo ridiculed the talk: "Huey's been talking about murder plots. He says they haven't had much luck. But I'll tell you how he can be put out of the way. Let him come into Mississippi to make speeches, disarm his bodyguards, and that coward will run himself to death trying to get back out of the state." But in Baton Rouge there was talk of a mob storming the capitol when Huey got there, of an uprising by the old Square Dealers. No chances were taken. Extra state troopers were alerted for the opening of the special session, Sunday, September 8. Huey would appear as scheduled, with his friends and bodyguards, but visitors, for the first time, were to be moved to an upper balcony. In addition, two of the three doors leading to the House were to be closed and guarded, and only legislators and witnesses were to be allowed on the floor.

The Legislature convened at ten Sunday morning. Huey,

dressed in a white suit and black and white shoes, appeared grinning, waving a hand, shaking hands and laughing with friendly legislators. Greetings over, he walked to the meeting of the ways and means committee to present his proposals for the day. He was interested chiefly in an act designed to regulate the spending of federal patronage money in Louisiana. There was only faint opposition. One legislator asked if the act would keep needed federal money out of the state, but Huey brushed the question aside by declaring that the bill was designed to "carry out the principles of the United States Constitution." Roosevelt and Ickes might have federal money to spend in Louisiana, but they would have to spend it through Huey or not at all.

That bill and routine business took up the morning. The committee recessed for the afternoon, ready to return for a full session at eight that night. Huey went to his private suite on the twenty-fourth floor for meetings and telephoning. The afternoon passed uneventfully.

In another part of the city a young man whose name would have been foreign to most Louisianians spent a quiet Sunday with his family—church in the morning, lunch and swimming in the afternoon, the ride home in early evening. He was thin, aesthetic, bespectacled Dr. Carl Austin Weiss, thirty, an ear, eye, nose and throat specialist with an impressive background and a promising future. He had graduated from the Tulane School of Medicine, had done postgraduate work in Vienna, was regarded as an able and sensitive physician who had not become hardened to personal suffering. Normally, as a professional scientist, he would have had little truck with politics or politicians. But there was one compelling factor that put Dr. Weiss in a separate category.

He had married the daughter of Judge Pavy, the same judge who, after thirty years on the bench, was about to find his district gerrymandered out from under him. Judge Pavy had been one of the last of the anti-Huey jurists, and Huey had vowed to remove him. Already another hostile judge, this one from Baton Rouge, had been removed from the Legislature, and Judge Pavy was next on the schedule. Even worse, Huey had threatened to take to the radio to tell what he allegedly knew about "nigger blood" in the Pavy family. For young Dr. Weiss, it was a time of brooding, of deep personal conflict. That evening, back from the day's outing with his family, Weiss told his wife he had a sick call. Shortly before nine, he left his home and rode to the capitol.

The night session, which had convened promptly at eight, took up Huey's federal patronage bill, passed it, heard routine matters and, by nine-thirty, adjourned. It had been a speedy, unimpeded session—one or two questions, the introduction of the bills, the roll call, the gavel. Visitors watched the proceedings from the upper balcony. State police stood guard, along with the sergeant at arms, at the lone open door to the House floor. Huey's bodyguards waited for him to emerge.

Out he came, striding briskly, his entourage a step behind him. In the group were John Fournet, now risen to chief justice of the Louisiana Supreme Court; James O'Connor of the Public Service Commission; Gerald L. K. Smith, the Share Our Wealth organizer; a legislator or two; and, flanking Huey, the bodyguards. He kept them trotting behind him as his black and white shoes tapped along the polished marble corridor.

At the door to Governor Allen's office, Huey started in, changed his mind, stepped out again and issued a businesslike, final command: "Tell everybody to be here in the morning." Another session was scheduled and Huey wanted everybody on time. He turned to pass through the door again.

From behind a pillar near the door, straw hat in hand, stepped Dr. Weiss. He took a few cautious steps toward the Kingfish, stopped momentarily, put out his hand as a prelude to speaking, then pulled the hand back and under his coat. Out came a revolver, which he pushed close to the dictator's side. The gun barked once. Huey, a pained but surprised look on his face, stumbled back toward Fournet, reaching for his side. "I've been shot," he gasped.

The sound of the shot still reverberated through the corridor when bodyguard Murphy Rhoden leaped forward, an arm outstretched. Weiss pulled the trigger again, but this time there was only Rhoden's sharp cry—the trigger had caught the webbing between his thumb and forefinger. Pulling loose, he jerked out his gun and fired once. Weiss slumped to the floor, the gun dropping from his outstretched hand.

Rhoden's shot galvanized the other bodyguards. Unlimbering their weapons in a blazing staccato, they poured bullets into the form on the floor. A later examination showed that sixty-one bullets had entered the body—thirty in front, twenty-nine in back, two in the head.

Even before the shooting ended, the Kingfish was hospital-bound. While the bullets were ripping into Weiss, Huey sagged first toward Fournet, then into O'Connor's arms. With O'Connor supporting him, Huey limped down a stairway to O'Connor's parked car, then sat, breathing heavily, while O'Connor drove him the few blocks to Our Lady of the Lake Sanitarium. As they drove up to the hospital entrance Huey, his hand pressed to his side, asked softly, "I wonder why he shot me?"

Huey had appointed Dr. Arthur Vidrine to head the New Orleans Charity Hospital five years before. Now, visiting in Baton Rouge, Dr. Vidrine was at hand to care for the Kingfish.

A quick examination showed that the wound was serious, but not critical. Surgery would be required. A call went out for two New Orleans doctors, reputed to be among the best surgeons in the state. They tried to charter an airplane, found none available, then set out by automobile. En route over Huey's Air-Line Highway, they met with an accident. It was too late to call other specialists. At 12:30 Monday morning, September 9, Huey underwent surgery.

The bullets had ripped into his side, torn through three intestinal loops, grazed a kidney. Surgery was needed to remove the bullet and to stop the hemorrhaging. Dr. Vidrine announced that Huey's condition was satisfactory, but that it was too early to determine his real condition. Huey went into an oxygen tent.

As he hovered between life and death, thousands descended on Baton Rouge from across Louisiana. From the north streamed the same hill folk and farmers who had come to watch Huey's inauguration seven years earlier. In the city state police reinforcements were called out to reroute traffic, mount road blocks, keep motorists and pedestrians away from the hospital area. Governor Allen ordered a Baton Rouge contingent of national guardsmen placed on alert. Meanwhile, on Monday, with Huey still fighting for his life, Dr. Weiss was buried in a closed-coffin ceremony attended by hundreds. The Archbishop of New Orleans, agreeing that only a temporary mental derangement would have permitted Catholic Dr. Weiss to commit murder, sanctioned a Catholic burial.

By mid-Monday, the drama inside the hospital edged toward a climax. A worried hospital official announced that Huey was not responding. Most of the time, the Senator was delirious. Shortly before midnight, as Louisiana waited, came another bulletin: "Senator Long is dying." Huey's family—Rose, the children, Earl, Julius, the sisters—arrived for the death watch, as did Governor Allen, Seymour Weiss, others close to Huey. At 4:10 on the morning of September 10—thirty hours after the shooting—the Kingfish died. According to Earl, Huey's last thoughts were with his LSU students. His last words, said Earl, were: "What'll happen to my poor boys and girls?"

Dressed in a tuxedo, his stormy features at last immobile, the country boy who had become a king lay in a great bronze casket in the capitol he had built. For two days thousands streamed past his bier; men wept, women fainted; troops stood guard. State police shuffled the throngs into orderly lines for a final walk past the coffin. Telegrams, messages of condolence, flowers by the truckload, poured into Baton Rouge. They came not only from Louisiana, but from every section of the country.

On Thursday, September 12, while drums rolled and bands played, the Kingfish was buried in the landscaped capitol grounds, a stone's throw from the skyscraper itself.

Gerald L. K. Smith, whom Brother Julius had dubbed "Gerald Lucifer Kodfish Smith," delivered the principal eulogy:

"He fell in the line of duty. He died for us. This tragedy fires the breast of every comrade. This untimely death makes restless the souls of us who adored him. Oh, God, why did we have to lose him . . . he has been the wounded victim of the green goddess; to use the figure, he was the Stradivarius whose notes rose in competition with jealous drums, envious tom-toms. He was the unfinished symphony." Smith ended the oration by reciting the whole of "Invictus."

Both houses of the Louisiana Legislature, in passing the resolution that authorized burial on the capitol grounds, called him a "statesman of national and international caliber as well as the political genius of the country," and deplored "the sad and tragic passing of our leader and friend whom we so profoundly loved and respected."

They built a great bronze statue of the Kingfish and placed

it over his grave, inscribing on it some of the words that had made him famous in the Senate:

> I know the hearts of the people because I have not colored my own. I know when I am right in my own conscience. I have one language. Its simplicity gains pardon for my lack of letters. Fear will not change it. Persecution will not change it. It cannot be changed while people suffer.

On the monument, the state inscribed a simple message:

> Here lies Louisiana's great son Huey Pierce Long, an unconquered friend of the poor who dreamed of the day when the wealth of the land would be spread among all the people.

All too soon, indeed, Huey's political heirs were busily sharing the wealth—not among all the people, but among themselves.

PART 2:

Death and Rebirth

8

The Heirs

THE Kingfish left no heir apparent. While he lived, Huey had been the undisputed master, the "Emperor of Louisiana," as Harold Ickes had snidely, but accurately, dubbed him. Now the Kingfish was dead, while the term of his prime minister and Longism's titular head—Governor Oscar K. Allen—was drawing to a close. By law, Oscar could not succeed himself. With Long dead, Longism needed a leader.

There was no doubt, in that fall of 1935, that there was political mileage aplenty in the magic name of the dead dictator. A crushing political force in life, Huey in death became a martyr and a saint. The tears shed by the thousands who attended his funeral, the eulogies in the Legislature, the letters to newspapers from all sections of the state—all these attested to the potency of the Kingfish's memory. None of these reactions escaped the notice of Louisiana's would-be kings and kingmakers. Indeed, the Kingfish's sainthood was there for anybody with eyes to see. For years after his death, notices like the following appeared in the classified columns of metropolitan newspapers: *Thanks to Huey P. Long for answers to my prayers.*

In the wake of the Kingfish's death, his heirs seized upon the magic of his memory to install themselves in the state's choicest offices, then to embark on a program of plunder so vast that Louisiana probably will never see its equal. The official thievery —effected at times with outrageous ease—went undetected for four years, while the heirs stuffed themselves at the public treasure trough. Men who had quaked when Huey had walked into a room became oil tycoons, securities manipulators, country gentlemen living in baronial splendor, possessors of elaborate hunting retreats and mansions with bathroom fixtures of gold. In the end, most of them—including the governor-successor to Huey's mantle—were found out, dishonored, convicted and sentenced to jail terms. In a moment of rare lucidity, Huey, casting an eye about him, had remarked casually, "If those fellows ever try to use the powers I've given them without me to hold them down, they'll all land in the penitentiary." Unwittingly, the heirs were to make their political patriarch a prophet.

But before they could divide up the state, they had to take official title to it. If an heir apparent was lacking, one had to be created. The question was: Who would be the new Kingfish? Before the echoes of the eulogies had died away, the ranks of the Kingfish's closest followers were riddled with dissension.

On one side stood the Share Our Wealth men: Gerald L. K. Smith, the preacher-orator; Earle Christenberry, Huey's secretary and the man who directed the SOW Washington organization; and James A. Noe, an oilman risen high in Huey's favor. He had been president pro tempore of the state Senate when John Fournet vacated his lieutenant governor's post to ascend to the Supreme Court. When that happened, Noe became lieutenant governor, a man close to the seat of power.

Although this group was regarded by the others as a Johnny-come-lately addition to the Huey clique, it possessed some formidable assets. Smith had been closely identified in the public mind with the Kingfish and had stood in the limelight at Huey's funeral. Moreover, he had continued to stay in the limelight with repeated assaults on the federal administration by hinting darkly that the Kingfish's assassination had been a political plot. By speech and by wire, he assailed Washington for its failure to help in "bringing to justice the perpetrators of the assassination of Senator Long." In the cases of Christenberry and Noe, their relations with the deceased Huey were as obvious and as formidable. One, as secretary to the Kingfish, knew all the master's secrets; the other could not have risen to his official position without Huey's complete endorsement.

On the other side were the hard party professionals, the money men and the organizers who had gone down the line with Huey from the earliest days. These were men of a practical bent who had frankly recognized SOW as a purely political vehicle, who had been content to espouse it as long as Huey reaped political capital from it. With Huey gone, the need for appearances was gone too. Who would believe that these men—for the most part men of means—would seriously insist on a program designed to deplete their own fortunes?

Heading the list was Robert S. Maestri of New Orleans, a wealthy real estate man, who had come to Huey's defense during the dark days of impeachment, who had been rewarded with the chairmanship of the State Conservation Commission, and who had become the single most powerful figure within Huey's inner circle.

Behind Maestri stood Seymour Weiss, the Alexandria shoe clerk turned Roosevelt Hotel director, the machine's treasurer and loyal fund raiser, the man who had pointedly reminded the United States Senate investigating subcommittee to mind its own business; Abe Shushan, the New Orleans money-raiser-lender, president of the Orleans Levee Board; Jules Fisher, a Long leader in the state Senate, signer of the famous "Round Robin," a man who had grown wealthy in the shrimp business and as political boss of Jefferson Parish, Louisiana's gambling mecca.

In addition, there were John Fournet, one of the Kingfish's staunchest early supporters; O. K. Allen, Huey's governor; Allen Ellender, speaker of the House and one of Huey's chief impeachment defenders; Wade O. Martin, Sr., chairman of Huey's Public Service Commission; and, in something of a dark horse's position, Brother Earl, who had come to a meeting of minds with Huey before the assassination. Huey had jokingly remarked, following the brotherly *rapprochement,* that Earl was "on probation." Nevertheless, Huey had taken him back into the official family by giving him the job of attorney to the Kingfish's State Tax Commission.

For a week following the assassination, the question of succession hung in the air as the talk centered, instead, on the passing of the leader. Fantastic rumors swept the state: that Huey's assassination had been known beforehand in Washington's ruling circles; that his political enemies had decided on Huey's elimination, had drawn straws, with the short one going to Dr. Weiss; that his bodyguards had deliberately or inadvertently fired the fatal bullet. The Kingfish's legislative allies promised to spend $100,000 investigating the murder. There were hints, particularly from Gerald Smith, that the probe would result in spectacular disclosures. Then the spotlight shifted.

At four one morning the press was hurriedly summoned to a Baton Rouge hotel where copies of the "Long ticket" were distributed. Noe would run for governor, Wade Martin for United States Senator. Gerald Smith would become Martin's secretary in Washington and continue the SOW program.

The ticket appalled the rival group. For one thing, it left out Earl Long, who had already indicated that he wanted the governor's job. Maestri, knowing that a Long name on the ticket would only help, and being an old Huey and Earl friend, supported Earl's contention.

More importantly, however, the practical politicians among the heirs looked on the SOW clique as little more than daydreamers, men who thought they could ride to power simply by proclaiming their intentions to carry on Huey's SOW scheme. The Maestri-Weiss faction knew better. In addition to Huey's good name, the job of electing top officials would require organization and money.

There was still another reason. Weiss, Shushan and Jules Fisher were under indictment by the federal government for income tax evasion. As long as Huey stood between them and the federals, they had one measure of protection. With Huey gone, that protection was gone, too. The more prudent course, now, would be to negotiate a peace with the Washington administration in the hope that the indictments could be dropped or delayed. With Smith attacking Washington at every turn, the chances of negotiating peace were deliberately threatened.

No sooner had the Noe-Martin ticket been announced than the Maestri faction rolled into action. Maestri drove from New Orleans to Baton Rouge for a war conference. He was followed by Weiss. Earl Long appeared to take his part. The Noe-Martin delegation appeared. The doors were locked, the cigars lit, the negotiations began.

Hours later, when the doors opened and the smoke cleared, two changes had taken place. The Noe-Martin ticket was withdrawn. In its stead, the heirs produced a new "Long ticket"—a compromise slate that all parties solemnly agreed contained the names that Huey himself had selected for office before his untimely passing.

For governor, the now-united group popped out a strange name: Richard Webster Leche, former secretary to Governor Allen, now a district judge, and a fervent Huey supporter. Up to this point, Leche had been lightly regarded as a good member of the second string, not one of the top-flight inner circle by any means, but a handy man to have around. He had two distinct advantages. He had the least number of real enemies; and, being a second-stringer without unseemly delusions, he was not likely to become a runaway candidate, one trying to become a Kingfish in his own right. Now he had the biggest advantage of all. He had the united support of Huey's heirs, all of whom stoutly affirmed that he was the man Huey had selected to succeed Oscar. Said Allen, "Fortunately, there was no doubt in the mind of Senator Long as to who his candidate for governor would be." Into the number two spot as candidate for lieutenant governor went Earl Long, who grudgingly confirmed that Leche had, indeed, been Huey's choice. Later, Earl was to cry despairingly that he had fought the Leche selection, only to find himself overpowered by the other heirs.

Dick Leche and Earl Long appeared on the ballot, but it was Huey who did the campaigning. Touring the state, the Leche-Long ticket played recordings of Huey's old speeches, tacked his portrait to telephone poles and speaking platforms, pleaded that only by electing them could the people hope to continue the "general program of Huey P. Long."

There were some embarrassing moments. The opposition candidate for governor, Congressman Cleveland Dear, derided Maestri as the "king of the tenderloin," implying that Maestri headed realty firms that collected rents from New Orleans' red-light district. In the beginning, Noe, not content to lose the governorship to Leche, had declared that Gerald Smith had promised to support him, then had double-crossed him by going over to the Leche camp. Noe's voice was soon drowned out by Huey's recordings, but he never completely forgave. Later, Huey's heirs were to discover just how warmly Noe nursed his grudge; Jimmy was to play one of the leading roles in exposing corruption in high places.

Then there was Earl. Although he loudly and persistently

proclaimed his devotion to Huey and his memory, the rednecks who had idolized the Kingfish never quite swallowed his abrupt and complete about-face. In places, Earl was heckled when he evoked the name of his dead brother.

"If you loved Huey," he shouted at one meeting, "you should love Bob Maestri."

"Did you love Huey?" a voice in the crowd asked.

"Well," said Earl, "I didn't agree with everything he said."

"We did," came the rejoinder.

The Kingfish's memory was too much for ordinary mortals like Candidate Dear to overcome. The people swept Huey's self-styled heirs into office by crushing margins. In as governor went Leche, with an overwhelming 67 per cent of the vote, while Earl, winning easily, got 12,000 fewer votes than Leche, a slap from voters who remembered his earlier opposition to the Kingfish.

Into the United States Senate, to complete the short term vacated by Huey, went Governor Allen, by almost 69 per cent of the vote. Named to a full term in the Senate, with a comfortable 68 per cent of the vote, was Huey's state House leader, Allen Ellender. Nowhere could the anti-Longs dent the drawing power of the dead Kingfish, as pro-Longs gobbled up most of the legislative seats, all of the disputed Congressional seats, an open seat on the state Supreme Court and a vacancy on the Public Service Commission. In death, Huey had routed his opponents more completely than he ever had in life.

Suddenly one of those unforeseen quirks, so typical of Louisiana politics, threatened to undermine all that Huey's heirs had won in the elections. Following the election, but before he could take his new, short-term U. S. Senate seat, O. K. Allen, Huey's rubber-stamp governor, died suddenly. Noe, who had gracelessly withdrawn his own gubernatorial candidacy in the face of the Maestri-Leche faction, was now governor.

At first it appeared that Noe might utilize the remaining few months of the late Allen's term to solidify his own political future. He proclaimed himself as the real leader of Huey's SOW heirs, then prevailed upon the Democratic State Central Committee to appoint Huey's widow to serve out the unexpired Senate term, thus showing that he had only the Kingfish's warmest interests at heart. For a time, Maestri-Leche-Weiss & Co.

held their breaths. But Noe's good fortune had come too late to do him much good. He served out Allen's term uneventfully.

Suddenly the seven-year storm was over. Huey had roiled the state, shaking it to its foundations. He had been against the New Orleans Ring, against the early Legislature, against big business, against the federal administration, against some of the Congressional incumbents. Now the sun broke through, beaming brightly, bathing Louisiana in the clear light of peace and promised prosperity. There was no more turmoil or tension. The heirs had come into their inheritance.

To Washington went Congressman Paul Maloney to negotiate a peace treaty with the United States Government. Louisiana offered repeal of the anti-federal state statutes pushed through the Legislature by Huey, twenty Roosevelt votes at the next Democratic National Convention, general and sympathetic support of the Roosevelt administration and its policies. In return, Louisiana wanted federal money—PWA, WPA, relief funds—and, most importantly, an end to the income tax harassment. Some of the heirs were already under indictment. They little relished the idea of prison terms, especially now that new opportunities beckoned to them.

While Washington considered the offer, the government made its big push. It pressed the trial of Abe Shushan, charged with failing to report $500,000 in income. The trial record swelled with evidences of shakedowns, kickbacks, illegal operations on the part of companies doing business with the Orleans Levee Board, which Shushan, with Huey's blessing, headed.

Huey's old law partner, Hugh Wilkinson, saved the day by employing logic as brazen as it was unique. If the government was right, contended Wilkinson, Abe got his money via extortion. Therefore, the money was illegally received—not income at all. If it was not income, certainly there were no taxes to pay on it. Shushan was acquitted to the courtroom cheers of the "payroll squad," and the government prosecutor, Rene Viosca, announced that the remaining indictments against Huey's heirs would be dropped. Said Viosca in effect: Since Shushan's was the best case the federal government had compiled, and since the government had failed to convict, it was little use pressing the matter. Nine of the twenty-three U. S. Grand Jury members who had indicted Huey's heirs filed a protest, declaring the government was derelict in not pressing the other cases. In Washington, where the peace treaty had by now been ratified, Attorney General Homer Cummings came to the defense of Prosecutor Viosca, affirmed his confidence in him, called the dismissals "routine."

The mutual assistance pact (or nonaggression pact) of Washington and Baton Rouge soon burst into full bloom.

In the regular session of the 1936 Legislature—the first under Leche—the old Huey laws that gave the state regulation of federal spending in Louisiana were repealed with only minimum opposition. In June the Louisiana Legislature recessed, convened in Texas as a body, and there cheered in unison when President Roosevelt delivered an address commemorating the Texas Centennial. (It was a unique gesture, the first time a legislature from one state had convened in another.) Roosevelt responded by appointing a Leche nominee as collector of customs at the busy Port of New Orleans.

In June, also, the Louisiana delegation to the Democratic National Convention got the honor of seconding Roosevelt's nomination for a second term. Casting its twenty votes for the President, the delegation then fought vigorously—and successfully—for the elimination of the two-thirds rule, by which it would have been possible for a bloc of southern states to impede Roosevelt's renomination. The man who headed the delegation was Seymour Weiss, now breathing more easily as a result of the government's enlightened action toward his income tax indictment.

By the fall of 1936 federal money, so hard to come by under Huey, poured into Louisiana, to be spent on roads and free bridges, for widespread construction at LSU, to enlarge the New Orleans Charity Hospital into one of the finest medical centers in the South. FDR visited New Orleans, where he rode in an open car with Maestri and Leche. Postmaster General Jim Farley, the target of Huey's unrelenting abuse, was welcomed to Louisiana as the chief commencement day speaker at LSU. Leche announced he was four-square behind Roosevelt's famous "court packing" plan, explaining, to the bewilderment of some, that to oppose it would be to quit the ball game "with the winning run on third base." As explanations went in those days, it was good enough.

At the state level the machine hummed along smoothly. Huey's oppressive laws against New Orleans were still on the books. Leche's Legislature repealed them, but for a price. In mid-1936 New Orleans Mayor T. Semmes Walmsley suddenly resigned, then backed Maestri for election without opposition. The heirs took title to New Orleans. But Maestri, a behind-the-scenes power, was hardly the man to stand before an audience to explain a platform. His unique handling of the king's English was legendary. One story had it that during Roosevelt's visit Maestri's sole contribution to the conversation had been to ask the President at the end of an official luncheon, "How do you like them ersters?" Obviously, it would not do to have Maestri run for re-election in 1938.

Dick's Legislature took care of this troublesome detail. By law, they "postponed indefinitely" (that is, eliminated) the 1938 mayoralty election. Bob now had clear title to the office for six long years.

Leche kept most of Huey's powers. But some of the more overt manifestations of dictatorship were eliminated—the Criminal Investigation Bureau (Huey's Cossacks) for example. And the theme now was peace, not war. The occupational license tax set on Standard, a measure that had once almost killed Huey politically, was cut from five cents to one cent. Although Allen, under Huey, had never collected the five cents and had settled for the penny, the one-cent tax now became law.

A legislative act made Huey's birthday a legal holiday at Leche's insistence. A perpetual light, located in the tower of Huey's capitol, bathed his statue at night. Leche reaffirmed his belief in some of Huey's principles: free textbooks, the homestead exemptions (indeed, these were increased), the "debt moratorium" statute by which farmers could arrange for easy loan payments. In addition, the Leche administration issued another thirty-five million dollars in road construction bonds to continue Huey's program.

In other areas, however, Leche and his backers quietly repudiated some of the inheritance. The "roving attorney" license, by which Huey had collected fees from the State Tax Commission, had been passed to his law partner, Wilkinson. Leche did away with it. Huey had kept city police and fire departments under his thumb. Leche gave them more authority, insurance against summary state interference. Dick set out to woo busi ness, to let the vested interests know that the old feud between Huey and Louisiana's big commerce was at an end. Grateful businessmen, free of state harassment, gave him a $13,000 40-foot yacht as a token of their appreciation.

Huey had regarded a sales tax as a "disaster." Leche had the Legislature pass a 2 per cent "luxury tax," in all respects a sales tax except in name. Later, the Legislature slashed it in half and called it what it was, a sales tax.

The Legislature was easy to manipulate in those days. In the 1938 session, Leche's floor leader, assured that an amendment to the existing sales tax had Leche's blessing, introduced the amendment. It was promptly passed, 24–9. Next day the Senate discovered that Leche actually opposed the amendment. Back it went to the Senate. This time it was defeated, 35–2. There was, perhaps, a reason for the ease with which Leche, like Huey, handled the lawmakers. Later, much later, when the Scandals burst and a reform administration took over, the books of the Debt Moratorium Commission were opened. They showed that between 1936 and 1940, thirty-seven legislators drew nearly $300,000 in salaries and fees from the commission. Thirteen of the twenty-eight New Orleans legislators, later examination showed, drew salaries from the city.

Leche himself became a man of commerce. Taking over the dormant *American Progress,* he quickly converted it into one of the most solvent publications of its kind in America. Huey had used the *Progress* as a purely political organ. Leche used it for political purposes, too. But now its chief function was the making of money. It developed into a fat, obviously profitable journal, crammed with advertisements, mainly from contractors doing state business. Most of the ads were glowing endorsements of Leche's policies and of his administration. Later Dick was to tell under oath just how profitable the *Progress* really had been for him. In the three years he operated it, he had made $185,500. He had paid $38,000 for it, had collected $36,000 in "dividends," then had sold his stocks for $187,500. It was a publication at which more hard-pressed publishers could only marvel.

The term "dee-duct" became an everyday expression in Louisiana. Under this system, state employees found that they had automatically taken a *Progress* subscription when they took their jobs. To pay for the subscription, $2.00 was deducted from their pay checks as a routine matter. In New Orleans, the *Times-Picayune* revealed that Charity Hospital employees were victims of the "dee-ducts." Questioned, the hospital auditor grumbled that it was a "mistake." But the employees soon found that, in addition to their own subscriptions, they were expected to sell or pay for five others. Sometimes they were asked to sell more, depending on the jobs they held. Leche purchased a 250-acre retreat in Tammany Parish, admitted blandly that during his first year as governor he had grossed $90,000 in income. Asked by newspaper reporters how he could gross $90,000 on his state salary of $7,500, he replied somewhat testily, "When I took the oath as governor, I didn't take any vows of poverty."

Governor Dick's star seemed to be always in the ascendancy. By mid-1938 he and the other heirs had succeeded in re-electing all the incumbent pro-Long congressmen. U. S. Senator Overton, whom Huey had put in office in 1932, was re-elected without opposition.

Dick became a jovial, smiling figure of growing national importance. Two new federal judgeships were created in South Louisiana. Immediately, old rumors—that Dick would take a federal bench job and let Huey's brother Earl have the governorship—began to fly again. Dick fended off queries about his plans with an easy smile and a noncommittal answer. Meanwhile, with the double blessing of the machine and the allies in Washington, the other federal judge was named to the hearty acclaim of all: Gaston Porterie, Huey's ex-attorney general.

Dick took frequent trips to Washington where he conferred with the junior Senator from Louisiana, Allen Ellender. He appeared before a House committee hearing evidence on the uses of WPA money to declare that Louisiana was a "model" of efficiency in that respect. He let it be known early that he had no doubts about who should be President in 1940—Roosevelt, third term or no third term. Suddenly, the talk about a federal judgeship was forgotten and new tales reached Louisiana. Dick was being considered as a running mate for Roosevelt in 1940. "Dick for Vice-President," went the talk in the right circles. Dick, as usual, refused hard comment. He had a state to run, he told inquiring reporters.

But the state appeared to be running itself most of the time. Governor Leche spent more and more of his time in his luxurious retreat on the St. Tammany "Gold Coast," conducting the more routine business by long-distance telephone. Soon he had neighbors. Abe Shushan built a colonial mansion within easy reach of Dick's. Big George Caldwell, recently named as the full-time construction superintendent at LSU—the first in the school's history—built another. Guests to George's house admired the wide verandas, the meticulously landscaped gardens, the huge rumpus room. But it was George's bathroom that became the conversation piece, what with its black marble, wide mirrors and—best touch of all—gold toilet and bath fixtures. Others of the growing political hierarchy planned or began homes in the suddenly exclusive section.

The stream of federal dollars, now reaching the $51,000,000 mark, flowed into every corner of the state. And under a flood of federal largesse, LSU expanded impressively. Thirty new buildings went up under Leche's regime, including Leche Hall, a replica of the United States Supreme Court building. WPA workmen dug a lake for student canoeing. LSU bought a new mascot, Mike the Tiger, then added a $12,000 "personal cage," air-conditioned, steam-heated, manned by a student attendant. Huey had always liked the football team. Now two airplanes were purchased to hunt football talent. Off season, the planes were handy for quick excursions by men high in public life. LSU became a social magnet, as well as a center of learning, and the elite of Baton Rouge and Louisiana society suddenly found themselves gravitating toward the delightfully lavish parties of President James Monroe Smith and his wife, Thelma.

Smith had never really aspired to social distinction because Huey had discouraged that sort of aspiration. Elevated by Huey from country educator to preside over a university that Huey regarded as his personal property, Smith knew his place and kept it. At any moment Huey might order Smith to the executive mansion for a discussion. Arriving, Smith would discover that the Kingfish merely had in mind a new color scheme for a building or a suggestion on how to improve the school band.

But sometimes the Kingfish could be downright rude. At one of the earlier parties Thelma had hung a replica of the moon from the ceiling of the Smith home. It swung like a pendulum across the crowded room, delighting the assembled guests. Huey, dropping in unexpectedly, glanced at the tuxedos, fine gowns and especially the moon, then bawled poor old Jim out right in front of the guests. His final words: "Get rid of that goddamned moon." On another occasion Thelma opened a riding stable at LSU, only to have the idea backfire. A student was killed while riding a horse. Huey, speaking in North Louisiana, wired angrily: SELL THEM PLUGS. The horses went. "The Doc," as Smith became known, endured the little humiliations and bided his time. It came after Huey's death, when the heirs took over. Before long, the Doc knew he too had come into his inheritance.

He began in a small way—a kickback on a bid for some building fixtures, a few hundred dollars under the table from a friendly architect or subcontractor, a dip into the university's food lockers. Doc lived in an LSU house and helped himself to LSU services. Once, when a clerk billed him for food taken from the cafeteria, Smith fired the clerk.

Doc soon found that he could get away with practically anything. He hiked his own salary by $3,000, forging the minutes of the Board of Supervisors' meeting to do it. He took out a substantial life insurance policy and regularly billed LSU for the premiums. Daughter Marjorie was sent to Mexico on a "study tour." LSU paid the $1,000 bill.

Smith graduated to a bigger league almost before he knew it. The board hired Caldwell as construction superintendent, giving him a one per cent fee on all building at the school. Doc altered the board's minutes and doubled George's rake-off to two per cent. While he was at it, he gave Caldwell and Business Manager E. N. Jackson unauthorized pay raises.

Kickbacks became common, bids nonexistent. State law called for all expenditures in excess of $1,000 to be awarded by competitive bids. Doc let them out to favorites without bids. A $75,000 building went up after Doc simply picked up the telephone and called a favored builder. LSU's cafeterias bought food at retail rather than wholesale prices. Architects submitted estimated costs that multiplied mysteriously when the final bills came in. One building, approved at an estimated price of $101,000, cost a tidy $202,000 in the final tally. Superintendent Caldwell, it turned out later, once put up a building that no one had ordered or approved. Doc, after hesitating, blandly assured inquiring newsmen that it was the university's new "school of aeronautics." Caldwell got his 2 per cent. Again, the state's architect was paid $24,000 in connection with the construction of one building. Several years later, he was paid another $24,000 for the same job. There were extraordinary ramifications to Doc's system, but basically the story was essentially the same in every instance. Doc and others were stealing LSU blind. Either no one noticed, or no one cared.

Doc Smith decided to branch out. He bought nearly 1,000 cases of bourbon in hopes that the whiskey, if allowed to mellow, could be sold at a neat profit. The whiskey failed to mellow and Doc lost money. So he needed to recoup. It was not for nothing that Doc, errand boy though he might have been, had been selected to head a university. He had studied economics, had taken a degree at Columbia. He knew a world crisis when he saw one, and there was no doubt that one was developing between Germany and England in late 1937. War looked like a sure thing. Doc decided it was time to act. He leaped into the commodities market, specifically into wheat. If war came, he reasoned, his market would soar. But heavy capital would be required for a killing of any real size, and Doc lacked the hard cash. Almost by habit, he turned to LSU and there, as always, he found the answer.

Soon he appeared before New Orleans broker J. M. Brown. Assured, poised, confident, the Doc talked of economics, of the worsening crisis. Then he turned to wheat futures, the opportunities there, and the "syndicate" he represented. The broker was impressed, not only by the logic but by Doc, too. The broker knew that Doc was more than just a mere university president. He was "one of the boys," an insider, one of the heirs. As he explained later, "I could hardly restrain myself from asking him to take me into the group." And Doc took the plunge. He ordered the broker to buy up all the wheat in sight, two million bushels. The money, he said airily, would be along shortly. Meantime, Doc sent $300,000 in LSU bonds as collateral.

But Hitler and Chamberlain dealt Doc a dirty blow. They negotiated peace, not war. The bottom dropped out of the wheat market and Doc found himself in a hole, desperately trying to recoup. He decided to double his bet. Taking a $1,000 LSU bond to a Baton Rouge print shop, he ordered, "Print me up three hundred of these as fast as you can." Back to the broker he took the new batch, but this time the broker was wary. There had been no legal opinion accompanying the first batch, he had discovered, and without a legal opinion from the State Tax and Bond Commission, the bonds might not be good. Doc brushed the complaint aside. He went to a New Orleans bank, brazenly told the banker he had been authorized by the board to borrow $300,000, got the money and left. The next day, the broker had a $300,000 cashier's check and Doc had his bonds back. Returning to Baton Rouge, he found that news of his financial activity had preceded him. A Baton Rouge banker, a friend of long standing, called to reproach him gently for not giving some of LSU's business to the home-town bank. "You're right," said Doc contritely, "I haven't been fair. I'll take $100,000 from you." With time and an even break in the market, Doc might have covered up long enough to recoup or to borrow enough to replace the shortage. But two incidents conspired against him.

In New Orleans, Rufus Fontenot, district director of the Internal Revenue Service, got wind of Doc's plunging. Convinced that this was the opportunity he had been waiting for, Fontenot went to Washington to plead for a full-scale investigation of Doc's finances. Soon special intelligence agents were roaming the state, poking into Doc's finances. Three weeks later, Washington got the report: Doc was in trouble up to his neck; the investigation should be pressed, even broadened. Washington gave a green light.

In Monroe, Jimmy Noe, bitter at being forced to take a back seat while the self-appointed heirs ruled Louisiana, received a tip that LSU workmen were hauling school materials to a friend of the administration in New Orleans. Noe alerted the New Orleans *State,* which exposed the transaction. Tongues began to wag.

As such matters went, the exposé was a small item. Noe had been calling attention to alleged irregularities for months. He had amassed a fearsome set of documents to back up his charges —980 of them. They became known as "Noe's 980." The LSU incident at first seemed like just another of the pesky charges. No one paid much attention to Noe or his "980." But this time the atmosphere was different. A federal investigation was under way. Leche began to hear reports about Doc Smith. The small, irritating charges were heard more frequently. Something had to be done, for show if for no other reason. Leche startled everybody by ordering a general investigation of all government departments. To make sure it went right, he added, he would conduct the investigation personally. All over the state eyebrows were raised. This was something new—an investigation. A few days later, the eyebrows lowered again. Leche announced that, after looking into the LSU building materials incident, he was convinced that no one had erred. Investigation finished. The governor, however, had a postscript to the announcement. Calling reporters to the mansion, where he lay propped up in bed, Leche announced almost casually that he would resign the following week. Ill health, he explained.

The announcement threw Louisiana into mild consternation. A governor had never resigned before. What would the procedure be? Dick laughed easily. He didn't know, he said, except that he had made up his mind to leave. "I'll do anything short of dying," he joked. "If they don't find a way out for me . . . I'll just walk out."

Four days later, on June 25, 1939, the carefree kingdom of the heirs began to topple. Leche summoned the press to the mansion once again, this time to say that he had ordered the arrest of Doc Smith for "possible irregularities" in financial matters at LSU. Police were even now on the way to Doc's house to make the arrest, he added. Pressed, Leche bared the whole story. The Doc, obviously agitated, had called him for an appointment "this very day." When he arrived, he had told Leche all—that he had taken $200,000 of LSU's money. (Later, he admitted it was closer to $400,000.) Doc wondered, said Leche, if the board would approve the "loan" retroactively. Leche had called in Attorney General Allison and Supreme Court Chief Justice Fournet, who was a member of LSU's board. They turned the idea down. Leche told Doc, "Well, Doc, do you want it the hard way or the easy way? I think you ought to resign and let the board look into it." Doc refused to sign a confession but did sign a resignation dictated by Leche. That was when Leche called in reporters and Doc returned to his home.

But police who arrived at the Smith home found the place a shambles. The Doc and Thelma had wasted no time in getting away, leaving behind Thelma's expensive silver, her custom-made gowns—everything but clothes, jewelry and cash. Gone, the police discovered, were Smith, Thelma, and Thelma's nephew, J. Emory Adams. Doc suddenly became a hunted man.

Baton Rouge police, state troopers, the FBI, joined in the manhunt, but Doc and Thelma had vanished. The search became a national *cause célèbre*. In California, a Louisiana official on vacation was detained by police who noted his low license number. Reports came in from all over the country about a couple answering the Smiths' description. Adams returned in two days to reveal that he had driven Doc and Thelma to Memphis, where they had registered at a hotel as "Mr. and Mrs. J. M. Southern." Where they were now, said Adams, he didn't know.

Louisiana, especially Baton Rouge, was in a frenzy. The news of Doc's departure was the day's only story. Politicians hurried to the capital from every direction. The big question was: What next?

Leche reversed himself, announcing that because of the new development he would not resign as planned. The next day he resigned anyway. In a subdued, almost tear-filled ceremony, Earl Long became Louisiana's governor. He announced his immediate plans: to co-operate with every investigating agency. "Let the chips fall where they may." Earl added: "Better a little righteousness, than a great revenue without right."

Smith became the most talked-about man in Louisiana. Newspapers dubbed him the "Absconding Academician," "America's Scholastic Lamster No. 1." His enemies had sometimes contemptuously referred to him as "Jimmy Moron." Now he became "Jingle Money Smith," or simply "Jingle Money."

The great chase ended abruptly. From Canada came word that Doc was ready to return and face the music. Canadian police reported that the Doc had told them he and Thelma had been on a quiet vacation (under an assumed name) when he'd read the papers and found out he was a wanted man. He had immediately made plans to come back.

Authorities wanted to send one of the LSU football planes for Smith. He would have none of it, muttering something about not feeling safe up there in a private plane with all those cops. The police brought him back by commercial airliner. At New Orleans the Smith plane was met by an aroused citizenry. "Hello, folks," said the Doc wanly. "I'm glad to be back. I was ill-advised." He and Thelma posed bravely for pictures.

Whisked to Baton Rouge, the two were fingerprinted. Thelma lost her composure and cried. The Doc was hustled off to a cell and Thelma went home. Police found $315 in cash in Doc's pocket, $9,400 in Thelma's purse. Soon Doc was making long and detailed statements to investigators who had begun a meticulous rummaging in LSU records. They found forged board minutes, mutilated LSU bonds, damaged athletic receipts which should have shown football and other revenues received by the school. LSU became a police outpost, as city, state and federal officials swarmed over the campus. The investigation spread.

Two days after Doc and Thelma arrived at New Orleans, another passenger arrived. This time, no crowds and only a few newsmen were there to witness the arrival. Talking easily, the young six-footer identified himself as O. John Rogge, newly appointed chief of the Justice Department's criminal division, newly appointed special federal prosecutor for Louisiana. It was an infamous day for Louisiana. Never before had the Justice Department sent the head of an entire division to investigate a state. It was a day to remember.

Rogge announced when he arrived that he planned to stay as long as he was needed, but that he hoped his stay would not exceed one week. He stayed eight months. A Phi Beta Kappa, a graduate of the Harvard School of Law at twenty-one, Rogge had compiled a record as a brilliant prosecutor. Now, at thirty-five, he headed an entire section of the Justice Department.

Rogge surprised and dismayed some Louisianians who had become accustomed to easy amorality, to investigations that started, went nowhere, then stopped. He talked curiously (for Louisiana) about bringing wrongdoers to justice. Once, during a conference with Leche, the ex-governor had pulled a fat roll of bills from his pocket. Rogge noted that they were all of the $1,000 denomination. Said he in a later newspaper interview, "It made my blood boil."

During Rogge's eight months, his men blanketed the state. The earlier income tax indictments had made Huey's lieutenants leery of government investigations. The boys had learned early not to manipulate their tax returns, nor to send incriminating documents through the mails. So Rogge applied a new technique, stretching the application of federal law to its limits. He knew he could not convict on income tax charges. He decided to use the postal laws. Defense attorneys protested that nothing had been sent through the mails, no deals, no instructions. Checks had gone through the mails, retorted Rogge, money that had been obtained fraudulently. But, said the defense lawyers, checks had been delivered to banks only in person, not through the mails. Yes, answered Rogge, but the United States mails figured in the transaction eventually. The checks went from bank to bank, then from bank to clearinghouse by the mails. This meant that illegally obtained money passed through the mails. And this constituted a use of the mails to defraud. The attorneys cried foul, charging that technicalities were being used to hang big crimes on their clients. Rogge's retort, delivered at a business luncheon, became a Louisiana classic: "Major criminals should not commit minor crimes."

Rogge's men shook down every suspected department, frequently turning up evidence to the effect that some of Huey's heirs had, indeed, looked on their inheritance as a cold cash proposition, on the state as one huge cash drawer which they could loot at will. In the Conservation Commission, once headed by Maestri, they found that Leche and Seymour Weiss had manipulated, for a $134,000 profit, the sale of a half million dollars of "hot oil." Louisiana, like other oil-producing states, allows a set amount of oil to be pumped from its wells each month. Excess oil, illegally pumped, is called "hot oil." If it is shipped in interstate commerce, it is a federal violation of the Connally Act, the so-called "hot oil act."

In New Orleans, the federals uncovered a case that shocked even hard-boiled Louisiana. Monte Hart, a favored contractor, and Seymour Weiss owned an unprofitable hotel, the Bienville.

It had cost them $541,000. They decided to sell it. But to whom? Why, to the giver of all good things—Louisiana. Hart and Weiss, with Jingle Money Smith's aid, sold the hotel to LSU, to be used as a nurse's home for the LSU Medical Branch. LSU paid $575,000 for the structure. Then the boys turned the venture into a classic "double dip." Having sold the hotel, they sold its furniture for another $75,000. The first "contract" had specified that the hotel came intact, furniture and all. But that was a technicality which didn't bother the boys. Jingle Money Smith got a $25,000 "loan" out of the arrangement.

Disclosure followed disclosure. The yacht grateful businessmen had given Leche had come starkly appointed. Leche had furnished it lavishly. The Conservation Commission paid the $12,000 bill.

LSU's books showed nearly $300,000 in uncollected "student loans." Some of the students said they'd never seen the money and hadn't applied for the loans in the first place.

A Charity Hospital building had been put on rollers, moved two hundred feet, then moved back again to the original site. The movers had charged the state $500,000. No one had complained.

The Conservation Commission had been authorized to erect a new geology building. The final cost came to $75,000 more than the original authorization. No one could explain what happened to the $75,000. It had been "lost."

Dr. J. A. Shaw, head of the proration division of the Conservation Commission, cast light on the extent to which the heirs held absolute power in business matters affecting the state. An oil deal involving a favored oilman had come to the heirs' attention. Weiss wanted an order signed to allow the friend to pump extra oil. Maestri told Shaw to sign the order. It turned out to be illegal.

"You signed that order without investigation?" asked the judge.

"Yes."

Judge: "Do you still hold your position?"

Shaw: "That's the only way I hold my position. I do what they tell me to."

Judge: "You mean you would sign such orders without investigation?"

Shaw: "I would sign anything they stuck in front of me, except an order to hang me."

What, Rogge demanded, did the public think about all this?

Answered Shaw: "The public didn't think anything of it for the very good reason that they never knew anything about it."

The investigation, by now a virtual free-for-all, reached into unexpected areas such as New Orleans high society. There the investigators ran across the names of Bobby Newman and Norvin Harris, bluebloods, members of two of New Orleans' oldest families, partners in one of the city's most respected bonding firms. Bobby and Norvin had, with some inside help, taken the outstanding bonds of the Orleans Levee Board (headed at the time by one of Huey's lieutenants, Abe Shushan) and "refinanced" them. The refinancing "saved" the state $700,000 over a three-year period. Bobby and Norvin took $500,000 of the savings. What did they do with the money? Of the $500,000, $132,000 went to Shushan, described as a "silent partner." Bobby and Norvin got $99,000 each; Herbert Waguespack, chairman of the Levee Board's finance committee, got $46,000. The board's accountant took $19,000. Another $12,000 went to a minor board employee. The rest went for "entertainment." Rogge termed the plot "a raid put over as an inside job, made possible by bribery." Shushan, Bobby Newman, Norvin Harris—and all the others involved—were indicted for bilking the state.

The disclosures had almost comic overtones. Abe, while riding high as one of the legitimate heirs, had been honored when the New Orleans municipal airport was named after him. Shushan Airport, it was called. Abe had seen to it that the name *Shushan* was prominently displayed on the airport building, on fixtures, on signs—everywhere. Where the fixtures, such as doorknobs and seat handles, were too small to accommodate *Shushan,* the letter *S* had been inscribed. In the wake of the Levee Board disclosures, the names and the initials were ordered removed. But the job was too big and too costly. By late 1940, workmen were still scraping the names and the initials from the buildings and fixtures. They never removed all evidences of Abe's prominence, for within a few years a new airport—named this time New Orleans Municipal Airport—was built and the old one went into moth balls. Abe, too, was put away.

1939 came to be known as the year of the "Louisiana Scandals." In all, some 250 indictments—the great majority of them federal cases—were handed down. Men went to prison by the score. The accepted estimate is that Louisiana was looted of $100,000,000. And nobody has ever questioned the figure.

The heirs, who had become Louisiana's new aristocracy, went to jail en masse. Leche, convicted of defrauding the State Highway Commission of $31,000, as well as of mail fraud, got one of the stiffest sentences—ten years. Faced with disbarment, he resigned from the Bar Association.[1] Weiss and Jingle Money Smith got thirty-month sentences in connection with the Bienville Hotel sale. In all, Smith was convicted on four of the twenty-seven charges against him. His total prison time was set at from eight to twenty-four years, in addition to the thirty-month sentence. Shushan, Bobby Newman, Norvin Harris, Waguespack and the others got two and a half years for the bond idea. Big George Caldwell, J. Emory Adams and a host of lesser lights departed their elegant villas for prison cells. Four of the indictees committed suicide before coming to trial. Leche Hall and Smith Dormitory on the LSU campus were renamed. One hundred forty-five plaques bearing the name of Leche, slated for buildings, bridges and other public structures, were destroyed. Louisianians with political pull and entitled to low license plate numbers traded them for ordinary ones. The inheritance had been squandered, the state sacked, the heirs dishonored and expelled. The great gouge was over.

On the fringes, keeping his own counsel, stood Earl Long, now governor by default. He had been investigated, as he put it, "from top to bottom." He had come out clean. Neither had the Long name been touched directly. The newspaper notices thanking Huey for "favors" continued. The light on his bronze statue burned brightly, as did his memory. Not once during the Scandals had Huey's reputation been smeared.

Now the interim had passed. In office on a fluke, Earl set out to make his own mark. It took eight years, but in the end the continuation of the Long dynasty became a reality.

[1] Leche served half of his term. Paroled in 1945, he was pardoned by President Truman in 1952. He was subsequently readmitted to the Louisiana Bar.

9

Country Boy

"I AIN'T like Huey. He could go a-champing around and get away with it. I've gotta go slower. I might get my head knocked off. Maybe I ain't as much a genius. But I got more horse sense."

The man who conceded genius for horse sense is Earl Long, the second link in the dynasty, a man who took Louisiana's Longism to its dizziest heights, then plunged it to its lowest depths. Huey wrought a revolution and gave the dynasty its initial impetus. Earl gave it continuity and an unmistakably modern flavor. Huey's heirs inherited his sweeping powers, but lacked his vision and personal dynamism. A reform-minded electorate, sick of the mammoth public looting, turned them out. Longism went into political eclipse for eight years. To Earl Long, a relative by blood but an heir by default, went the job of picking up the pieces.

"Earl," said *The New York Times* of November 7, 1948, "is trying mighty hard to wear Huey's shoes, but he sort of rattles around in them. He hasn't got Huey's brains and he hasn't got Huey's finesse. Where Huey was fiery, this fellow is just loud. Where Huey outsmarted his opposition, Earl just slams into the center of the line."

The fact is that Earl, who made Louisiana his personal political football field since 1918 (when he helped Huey become a railroad commissioner), chalked up some impressive yardage. Since 1918, he has been in the thick of every political campaign in the state. He took leading parts in Huey's campaigns of 1924 and 1928. Rebelling against the Kingfish, he ran for lieutenant governor in 1932 and for the same office in 1936, then slipped into the executive mansion via the back door when

Leche resigned in 1939. He has been governor of Louisiana three times—more times than any other man—and win or lose, he has inevitably been the chief target of the combined opposition. Since 1940, when he made his first independent bid for governor, the political history of Louisiana has largely been the political history of Earl Long. Without question, he is more deeply rooted in Louisiana's pyrotechnic politics than any living man.

"Just say I'm *sui generis,*" said Huey in explaining himself, and nobody ever doubted it. Earl is *sui generis,* too—only there's a difference.

Huey was a country boy by accident of birth and geography. As soon as he learned something about big-city ways, he took to them like a Long to politics. After he left the farm, he came back only to campaign. Campaigning, he was careful to say "ain't" for "is," "them" for "those."

Earl was and is a country boy at heart. The "ain'ts" and the "thems" came naturally to him and he made no apologies for them. On any given weekend while in office he would succumb to the urge to get back to the farm. Out would come the governor's personal Cadillac, to be loaded with baskets of fruit, groceries, vegetables. Tied to the back of the car would be two big garbage cans of accumulated slop. At the farm Earl would feed the chickens, slop the hogs, eat a breakfast of freshly laid eggs, then sit around in an undershirt, receiving his country followers. Earl held court in the four-room house he affectionately calls the "shack" on his "pea patch," a shack with linoleum floors, naked light bulbs and the picture calendars on the walls. Here, Earl feels most at home.

Huey's feel for the poor country voter was instinctively shrewd. Earl's was just as instinctive and shrewd, but forty years of direct political contact honed it to precision. He knows how to talk to the folks and he knows how to look when he talks.

There you would find him, in any of a score of backwoods parishes in the heat of an election campaign, standing on a platform or the rear of a panel truck. The steaming Louisiana sun would heat up and Earl would get hot with it. Hands jammed into hip pockets, coat off, sleeves rolled to the elbows, the galluses showing, he would roar his message with a gravel-tinged voice that took on a tremulous falsetto when he became excited.

That other candidate? "He's High Hat Sam, the High Society Kid, the High-Kicking, High and Mighty, Snide Sam, the guy that pumps perfume under his arms." The straw-hatted audience would snicker and Earl would pour home the devastating indictment: "He sleeps in silk pajamas."

Why does he want to be governor? someone in the crowd might ask. Earl would guffaw, grin, shift. That's easy, he'd confide. "You live in the best house I ever lived in. You have servants and you don't have to buy even your own food. Every time you open the door, someone hands you a turkey or a blanket or all that free stuff. Well, I like that free stuff." There would be a whistle, a rebel yell, a scattering of applause, and Earl would lean into the microphone again. "When I'm elected, I want y'all to come up to the mansion for a cup of coffee. You might as well. You're payin' for it." Cheers and more applause. Earl would grin, slump into a chair, stay there to talk to the folks streaming by. If they felt like singing, Earl would gladly join in the songfest—"I'm Looking Over a Four-Leaf Clover," or some such lyric.

Huey treated legislators like servants, the Legislature like his personal property. "We bought that guy just like you'd buy a carload of potatoes," he said of one representative. Earl never bought anyone. "I just rent 'em," he laughed, "It's cheaper that way."

Earl prowled the legislative halls just as Huey did twenty-five and thirty years before. He knew exactly how many legislators he had in his hip pocket. But his best shows, unlike Huey's, were reserved for the rostrum when he addressed joint sessions. It was then that Earl talked at the legislators—and to the people over the Legislature's head. He treated the lawmakers like a group of recalcitrant schoolboys caught playing hooky. He was the old man, talking to his boys.

His face thrust close to the microphone, a pop bottle propped beside him, Earl would alternately chide, scold, threaten and cajole his legislators like a stern father laying down the law.

If he found himself blocked on an amendment to a sulphur bill, it would be time for a gentle scolding:

"Last few days it's kinda hard to get sixty-eight votes. . . . There's a man here that's a big man. He's almost running this Legislature whether you know it or not. He can't get sixty, but he can get thirty-five or forty or thirty-six or thirty-four, which in some cases is as good as a hundred. Cause when you're stopped you're stopped, huh? When you're bogged down you're bogged down." Was there any doubt about who the mysterious figure running the Legislature was? The lawmakers squirmed as Earl told them, "You know who's from that parish, doncha? Is there anybody here doubts who's from that parish . . . ? Is they? Hold up your hand and I'll tell you." No show of hands.

If the legislators needed a lecture or a spanking:

"This bill has no more business in the constitution than I have . . . she went in there because she's paid for—C.O.D.—C.O.D.—C.O.D.—and if you don't think there's been some C.O.D. goin' on around this Legislature in the last few days you're dumber than I think you are . . . and I believe we comprehend each other . . . and I think you men oughtta join with me to help stop this kind of skulduggery."

Leander Perez, Earl's implacable enemy, the political boss of Plaquemines Parish, would be pushing the sulphur bill. And Earl would want the Legislature to know he opposed the bill, not Perez:

"Judge Perez is a fine man—a man that I stopped a fella from jumpin' on in the Senate in 1942. He lost his temper and he rushed down there and a policeman grabbed him. I said, 'You leave Judge Perez alone. Don't you put your hands on him. This is a free country. If Judge Perez wants to call Earl Long a goddam liar, let him. That don't mean Earl Long is a goddamn liar.' "

The Legislature would be softened up, ready for Earl to deliver the punch line:

"I'm willing to call a spade a spade, and an ace an ace, and a falsehood a falsehood, and a fraud a fraud, and that's what I say about the way that sulphur bill was injected into the constitution of this state. I wanna say this—if I go down fightin', that don't worry me—that don't worry Ole Earl. I wanna go down fightin' for what's right, what's just. Be decent with me and I'll be decent with you. I wanna get a little cocky. I dare you to answer me somethin'."

There was rarely an answer. Earl knew his legislators too well. Said he in explaining the art of refined political contact, "Don't write anything you can phone, don't phone anything you can talk face to face, don't talk anything you can smile, don't smile anything you can wink and don't wink anything you can nod." In the next breath he'd say with equal conviction, "Maybe my weakness is that I spout off too much. But if I ever closed this mouth, God help Uncle Earl."

As long as he kept his mouth open and the explanations flying, Earl did all right with the voters of Louisiana. Until 1959 and except for the ill-fated bid for lieutenant governor, when Huey had to spank him at the polls, Earl never received less than 40 per cent of the popular vote. In his unsuccessful bid for governor in 1940—at a time when many of Louisiana's voters identified him with the Scandal administration—Earl trounced his opposition in the first primary, but was beaten by a coalition in the second. In the 1944 race, when he ran for lieutenant governor, he far outdistanced the ticket leader, Lewis Morgan. Morgan got 27 per cent of the vote. Earl got 41 per cent. In his 1948 victory he got the largest majority any candidate for governor, including Huey, ever commanded in Louisiana. In his 1956 victory, he established a precedent. He became the first governor of modern Louisiana to win his seat in the first primary, sweeping into office a ticket that lagged behind him.

Despite his impressive showings at the polls, Earl was roundly denounced for his crudities, called a "disgrace" to his state by national and Louisiana publications alike. His raging temper, his uninhibited spitting, rump scratching, nose blowing and public cursing tactics resulted in anger, despair and a largely hostile press. To all this indignation Earl thumbed his nose and snorted: "I may be rough and tumble . . . you've got to be rough some times. One of those namby-pamby hustlers [governors who have preceded him], how long would he last up here? About as long as a snowball would in heaven."

Sitting at his gubernatorial desk, Earl was just a few feet from the spot where a mortally wounded Huey fell. He had only to glance from his office window to see the Kingfish's grave. At night, from virtually any point in Baton Rouge, he saw the perpetual light beaming down on Huey's bronze statue. Earl lived and labored, in short, in the lengthy, omnipresent shadow of his late brother. For him, it was that way from the beginning.

He was born August 26, 1895, two years behind Huey, on

Father Long's Winnfield farm. Growing up, he slept in the same bed with Huey, fought Huey's early fights, saw Huey quit school to hit the drummer's trail, then followed three years later. Selling hardware, drugs, groceries and shoe polish, he developed as intimate a knowledge of backwoods Louisiana as Huey did and put it to good use during his later campaigning. Like Brother Julius, Earl has a predilection for taking credit for Huey's early victories. Says Earl, "I did more talking for Huey than I did for my company and I sold him a lot better than the baking powder I was supposed to be selling. He'd never have been elected if it hadn't been for me. He said so himself."

Profiting by Huey's example, Earl decided to combine work with education. For a short time he attended Louisiana Polytechnic Institute, then, like Huey, switched to law. Two years of night school at Tulane and Loyola, a bar examination, and Earl became what he later called a "jackleg lawyer." Apart from his stint with the Home Owners Loan Corporation and a few state lawsuits, Earl never made a living out of law. He never had a private practice and never tried a lawsuit that didn't involve a state agency.

The folks around Winnfield never had trouble distinguishing Earl from Huey. Huey was the shorter, a rumpled, fire-breathing talker. Earl was the taller, quieter fighter, a shade behind his brother in brain power, but miles ahead in physical courage. Earl's reputation as a handy man with his fists stood him in good stead during his political development. At the height of a campaign he administered a severe beating to a New Orleans attorney who opposed Huey. In the fight, he almost bit off one of the attorney's fingers. Earl's attack on the anti-Long legislative leader during Huey's impeachment fight enhanced his reputation. In a state where a man's willingness to shuck his coat and step behind the barn is held in great esteem, Earl's physical courage was never a liability. No one ever called him coward.

In one instance Earl might have had second thoughts about jumping into the fray. During the 1934 campaign to elect John Fournet to the state Supreme Court, Earl came upon Brother Julius—by this time as disillusioned with Earl as he was with Huey—campaigning for Fournet's opponent. Earl stood in the audience, taunting Julius. Julius shouted back. The exchange became heated and personal. Earl started for the platform, yelling, "I'll clean your plow." But onlookers intervened. Julius claimed that Earl didn't need to be stopped, that he knew better than to get closer. Brother Julius, Earl knew, was in the habit of making speeches with an impressive briefcase beside him. Inside the briefcase he carried a revolver—"just in case I had some trouble."

Earl Long, making his first bid for governor in 1940, faced a dilemma. If he denounced the Leche administration too strongly, he would be indicting himself by indirection. Moreover, he would alienate some of his most important backers, principally Maestri of New Orleans. If he soft-pedaled the Scandals, he would be accused of covering up. Earl chose a middle course.

The Scandals centered on Jingle Money Smith, observed Earl, but Smith was only one man. Why call the whole administration rotten? "Look at Jesus Christ," said Earl, "he picked twelve and one of 'em was a sonofagun." When the list of indictments grew, Earl changed his tune. "I'm determined to remove from the seat of authority every man who in any degree worships Mammon rather than God." To which the opposition replied that Earl had been doing a little Mammon worshiping himself by selling hogs to the state at fancy prices.

Earl protested that he didn't know anything about the Scandals, that he would have acted if he had known. The opposition replied that if Earl didn't know about the thievery he was too stupid to be governor; if he did know, he wasn't fit for the office.

Earl imported ex-Share Our Wealther Gerald L. K. Smith to help his campaign. Then, to show that he meant to push Huey's old program, added Huey's ex-secretary, Earle Christenberry, to the ticket as candidate for state treasurer. "Earl says he believes in the principles of Huey Long and O. K. Allen," charged reform candidate Sam Jones, "but both of them said he wasn't fit even to be lieutenant governor." State Treasurer A. P. Tugwell, harking back to Earl's split with Huey, issued the most damaging comment: "Earl Long posing as a leader of the Huey Long people! That's like Judas Iscariot running on the platform of Jesus Christ." Replied Earl, somewhat lamely, "God knows I'm sorry I fell out with Huey. What more can I say?"

The opposition centered all its fire on Earl. Candidate James

Morrison, campaigning with a monkey named Earl Long, paraded his campaign workers through New Orleans. The paraders were dressed like convicts, each of them bearing the name of a discredited Leche administration figure. The newspapers helped in reducing Earl to a buffoon. Cartoons showed Earl playing a piano, remarking happily, "I just work here. I eat out." Earl looked like a hasbeen before he had even started. But there was still that solid bloc of Long country voters to be heard from.

In the election, Earl led the five-man field with 40.9 per cent of the vote, sweeping 41 of the 64 parishes. Reformer Jones, in second place, netted 28 per cent, while the third man, Jimmy Noe, got 21.1 per cent. In the Long-Jones runoff, the deciding factor would be Noe of "Noe's 980" fame. Noe tossed his support to Jones, cementing Earl's fate. In the February 1940 runoff, Jones beat Earl by 19,000 votes, sending Earl Long and Longism into political eclipse for eight years. Running for lieutenant governor in 1944, Earl led his ticket in the first primary but went down to defeat in runoff strategy. By 1948 he was ready again, this time to try for governor.

The biggest assets Earl Long had in his 1948 comeback were the two governors who preceded him, Sam Jones and Jimmie Davis.

Jones, billed as the "Liberator of Louisiana," took office pledged to a sweeping investigation of the Scandal administration. "I said that I intended to destroy the state machine—and I meant it. I propose to uproot it, rip it limb from limb, branch from trunk and leaf from twig," said Jones.

But if Jones and his followers were ready for reform, a good bit of Louisiana was not. The Legislature, rarely friendly to Jones, cut his request for appropriations for a crime commission to root out graft and corruption. Parish officials, who had called for a cleanup during the campaign, became strangely reluctant to prosecute exposed officials. And Jones, a brusque, matter-of-fact former judge, did little to contribute to his popular appeal. "I'm not in this job to make myself a popular hero . . ." he said. "I'm not governor because I want hooray and applause. I'm governor because someone had to clean up the mess Huey and his successors left." For Governor Jones, who had solicitously declared during the campaign that his "pappy was for Huey," this was something of an about-face. For a people who liked their governors on a first-name basis, Honest Sam became Frigid Sam. He made two tactical mistakes which Long-pampered voters viewed with skepticism. During the campaign he had promised to abolish the sales tax imposed by Leche and to provide $30-per-month pensions for the state's oldsters. When he failed to deliver on both counts, his political stock plummeted. In direct proportion, Longism's went up.

After the factional wrangling of the Jones and anti-Jones forces from 1940–44, Jimmie Davis rolled into office as a compromise governor on a program of "peace and harmony." In contrast to the stuffy ones, Davis was well liked. At the end of the 1944 session of the Legislature, Davis led the lawmakers in singing "You Are My Sunshine," a popular tune he had written, as a representative released two pigeons labeled PEACE and HARMONY. Davis left the legislative chamber to the applause and cheers of the legislators. But if he was a popular figure, Davis still was a weak sister as governor. He spent a great deal of his time outside the state: 44 days in the fiscal year 1944–45; 68 days in 1945–46 and 108 days in 1946–47. While the state called for leadership to guide it through the immediate postwar adjustment, Davis was busy in California making a movie. For a state in which the governor had—since Huey's time—traditionally acted as a leader and a mover, Davis acquired a reputation as a "do-nothing" chief executive. In some measure, the reputation helped Earl's 1948 comeback.

Eight years of exile taught Earl some important lessons. In the 1940 campaign, for example, he had promised to double old age pensions. This would have brought them to about $27 monthly, while other candidates were pledging $30 pensions. In the 1940 campaign, Earl had made promises that he knew he could keep with existiing revenues. If new revenue was needed, Earl spelled out the details. This time he made no pretense of fiscal responsibility. From the moment he took the stump it was evident that Earl was determined to out-Huey the Kingfish in welfare matters. He had little in the way of an organization. As he described it: "When I started out, practically every politician in the state gave me the cold shoulder." With nothing to lose and everything to gain, Earl whistled through Louisiana, a political hurricane after the soft sea breezes of the previous eight years.

Was Louisiana sick of these "do-nothing" administrations? asked Earl. Oh, yes, and he was sick of them too. The only way the people could get back to the good things was to remember Huey and vote for Earl. To prove his point, Earl trotted out Huey's widow, Rose, pressed young Nephew Russell into service as a campaigner and turned, as Huey had, to Maestri of New Orleans for political and financial support.

Huey had built the highways? Earl promised to widen them, to complete all the farm-to-market, school bus and mail routes. Huey had given free schoolbooks? Earl would give free hot lunches to the school children.

It was Huey who had given the old folks a break by pushing pensions for them. Well, said Earl, he'd improve on that—$50-a-month pensions for everybody over sixty-five, homestead exemptions to be raised to $5,000.

In 1940 an independent-minded Earl had given the back of his hand to the state's schoolteachers. They had asked for a twelve-month salary, had inquired about Candidate Earl's stand on this. Imperiously, Earl had written a stinging letter, advising that he was "not ready to turn the affairs of the state over to the teachers—not by a devil of a lot." Added Earl: "To be brief, no one can put a pistol to my head because the election is a few days off and make me commit myself to something just because they are taking advantage of circumstances. I may be defeated—but I do not think so." Well, he had been defeated, and it was an older and a wiser Earl who announced his school pay stand in 1948: a minimum of $2,400 salary for all teachers, twelve-month salaries for all school bus drivers.

There was something for everybody: bonuses for veterans; improvements in the state's mental institutions, hospitals and prisons; a revitalized port for New Orleans; the repeal of an unpopular driver's license law; and—to help oil and gas men—the lifting of restrictions on natural gas exports. Taxes? What would it cost to pass all this? Earl didn't go into that.

But Sam Jones, back for another try at the Governor's Mansion, did. If only half of Earl's program went through, Jones said, taxes would have to be increased by 50 per cent, despite the fact that the state treasury boasted a record surplus. Other reform groups produced all kinds of estimates of what Earl's program would cost; one group put the cost as high as $892,000,-000 a year, an astronomical figure, even for a Long.

But Earl's rampaging campaign tactics, his pie-in-the-sky program—so reminiscent of Huey—the support of Huey's widow and son, and the largely negative tactics of the opposition were all Earl needed. In the first primary, with the hard core of the traditional Long supporters backing him, Earl polled 41.5 per cent of the vote to Jones' 22.9 per cent. This time, there was no coalition to snatch his victory from him, as the third candidate, District Judge Robert Kennon, remained neutral. In the runoff primary, Earl was nominated—that is, elected—by the biggest majority polled by a gubernatorial candidate in modern Louisiana history, swamping Jones by almost two to one. Into office, also, went a majority of pro-Earl legislators. It was, in all respects, a Long landslide.

The voters had shown they wanted Longism—or at least a Long—back in office and Earl lost no time in giving them both. As one of his first acts, he appointed Huey's son, Russell—fresh out of LSU's law school—as his "executive counsel," posing proudly with his nephew as photographers clicked away. Then he turned on the steam, just like Huey before him.

On his inauguration day, Huey had ordered buckets of cold water, complete with dippers, placed on the capitol grounds for the thousands of supporters who streamed in to see him take office. Earl announced that his inauguration would take place in LSU's football stadium. He invited all Louisiana to be there. Thousands from across the state attended. There were 140 high school bands, a two-hour parade, high-stepping drum majorettes, speeches and an all-prevailing cameraderie. Earl's supporters—and some who got on the bandwagon late—gulped down 16,000 gallons of buttermilk, more than 200,000 hot dogs, and drank as many bottles of soda pop. Baton Rouge had not seen an inauguration like it since Huey's heyday. Meanwhile, in the flush of victory, Earl made two significant gestures. The capitol light that used to shine on Huey's statue had been turned off as a "blackout precaution" during the reform administration. Earl turned it on again. And he held out a friendly hand to the Kingfish's son, Russell. U. S. Senator Overton, who had first been elected with Huey's help, died. A primary election was scheduled for August. Earl would have appointed Nephew Russell, but Russell was not yet thirty, the minimum legal age for a senator. Instead, Earl appointed his wealthy backer, Oilman William Feazel, but made it understood that in the August primary Russell would be in line for the seat. Cried Earl, "Happy days are here again. The Longs are back in the saddle. We'll improve on everything Huey did."

Taking office, Earl inherited a whopping $45,000,000 budget surplus. His first step was to call for new taxes. The $45,000,000, it turned out quickly enough, couldn't begin to meet the cost of Earl's welfare program.

With the help of his friendly majority in the Legislature, Earl shook up the state's tax system. The gasoline tax went up two cents per gallon. Two and a half cents of new taxes were added to each bottle of beer sold (which quintupled the tax) while the state sales tax was doubled. Soft drink taxes were cut in half, but a three-cent tax was added to each package of cigarettes sold. As usual, oil and natural gas came in for their share. The severance tax on oil was doubled; the gathering tax on natural gas was also doubled, although Earl originally wanted it quadrupled. Finally, in his search for additional revenues, Earl turned to the most unlikely quarter—slot machines. Although these were illegal, the Legislature taxed them, too. Said Earl to protests about the new taxes, "If you'll look these taxes over carefully, you'll find that they won't hurt anybody." Said the New Orleans *Item:* "It's what they [the people] voted for."

During the campaign, Earl had carefully listed the order of his new benefits. First on the list came increased old age pensions. Within seventy days after he took office, Earl's administration was mailing the new $50 payments to old people. But pensions were only the beginning.

Earl had promised to make the administration of hospitals and mental institutions "my personal concern." Within months after he took office he put through an expansion program for mental hospitals, free ambulance service for charity hospitals, an expanded dental trailer service, and more charity hospital beds.

In the schools, funds for the hot lunch program were quadrupled, other funds augmented. The teachers got their minimum salaries and, for the first time, Negro teachers got the same pay as their white counterparts. The veterans' bonus bill went through, as did increased home exemptions. Meantime rural parishes got healthy increases in road maintenance funds.

While he doled out the benefits Earl also took pains to extend his own influence and authority, as Brother Huey had done before him. With legislative help Earl reorganized LSU's Board of Supervisors and the Orleans Parish Levee Board (replacing their memberships with his own supporters). He virtually took over the state parole system (which had been liberalized during the reform administrations) and took a new and direct hand in administering the state's liquor industry by naming an Alcoholic Beverage Control Board answerable to the governor. He saved his most drastic, state-wide blow for last.

Along with other candidates, Earl had been asked if he favored keeping the civil service system, a built-in guarantee against patronage-hungry governors. Earl had answered yes like most of the other candidates. But under his direction, the Legislature repealed civil service, making the state's employment rolls a choice patronage roost once again. Said one Long legislative ally, in a cynical summation of the Legislature's attitude toward patronage, "Let's feed the horse that brought in the feed and the fodder during the campaign."

The strategy behind Earl's freewheeling tax and spoils program was transparent, the issues clear cut. Although dramatically increased taxes would meet with little approval, Earl hoped that the accompanying widespread benefits would more than balance resentment against taxes. By August of 1948 Earl had his answer. He had been too freewheeling in spending and spoils.

That answer came in the August 31 primary election, when Nephew Russell made his initial bid for a United States Senate seat—the two remaining years of the Overton term. During Earl's campaign for governor, Russell, as the son of the late Kingfish, had asked the crowds to forget Earl's split with Huey. Huey's family, said Russell, had forgiven Earl and was "satisfied" with him, "and if we're satisfied you ought to be too." Now that Earl had made his own comeback, he announced, too, that he was satisfied with Russell. Russell, without an experience record of his own, promptly fell back on Uncle Earl's program in his bid for election. It almost proved his undoing.

Russell's opponent was Judge Robert Kennon, who had run a surprisingly good third behind Earl and Sam Jones in the 1948 gubernatorial primary. A staunch anti-Long, he had the spirited backing of Reform Mayor deLesseps "Chep" Morrison of New Orleans.

By election day, the impact of Earl's $80,000,000 in new taxes was beginning to be felt, while some of the benefits were yet to come. Although Russell commanded respectful attention in the northern parishes, where his father had been a spellbinder twenty years before, the city voters regarded him as something of a curiosity, the Kingfish in the flesh once again. And when the vote rolled in, the Longs could see that Russell was in some trouble.

Despite Earl's backing and Russell's uninhibited references to his father's record, Russell beat Kennon by only 10,475 votes, a squeaky victory in terms of Louisiana's politics. A good indication of voter resentment against Earl—and Russell—was the difference in the total number of votes cast in Russell's race, as compared with the number cast in the other Senate contest, in which Allen Ellender sought re-election. Russell's race drew 517,811 votes; Ellender's only 460,799. Obviously, anti-Longs had gone to the polls in great numbers. Russell had no illusions about who made his victory possible. In a post-election speech he thanked "all my friends and supporters, especially those good boys who laid down their cotton sacks, plows and hoes and went to the polls. . . . I never would have made it without a heavy country vote."

The storm warnings were enough for Earl. With Russell due to face the electorate in another two years for a full Senate term, Earl had to mollify the opposition. A defeat for Russell would spell disaster in terms of Earl's personal prestige. At that early juncture in Russell's career, also, it might permanently remove him from the political picture.

Earl poured it on. Extra funds, on hand from the newly imposed beer tax, were thrown into the school lunch and farm-to-market paving programs. In the 1950 regular session of the Legislature, Earl, who had taxed to the hilt two years before, now solemnly declared that he would not ask for a single new tax. Said Earl, ". . . We in Louisiana have, at this time, reached a point where I feel that our economy can stand no new taxes." Meanwhile, he held out the olive branch to New Orleans (where Russell had been swamped by Kennon) by opposing a move to cut into the city's Levee Board funds. Most significant of all, however, Earl refused to oppose the passage of a home rule charter for the city, a measure that gave it the greatest control over its affairs since Huey took many of its powers away. As a final gesture Earl, who had allowed the Legislature to trample state civil service barely two years before, now declared himself in favor of a strong civil service law. The Legislature beat down this threatened invasion of its patronage rights, but Earl was clearly on record as favoring civil service.

Earl's moderacy paid off. Anti-Long Sam Jones anounced that he would not oppose Russell's re-election bid. Mayor Morrison of New Orleans, although pressured by reform groups in the city to oppose Russell, kept his opposition to a low level. Meantime, the anti-Longs put up a largely unknown and unspectacular candidate, Attorney Malcolm Lafargue. In the July 25 primary, with a moderate Earl backing him, with a respectable two-year Senate record behind him, Russell won his first full term by trouncing Lafargue. Rolling up heavy majorities in 55 of the 64 parishes, he mustered an impressive 68.5 per cent of the vote, a percentage significantly larger than either Huey or Earl had ever garnered. Said a proud Uncle Earl:

"He is a good boy. The fact is, I say, not because he is my nephew (I have several nephews), he is one of the most conscientious, tolerant, uncontrollable young men I have ever known in my life and is most respectful of the rights of other people.

"He will vote for what he thinks is right, regardless of what I say (I have already tried him) and what you say or what any pressure group says. He is an improvement on his uncle and his father, Huey P. Long. He is better educated and respects the other man's opinion more."

Two years later, the "boy" had grown up. With his Senate term secure for another four years, but with Earl a fading lame duck, Russell made his first overt bid to become the new leader of Louisiana's Longism. Just as Earl had challenged Huey, Russell now challenged Earl. By 1952, they were battling all over Louisiana.

10

Crown Prince

IT WAS a political extravaganza that even campaign-hardened Louisiana could enjoy. Leaflets bearing candidates' names streamed from overhead airplanes. Bands played while flat-heeled coeds, mixing with stockinged chaperones, danced the Big Apple. A platoon of shine boys perspired while polishing the shoes of one candidate's followers. Another candidate passed out dollar bills. There were parades and pep rallies and once a line of pretty girls in skimpy bathing suits strutted by, their candidate's name boldly emblazoned on bare backs. There was the usual charge and countercharge. One hopeful hotly accused another of trying to "monopolize" the lucrative "laundry racket." The accused angrily retorted that his accuser had offered him $1,200 cash and a part-time state job. Back came the usual campaign denial: "That's a damn lie." The voters would have to decide.

In the end the dollars and shoeshines and bribery charges were as nothing when stacked up against the political magic in the name of the leading candidate. Russell Billiu Long, son of Louisiana's political patron saint, romped to an easy 3–1 victory to take his first political office. The time was 1938, the place the LSU campus. Russell's new title: President of the LSU Student Body.

Since that day when he turned his first political trick as an LSU student, Russell has shown that the Long penchant for winning elections has been safely passed down to him. He has never lost an election in which he was a candidate, and only once has he come out on the short end in any political contest in which he took an active part. That was in 1952, after Russell himself was comfortably seated in the Senate in Washington, with two-thirds of his term still ahead of him. For that stain on his record, he can perhaps be excused. Part of the reason he backed a losing candidate stems from the fact that he found himself at odds with another Long, his politically wise Uncle Earl. On the other hand, Russell could gain some solace from the result of the election, for Uncle Earl, for all his political cunning and power, didn't push his candidate into office either.

As Huey's son and Earl's nephew, and as a politician with a demonstrated ability to command his own following, Russell Long is by birth, inclination and circumstance the inheritor of the Long political mantle. He is the third solid link in the dynasty that goes back to Huey's 1928 gubernatorial victory. With Uncle Earl out of office once more, Russell is the only Long left in a major political post. Whether Louisiana keeps a Long—if not the concept of Longism—in office now boils down to Russell's ability to keep on winning elections. He is, until the reinforcements grow up, the last of the direct line.

The current link in the dynasty was born November 3, 1918, in Shreveport in the midst of two memorable conflicts. One was the waning struggle in Europe. The second was the war Father Huey had declared against Louisiana's vested interests in his bid for a Railroad Commission seat. One war would change the physical map of Europe. The other would alter the political fortunes of Louisiana. Russell was destined to play a role in the latter.

Russell made his initial appearance under conditions somewhat different than those existing when Huey was born. Huey in 1918 was no poverty-stricken sharecropper, scratching out a bare existence, but an attorney with ambition and a rapidly growing reputation. Moreover, Russell was born in the city and not in the country to which his father directed his vote-getting appeals. Although Huey was far from a rich man at the time Russell was born, Uncle Earl, in a moment of political pique, would later complain that Russell was "born with a silver spoon in his mouth."

Predictably, Russell was born at a time his father was out campaigning. Hurrying home to be with his wife, Rose, Huey discovered that she had already named their first son Huey Pierce Long, III. Huey promptly changed the name to Russell, a fact neither Rose nor Huey bothered to correct on the official birth certificate. If the error on the birth certificate embroiled Russell in some exasperating Navy red tape during World War II, the name change came as something of a blessing, too. Young Russell, growing up in Shreveport, had his share of schoolyard fist fights because he happened to be Huey's son. As a Huey P., III, his early difficulties could only have been magnified.

Russell spent his early years in Shreveport, then moved to the Longs' Audubon Place mansion in New Orleans when he was twelve. A year later he moved to Baton Rouge, to live for a time in the home of LSU President James Monroe Smith. Returning to New Orleans, he finished at Fortier High School at sixteen. Three weeks before he began his classes at LSU, his father was assassinated.

In the 1935 campaign, in which Leche and Earl stumped on a promise to continue Huey's programs, Russell spent part of his Christmas holidays endorsing Leche and Uncle Earl. This was the first extensive look Louisiana's voters got at Huey's son and the verdict was unanimous. Although the boy obviously lacked the Kingfish's hell-raising fire, he was a dead ringer for his daddy, what with that curly, unmanageable hair, that fleshy face punctuated by a bulb of a nose. Just like Huey. Russell, at these appearances, said just enough to draw hearty applause—and to show that he approved of the heirs: "I'd like to meet all of you and shake hands with you, but I really came just to thank you for your friendship to my father." In post-Huey, pre-Scandal Louisiana, Russell's presence was as effective a vote-getting tactic as any the heirs employed. Soon, he was being asked to address civic groups, luncheons, fraternal associations. Everywhere he appeared the comment was unanimous: He looks just like Huey.

Married to his LSU sweetheart, Katherine Mae Hattic, in 1939, Russell got his law degree, became a Navy officer assigned to landing boats when World War II broke out, saw action in North Africa, Sicily, Anzio and Southern France. Back home, he practiced law for two years, stumped for Uncle Earl's election in 1947, became Earl's executive counsel by appointment shortly after Longism made its comeback.

As Earl's lawyer, Russell occasionally showed flashes of the economic bluntness that had characterized Huey. Having drafted a good share of Earl's mammoth tax program for 1948, Earl found oil companies hotly opposed to it. Defending the program after some oil companies brashly threatened to leave Louisiana, Russell declared matter-of-factly: "When the oil and gas are gone they are going to pick up and leave and that's the last we'll see of them. Some say they can't afford to pay the tax, but when oil was selling for eighty cents a barrel they were paying eight cents tax and were doing all right." The oil companies stayed, but Russell didn't. Two months after taking his state job with Earl, he announced, with Earl's undiluted blessing, that he would run for the United States Senate to complete the two years of the late John Overton's term. After squeaking by with a close win, Russell displayed what is probably his most significant characteristic, his earnest willingness to make friends of his enemies. Huey might have threatened reprisals against the groups who opposed him. Russell, invited to speak to a conference of industrial leaders, drew hearty applause when he declared, "I doubt whether a man in this room voted for me. But I'm going to try to do such a good job that you'll vote for me next time." Next time, when he polled a crushing 68.5 per cent of the vote to swamp his opponent, Russell could take satisfaction in the knowledge that some of them did.

With Uncle Earl running the state back home, Russell, by now caught up in the Washington whirl, gave every appearance of remaining a Long *in absentia,* except for election times. "I'm convinced," said a serious-faced Russell on July 25, 1949, "that I never want to be governor, that I'd rather be a senator. I'm going to try for re-election next year." Ten years later he would tell Hugh Mulligan of the Associated Press: "I've always had an ambition to be governor and someday follow my father in the mansion, but I have serious doubts at this time about leaving the Senate for the governorship. The normal political path is through the governor's office to the U. S. Senate, not the other way around. However, if it were the only way of keeping the Long faction together, I might consider running." But in 1949 Uncle Earl still ruled Louisiana and the Senate seat was a safe refuge. By 1952, secure in his first full Senate term, Russell indirectly challenged Earl's leadership in Louisiana. Perhaps unwittingly, it was Earl who gave both opportunity and impetus to the challenge.

By mid-1950 Earl Long could see tangible evidences of his programs. Benefits to schools, hospitals, veterans and oldsters had been delivered as promised. New construction was under way across the state. Moreover, Russell had just won a thumping victory, a condition that Earl rightly regarded as stemming at least in part from Earl's olive-branch tactics. At this point, Earl decided it was time to change the state constitution and, as the regular session of the 1950 Legislature met, he made his move. Under his prodding, the Legislature called a convention to revise the constitution. In August, Earl called the Legislature back into a special session to revise the original call and to insure convention control by a faction friendly to him. Earl's enemies, fearing another Long try at a massive power grab like the one Huey executed in 1934–35, reacted immediately.

A Greater Louisiana Citizens' Committee of New Orleans Chamber of Commerce members was formed to oppose the proposed convention. The New Orleans Dock Board charged that the real purpose behind the move was Earl's ambition to dominate completely the Port of New Orleans. Others viewed it as the first step by Earl toward skirting the constitutional clause that prohibits a governor from succeeding himself. Finally, there were those who felt that while Earl could not perpetuate himself in successive terms, the convention was designed to keep a good part of his machine in office. If successful, the move would give him a solid advantage in the 1956 elections, when he would again be eligible to run.

By September, under pressure from all sides, including some of his most important friends, Earl called a one-day session of the Legislature that repealed the convention law. In the meantime, however, his transparent bid for a grab at power had alienated such important allies as Russell, William Feazel, whom Earl had appointed as an interim United States Senator, and his New Orleans leader, Clem Sehrt.

The voters showed, too, that they viewed Earl's attempt at steamroller tactics in a dim light. In November they voted down a $14,000,000, Long-inspired road bond issue, a highly unusual move in benefit-conscious Louisiana. By March of 1951 Earl tried to undo some of the damage by calling a special session of the

Legislature to hike expenditures for highways and other state agencies. But it was too little and too late. When the gubernatorial primaries began, Earl's prestige was at low ebb.

Unable to succeed himself, Earl immediately named his "successor"—Baton Rouge District Judge Carlos Spaht, an able pro-Long jurist who, given a chance, might have run his own race successfully. But Earl never let anyone forget that Spaht was his candidate. Throughout the campaign the voters simply eyed Spaht as an extension of Earl. He was universally referred to as "Earl's boy." Earl's difficulties were enhanced, meantime, when his lieutenant governor, Bill Dodd, decided to run for governor. Dodd, a loyal Long follower, believed his record had entitled him to Earl's support. When Earl chose Spaht instead, Dodd broke with Earl to press his own campaign.

It was at this delicate juncture in Earl's strategy that Russell moved independently to establish himself as a separate political power by announcing that he would support a rival gubernatorial candidate, U. S. Representative Hale Boggs. It was a bold and calculated move. With Earl a lame duck, his popularity at an ebb because of his constitutional convention tactics, a Boggs victory would establish Russell as the most politically powerful Long in Louisiana. Moreover, Russell's Senate term expired in 1956. If he chose to run then, Boggs—unable to succeed himself—would be showing only elemental political courtesy in supporting him.

No one sensed the danger better than Uncle Earl, who campaigned with unrelenting vigor, directing most of his criticism at the Boggs-Russell combine. "Two young squirts down from Washington," sneered Earl as he hit the back roads. As they crossed paths in support of their respective candidates, Russell and his uncle hurled charge and countercharge, sometimes angering each other to the point that friends thought it advisable to keep them apart.

"He was Louisiana's leading deadhead," cried Earl, charging that Russell, as assistant secretary of the state Senate during the Leche administration did nothing to earn his salary. Replied Russell: "Earl Long is getting as bitter toward me as he was toward my father. I have always earned my salary in every job I have ever held. Certainly if Earl Long thought otherwise, he should not have recommended me to the people of Louisiana for the United States Senate." Nagged Earl: "Russell Long was picked too green on the vine." Retorted Russell: "If I was picked too green on the vine, then Uncle Earl is too ripe on the vine and should be picked at once." Earl denounced Russell for teaming up with a New Orleans "city slicker" like Boggs. Russell replied that it was time to "forget factional differences." Said Russell: "Blessed are the Peacemakers."

The results of the 1952 gubernatorial first primary confirmed a political principle. A Long traditionally has about 40 per cent of a hard core of Louisiana voters on his side when there is more than one opponent facing him. By picking up a bare 10 per cent of the residual vote in a second primary, a Long is pretty sure to win his election—unless the defeated candidates gang up on him.

Earl demonstrated this graphically enough in the three races he ran in the 1940's. In his first 1940 primary bid, he got 40.9 per cent of the total vote, and only a Jones-Noe combination beat him in the second primary. In 1944 he got 41.9 per cent in his first primary bid for lieutenant governor. When Jimmie Davis beat the leader of Earl's ticket, Congressman Lewis Morgan, Earl went down to defeat, too, despite the fact that he outran Morgan. In 1948 Earl pulled down 41.5 per cent of the first primary vote in his successful bid for the governorship. The same held true, to some extent, for Russell when he faced a single opponent in 1948; he won by a bare 51 per cent of the vote—the traditional 40 per cent plus a predictable 10 per cent from other quarters.

Now, in the 1952 gubernatorial first primary, Earl's candidate, Spaht, polled 22.8 per cent, while Russell's candidate, Boggs, polled 18.7 per cent to come in third. In short, the two Long candidates polled a combined total of 41.5 per cent—the traditional Long hard core. Spaht thus went into a runoff with the number two candidate, Robert F. Kennon, the erstwhile opponent of both Earl and Russell. With heavy endorsements from some of the displaced candidates, Kennon, a dark horse, swept to a lopsided victory over Spaht, capturing 61.4 per cent of the vote and taking a full ticket together with a majority of pro-Kennon legislators into office with him. For the first time since 1928, a Long or a Long-backed candidate had been overwhelmingly repudiated by the voters. The Earl-Russell squabble proved to be pretty expensive wrangling, a mistake they would not repeat when the stakes were higher in 1956.

In the gloom that settled over the Longs in 1952 a small ray of light went virtually undetected. At Pineville, in the Eighth Congressional District, Dr. George Long was elected to Congress on his third try. Said he, perhaps before the full import of the major state races dawned on him, "There is no question that my election represents a comeback for the Longs in Louisiana."

George Long, born September 11, 1883, at Winnfield ten years before Huey, was the second of the Long children. More fortunate than Julius, George came along at exactly the right time. By the time he was ready for an education, Father Long had sold some property to the railroad and George was sent off to dental school in Atlanta. Two years later, instead of turning to dentistry, George developed wanderlust. Successively, he visited in Memphis, Louisville, returned to Louisiana for a brief time, then set out again, this time for Tulsa, Oklahoma. Even at that remote distance the Long penchant for politics asserted itself. After establishing a dental practice, George plunged into Oklahoma politics, won two terms in the Legislature, then gave up his practice and politics to return to Louisiana after Huey's death.

For a time he stayed quietly behind the scenes, living first in Monroe, then settling in Pineville. After he campaigned briefly for Earl in 1944 and 1948, Earl offered him the job as superintendent of the Pineville State Colony and Training School. George took it, only to find his patronage position quickly whisked out from under him by an irate Earl. After a squabble with the colony's business manager, who accused him of buying food supplies from a friend at higher than minimum prices, George fired the business manager. Earl, hearing about the episode, fired George, who waited until 1952, then asked for Earl's support in the Congressional races. Earl, having refused to support George three times before—George lost each time—finally relented. George won.

By 1954 he was a well-established Congressional figure as well as a prominent businessman. Back in Louisiana, perhaps following the pattern established by political hopeful Dudley Leblanc of Hadacol fame, George invented a patent medicine named Vitalong. To publicize it, he frequently passed bottles of it among legislators. Re-elected to the United States House of Representatives in 1954 while Earl was in political exile, George refused to deny persistent and disturbing—to the other Longs—rumors that he would be a candidate for governor in 1955. Returning to Louisiana in 1955, George confirmed the rumors. He would be a candidate that year. Earl, meanwhile, made no secret of the fact that he too intended to run. Warned George with understandable solicitude: Earl should not run because a campaign would endanger his health. Pointing out that Earl suffered a heart attack in 1950, George cautioned newsmen and voters, "If you love Earl, don't vote for him. He's a sick man. It would be suicide." George added that he had the "kindest feelings" toward Russell and would support him for re-election to the Senate in 1956.

In Washington, meantime, Russell busily divided his time between becoming a full member of the Senate's liberal wing—headed by Hubert Humphrey and Paul Douglas, Russell's close friends—and explaining his late father's Senate performances.

"My main concern, just like my father's," said Russell when he first came to the Senate, "will be for social legislation. I think we ought to have wider social security benefits, more public health and hospital services, more federal aid to education, free school lunches and that sort of thing. We've got all of these things in Louisiana now, but many people outside of Louisiana don't give Huey Long credit for it. I think it's the sort of thing we've got to have for the country as a whole."

But, Russell emphasized, he would not turn the Senate upside down to get these things right away. "I guess the main difference between me and my father is that the only way he knew to get things he wanted was to fight and raise hell for them. He wanted all these good things to happen right now—fast. I know you can't get things that fast, and I'm satisfied to take my time."

He rarely lost an opportunity to extol Huey and denounce the Kingfish's critics. He told *The New York Times,* "I think my father was one of the greatest men of his time. He was certainly the greatest man I ever knew. He truly gave his life fighting for the poor and underprivileged, not only of this state, but of the nation. Naturally, he was cursed and vilified by every entrenched interest there is. They said he was a dictator and a crook. They tried to impeach him when he was governor and they did everything they could to blacken his character. But he figured if your enemies try to low-rate you the only thing to do is to low-rate them right back, only do it better. He did it better, too, and that's why they can't forgive him even after he is dead."

To another reporter Russell explained that his sustaining purpose in Washington was to emulate his father's deeds, if not his tactics: "I would not be in politics if his enemies, including the press, had given him credit for the good things he did. I am going to try to carry out some of his ideals, and if I can't do it, I shall help someone else who can."

As he had predicted, Russell took his time for the most part, stirred up few fires in Washington, soon climbed to seats on some of the more important committees. As a member of the Armed Services Committee, he roamed overseas inspecting American military bases, took time out on one trip to swim from Europe to Asia—over a one-half-mile stretch of the Bosporus—with U. S. Ambassador to Turkey George McGhee. Standing on the Asian shore cheering them on was Oregon's Senator Wayne Morse.

Back in Washington Russell strengthened his liberal reputation by denouncing Senator Joseph McCarthy, by plumping hard for small business, the farmer and increased social security payments. He strongly opposed the limitations on U. S. treaty-making power inherent in the Bricker Amendment, supported a strong national defense program and only infrequently showed flashes of his famous father's temperament.

Introducing an amendment to a social security bill to increase payments to people over sixty-five, he cried out against the philosophy of overspending abroad while clear-cut need existed in the United States. Said Russell, "A nation that can afford to spend more than five billion dollars each year in assisting the development of foreign nations and raising the living standards throughout the world can certainly afford to care for its own."

But his most celebrated outburst came when he, as a member of the Senate Foreign Relations Committee, became the lone committee member to oppose the nomination of C. Douglas Dillon as Undersecretary of State. Labeling Dillon a "Wall Street banker," Russell cried, "I shall feel compelled to engage in deliberate, dilatory tactics to slow down this steamroller. If the junior Senator from Louisiana lacks the courage to fight for his convictions, he did not get it from his father or his mother. Perhaps one of the reasons that I adore the U. S. Senate more than any institution on earth is that I had the privilege, as a boy, of sitting in the gallery and watching my father fight a one-man battle against hopeless odds." The Senate confirmed Dillon's nomination easily, but not before Senator Prescott Bush indignantly labeled Russell's tirade as "quite offensive."

By election time, 1956, it was evident to the Longs that by dividing themselves they succeeded only in conquering one another. Russell, who had been mentioned as a possible gubernatorial candidate, returned to Louisiana to announce that he would seek re-election to his Senate seat. Dr. George, in a sudden about-face, reported that he would try for a third term in Congress. Earl, to no one's surprise, declared that he would be back to try for another four years in the executive mansion. This time, it was a united Long front that faced Louisiana.

The results showed the difference. Russell was re-elected without difficulty, as was George. Earl, after refusing to campaign on television ("it makes me look like a monkey on a stick") conducted an intensive handshaking campaign that gave him the greatest victory in Louisiana's modern history. Walking off with an unprecedented 51.4 per cent of the first primary vote, Earl swept into offce with him a majority of his legislative allies together with his entire ticket. Blanche Long, Earl's wife, was elected Democratic National Committeewoman, giving the Longs still another voice in party councils. In his dramatic victory, Earl captured all but two parishes. In traditionally anti-Long New Orleans, he trailed by only 2,000 votes.

George and Russell returned to Washington while Earl reiterated his campaign pledges for greater old age benefits, more school and highway money, more aid to state institutions. In the spring of 1956, the all-conquering Longs appeared to have pumped new political magic into the ever-attractive name. But as they settled back to the job of running Louisiana again, new pressures over which they had little control were building up around them. A quarter of a century before, Huey had become the unwilling star of a major drama that ended in his death. When the curtain went up this time, it would be a pathetic, if not a tragic, Earl in the spotlight. Longism, strangely enough, was riding for its biggest fall even as it scored its greatest triumph.

11

Out-Kingfishing the Kingfish

BY THE spring of 1959, Earl Long faced a dilemma. Louisiana had undergone some changes since the 1955 election, when he swept to his unprecedented first-primary victory, and the changes boded ill for Longism. A new conservatism had sprung up in Louisiana in 1948, in the wake of the Dixiecrat resentment against President Truman and the national Democratic Party. But Louisiana had gone Democratic in both 1948 for Truman and in 1952 for Stevenson. By 1956, the picture changed, as conservative Democrats crossed party lines to vote for Eisenhower.

The new conservatism came at the same time another voice was being heard in Louisiana and the South—the militant segregationist, who in all probability was a member of the burgeoning White Citizens Council movement. Earl Long, Longism's liberal standard-bearer, a man who had enjoyed a heavy Negro vote in the 1955 primary, found himself besieged from two sides. He was loath to alienate his Negro support (sure to happen if he, like the new conservatives, became a militant segregationist) but he stood in acute danger of losing his conservative legislative support (which did happen when Earl failed to take a strongly prosegregation stand).

In post-1955 Louisiana, continued segregation of the races became a *cause célèbre* as, indeed, it did elsewhere in the South. The chief spokesman for the new movement was State Senator William E. Rainach, who quickly became Earl's chief legislative opponent. By 1956, Rainach and Earl had locked horns on a number of occasions.

Under Rainach's prodding, the Legislature passed one prosegregation bill after another: no mixed racial meetings, no mixed entertainment, prohibition of the use of public facilities, such as parks, by both races at the same time. Earl tried to straddle the issue, picturing himself as for segregation, but objecting, at the same time, that prosegregation legislation was useless in the long run. Said Earl to the Legislature, "I don't see any need to pass a lot of segregation bills even though I would favor them, when the Supreme Court [of the United States] probably would knock them out anyway." It wasn't good enough for the segregationists in the Legislature. They called for impeachment of the United States Supreme Court, particularly for its stand on the school segregation issue. Replied Earl, "You can't kick the Supreme Court in the slats on the one hand and expect a square deal on the other." To Rainach he said, "A lot of people are following you, not because they agree with you but because they're scared of you. I'm for segregation one hundred per cent, but I don't believe you should run for office on it."

In the 1959 spring session of the Legislature, the segregationists under Rainach made their boldest move. They introduced legislation designed to remove from voter registration rolls thousands of Negroes, most of whom had supported Earl in the last election. With one swipe, the segregation-minded Legislature was about to eliminate a big segment of Longism's voting strength. Earl decided to fight the move.

Meantime, however, Earl had been talking about running for governor again, although he mystified friends who pointed out to him that Louisiana's constitution prevented a governor from succeeding himself. Earl, however, told his friends that he had devised a way to get around that obstacle. He mentioned his intention to run again to his wife, Blanche, who strongly opposed the idea. Earl, however, had his reasons. If he failed to run for governor in 1959, he would be sixty-eight by the time the next election came in 1963—an age that would work against him. Moreover, by that time, who could tell what damage the prosegregation raiders might have done? Earl decided he could not risk not running.

With the compelling political image of his dead brother haunting him, Earl Long prepared to stake out his own claim to political immortality in Louisiana. In some ways, his credentials were more impressive than Huey's.

Huey had served only one gubernatorial term, but Earl had already been elected to two full four-year terms and had finished part of another—the unexpired term of the unlamented Dick Leche of Scandals fame. Not even Huey had been sufficiently imaginative to skirt the state constitution by attempting his own succession. But Earl blandly, almost indifferently, manufactured his legal loophole and began to inch through it. Huey had ruled indirectly, hand-picking his successor, then treating him like an office boy. Earl decided on the direct and the dramatic. He would out-Kingfish the Kingfish by perpetuating himself and the dynasty.

On newsprint and video tape it looked appealingly simple, even though the proposition threw Louisiana into a mild uproar. Could this be done? Could Earl, like Brother Huey before him, flick aside all precedent, "swallow the Pelican" and declare himself the state's unchallenged monarch? Even today, the questions are, at best, moot. Louisiana's constitutional lawyers never resolved the issues. As it turned out, Earl's political enemies could have spared themselves the mental anguish of dwelling on the various possibilities, while his political dependents should have had sufficient knowledge of the ring to begin their periodic drift to another corner. In fact, many of them did. Others stayed with the old campaigner. In the end, however, the flutter came to nothing.

The fact of the matter was that as he laid his political barricades to meet the challenge from a variety of quarters, Earl failed to recognize that he had become his own Fifth Column, his own worst enemy. Earl, to state it simply, became the victim of a twin obsession—a consuming dread of losing power and an unbridled passion to perpetuate himself as a latter-day Kingfish. With characteristic Long gusto, Earl flung himself into a resolution of the obsession. In the end, the effort almost killed him.

A man obsessed, particularly an old and physically failing specimen, is hardly a pretty sight. Earl, it quickly became apparent, ranked as one of the unprettiest, as well as one of the most pathetic. It took no time at all for official Louisiana and others close to the capital's freewheeling politics to spot the effects of the psychological tempest that churned within the governor. Physically, mentally and morally, Governor Long's deterioration grew plainer by the day.

Shortly after he suffered a thrombosis in 1950, Earl, who had been a nervous smoker, gave up the habit. Suddenly, however, he was puffing away again, this time chain-style. To his wife's pleas that he stop or cut down Earl turned a deaf ear. Soon, the nicotine habit paled in comparison as Earl exhibited newer, more disturbing symptoms of his unrest.

Always a garrulous politician with a quick sense of humor, Earl now began to tirade at the drop of an imagined slight. Close political friends, who had been accustomed to the rasping, gravel-coated voice that took on an adenoidal twang when Earl became excited, began to detect a new quality when the governor spoke. Before, the voice had been full of humor, the words usually punctuated with a low, rasping chuckle. Now the voice roared out harshly, the words cut indiscriminately. The closer the friend, the sharper the epithet. Few escaped the gubernatorial wrath as a sensitive Earl fancied himself hemmed in by political plotters and conniving traitors. In this group he included, especially, the members of his own family.

Newsmen, close friends, state employees and capitol buffs had long ago learned to smother their shock at some of the governor's milder idiosyncrasies, particularly the newsmen who came in for periodic tongue lashings.

"Them lyin', goddam newspapers," Earl rasped at a press conference as the reporters shifted uneasily. Eyes agleam, Earl emphasized his distaste for the press by tossing an offending journal to the floor, spitting on it, then wiping his mouth with the back of a sleeve as he glared triumphantly at the reporters. Nobody, by God, was going to tell him.

Had he been content to indulge himself in these peccadilloes, Earl might well have continued without surrendering a particle of his political prestige or power. But the brain that controlled the impulses was aflame; the obsession that consumed him steadily moved him farther from reality. In his own mind, Earl could do no wrong.

To Earl Long's wife, Blanche, the symptoms of her husband's crack-up became evident earlier and more clearly than to even his closest political supporters. Long before his manic fury erupted into open and uncontrolled rages, Blanche divined that Earl was being racked by an inner struggle. In a *Life* Magazine article, she described Earl's withdrawal from reality:

> I knew this was coming eight months ago, it was just as plain as day. Suddenly Earl started talking about running for a fourth term as governor and it got so that that was all he would talk about. He stopped eating and even though he had given up smoking years ago because of a thrombosis condition, he started to smoke cigarettes again. He started to drive himself unmercifully. After a long hard day at the capitol he would come home and go to bed. But he couldn't sleep. After an hour or two of tossing and turning he would get up and walk around the bedroom or perhaps sit up in a chair with a light on. I was so sick with worry over him that I called the family together and warned them that we would have to do something or Earl would drive himself to the grave.[1]

Other friends, acquaintances and political enemies began to tumble to the truth. One of Earl's closest political friends quit a state job to which the governor had appointed him after Earl, who had always been gruff but courtly with the ladies, persisted in shouting four-letter expletives in the presence of the official's wife. Asked to modify his language, Earl told his friend to go to hell. The official quit his state post, refused to take another Earl offered him, declared he was through with the governor.

Earl had never been a heavy drinker. But now he suddenly began to drink heavily, mostly gin camouflaged with grape juice, which he disguised in a Coke bottle. Earl, his unsteady gait and the Coke bottle soon became a familiar sight in the capitol corridors, even in the legislative aisles.

One newsman, a long-time observer of Earl's antics, described with surprise how he first tumbled to Earl's perambulating drinking.

"Earl had always taken a nip, he was what you might call a convivial drinker," said the reporter. "But nobody could ever accuse him of being a drunk. Well, one day I was standing in a capitol corridor when Earl walked up with his Coke bottle in his hand. He asked me how I felt and I told him I had a sore throat. Next thing you know he said, 'Here, take a swig of this. It'll help.' I took a swig and my eyes almost fell out. It was the first time I had ever drunk one hundred proof Coke."

[1] *Life,* June 15, 1959.

Outside the limelight, Mrs. Long fretted and Earl's family and friends grew more apprehensive. Then, in April and May of 1959, Earl exploded into an entire series of ridiculous escapades.

With the Legislature in session in Baton Rouge, Earl bundled cronies into a National Guard airplane, flew to Marietta and Atlanta, Georgia, to pick up a planeload of entertainers, then flew back to Baton Rouge for an official mansion party.

In New Orleans, two weeks before his crack-up, Earl, who had never been much of a ladies' man, took one look at a voluptuous night-club dancer named Blaze Starr ("the newly crowned queen of burlesk") and decided she had what he liked. Invited to Earl's table, the dancer spent the evening amusing him, ended by slipping a publicity photo of herself practically in the nude into the governor's pocket. Later, to reporters, Miss Starr confided that the governor and his wife separated over that picture when Mrs. Long discovered it in the governor's jacket pocket. Blaze's "confession" was ridiculous on the face of it. But she knew a good publicity gimmick when she saw it. Within weeks after she dissolved her association with Uncle Earl, Miss Starr—who had had second-rate billing—became the most publicized stripper along Bourbon Street's night-club strip.

In addition to drinking and playing in New Orlean's hot spots, Earl set out on man-killing speaking schedules. During most of his last term, he had assiduously avoided speaking engagements in order to rest as much as possible. But now he accepted any invitation that crossed his desk, insisting that he had to get out and meet the people in his bid for another term. Laughed Earl to legislators and friends alike: "The only chance I can get before the people is with this big mouth of mine. If it ever closes up, God help Ole Earl. God help him."

Earl had no intention of keeping his mouth shut. Instead, he cunningly injected himself into the speculation over the next crop of gubernatorial candidates wherever he spoke as he stumped the state.

As far back as December of 1958, Earl, with a dead pan and a tired shrug, had told a press conference that he was "too old and tired" to run for governor again. On January 7, 1959, he laughed outright at the possibility that he would try to succeed himself. If, said Earl, he found a man who was "hell-bent on running for governor," he would personally send him somewhere "to have his head examined." Clearly, Louisiana editorialists speculated, Earl had dealt himself out of the political poker game. Meantime, other potential candidates began to make ambitious gestures, among them former Governor Jimmie Davis, author of the popular ballad "You Are My Sunshine," which he used as his campaign song; New Orleans Mayor deLesseps Morrison (whom Earl had soundly thrashed in the 1956 elections); State Comptroller Bill Dodd; and State Senator Willie Rainach, an avowed segregationist.

Earl dropped his first political bomb—a low megaton blast—on April Fool's Day of 1959 by hedging a bit. Disregarding his earlier, adamant no-run stand, Earl blithely allowed that "if I ever run again I'll run now. No law on earth could prevent me from succeeding myself for a second term." Asked how he could succeed himself in view of the constitutional block that prohibits a governor from succeeding himself, Earl dropped his second bomb. Said he: He would resign at sometime prior to the filing deadline, run and win. That way, he would be succeeding not himself, but the lieutenant governor who, by that time, would be acting governor.

Two days later, on April 3, Earl hedged again. At a convention of the Louisiana Municipal Association—at which he appeared as a "surprise" speaker—Earl told the assembly, "I may or I may not be a candidate. You know what the old farmer said about the mule—you can't trust a mule sideways, or a politician noways."

Next day, Earl made another surprise appearance before the Association of Registrars, meeting at Alexandria in central Louisiana, with an announcement that verged on the positive.

"I'll run," he said, "if I think I can be elected—unless I spring a leak somewhere." At the same time, Earl took time to plug for a voter registration bill he intended to introduce to the session of the Legislature that was due to convene in a month. In essence, Earl's bill would have liberalized the voter registration requirements, thus allowing many Negroes and poor whites, until then excluded from the polls, to vote. The significance of the announcement escaped nobody, since Earl historically had drawn heavy support from these elements. It meant simply that Earl was preparing for a campaign to succeed himself and wanted to see as much of his bloc support as possible ready and able to vote.

From this point there was little doubt that Earl was an active, if not an officially announced, candidate.

By April 4 Earl was warming to crowds and charming them in the traditional Long manner, as he sang a duet with gubernatorial-aspirant Jimmie Davis at the Baton Rouge Gridiron Dinner. By April 7 Earl conceded formally that he would run "if my health stays good and if I can get the do re mi." At the same time Earl took a swipe at Segregationist Rainach (at this point the most vocal opponent of Earl's voter registration proposal) by charging that he was "running around" and "stirring up all that hell" only for political purposes. A few days later, Earl swung his attention to one of his favorite whipping boys, New Orleans Mayor Morrison (whom he frequently referred to as "Blue Boy Morrison," or "Sweet Boy Morrison"). Chided Earl: He would run again, if for no other reason than to "give that little squirt dee-le-soups Morrison one more beating." Later however, still playing the wavering politician to the hilt, Earl nostalgically announced that if he failed to run, he would, in all probability, forsake the big city life of the capital.

"If I leave the governor's office, I'll probably wind up in my pea patch in Winnfield looking after my billy goats." By April 13, however, all doubt about Earl's intentions had vanished. Addressing a convention of state police jurors, Earl revealed that he had made his firm decision. Only "death and the law," he said, could keep him from running again.

Despite this announcement, some editorialists still doubted that Earl would try to succeed himself. They speculated, instead, that his announcements were calculated to give him a stronger bargaining hand when the Legislature convened in May.

Earl soon dispatched this illusion by not only predicting that he would triumph in the December 1959 Democratic primary election, but by itemizing the standings of the various candidates. Earl put himself in the number one spot, with Morrison second. Then followed Rainach, Davis and Bill Dodd.

At least one politico had no doubts at all about Earl's intentions from the beginning. "Long," said Secretary of State Wade Martin, Jr., "lives for one thing—to be governor. He has no hobbies, such as hunting, fishing, reading or looking at television. He just goes to the horse races and runs for governor."

By the end of April, as he left Louisiana for a fling at the Kentucky Derby, Earl fired off one more volley, thus removing the final vestige of doubt about his candidacy. Before leaving Louisiana, he announced that he would begin his campaign June 9, right after the Legislature adjourned, and that he would resign his office to qualify for re-election between September 5 and September 15.

The die was cast. Earl would try to write a new chapter in Louisiana's political history.

PART 3:

The Crack-Up

12

The Breakdown

AS Earl Long moved from one gargantuan rage to another, a series of other, more subtle pressures worked away at him. Although Blanche exuded happiness over their move into the new $60,000 mansion she and Earl had built on Baton Rouge's exclusive "millionaire's row" ("the first one we had ever built on our own"), Earl fretted about "putting on the dog." Billed, like his brother Huey before him, as a "man of the poor people," Earl worried about the effects of plush living on his vote-getting prowess, grumbled that he was more at home in the starkly appointed cabin on his "pea patch" at Winnfield. Meantime, Earl received the surprise of his life when agents of the U. S. Bureau of Internal Revenue called to advise him that his income tax returns for 1956–1958 were being investigated. Exhibiting more gall than good sense, Earl flew to Washington for conferences with Nephew Russell, tried to persuade the tax investigators to postpone their probe until after the December 5, 1959, primary elections. He met with the same response any ordinary taxpayer would likely get. The investigation, said the agents, would proceed, election or no election.

By mid-May, it became evident to everyone but Earl himself that his breakdown was at hand. In the Legislature, Earl tried to block the voter registration bill, only to see the Senate pass it, thus handing him an ignominious legislative thrashing. The setback galled and stunned him.

Earl brooded. He called legislators at all hours, pleading, persuading, threatening and cajoling them to back his stand. He took to staying up all night, nursing a bottle, sometimes bursting into tears at an imagined or real injustice. In a few weeks, his pudgy 203-pound frame lost forty pounds and began to sag noticeably. The eyes that had danced mischievously now glared wildly; the dentures glinted and ground audibly as Earl gritted his teeth and kept his lips ajar. Soon he was talking again, and this time it was clear, from the moment he spoke, that he was a sick, dispirited and frantic old man.

The week of May 24, 1959, is one that the Long family and official Louisiana will remember in a sort of nightmarish haze.

On Monday, May 25, with a group of entertainers from Georgia and a dancer and jazz band from New Orleans, Earl entertained at an uninhibited party at his official mansion. Elaborately decked out in a red dinner jacket and polka-dot vest, Earl danced gaily, drank pink champagne from a water glass, startled the singer who stood before the band delivering "Basin Street Blues" by sidling up behind her and yelling, "Sing it, baby." He further disconcerted her by standing directly behind her until she finished her offering. That night he called a midnight press conference. In some of his saltiest language, he sailed into his political enemies in the Legislature, branding them liars, deceivers, opportunists. Ever the magnanimous man of the people, Earl, at one point in the press conference, called out one of the mansion's servants to shine the shoes of a newsman who failed to come up to sartorial expectations.

There followed two days of wild public behavior. On Tuesday, still hung over from the champagne, Earl bounded into the Legislature to address a joint session. As usual, he began calmly enough. But in minutes he was clutching the microphone, screaming wildly, cursing and abusing individual legislators who, for the most part, sat in stunned silence.

Roaming up and down the speaker's platform, Earl from time to time snatched the microphone to make a point or tell a story. When one of the legislators protested that Earl's stand on voter registration could only help integrationists, Earl lumbered to the microphone, glared about him for a second, then launched into some family history.

"About 1908 or '06," rasped Earl as the lawmakers stirred in embarrassment and the crowded galleries leaned forward, "I had an uncle who . . . got drunk one night, went down to the colored quarters in Winnfield, kicked a nigger man out of bed and he got into bed. That nigger man was so enraged he shot my pore ole uncle and he died. Do you know, that's what the colored people resent now most. They want their womenfolk left alone."

Once, during his two-day spree, Earl appeared before the committee hearing, toting his spiked grape juice, chain-smoking and perspiring profusely. As witness after witness appeared, Earl interrupted the proceedings, jeered, cursed, abused committeemen and witnesses alike. Once when a legislator tried to shush him Earl wheeled on him, screaming, "Don't tell me to shut up, you bastard." The lawmaker subsided.

At another point, during a burst of profanity, Earl glanced up to spy a group of school children who had come to observe the Legislature in action. Accompanying the pupils was a group of nuns. Smirking boyishly, Earl offered an apology of sorts. "I just sent for my Bible," he drawled, "and I'm going to swear off cussing. Let's you and I and the good nuns keep from cussing as long as possible." The nuns lowered their eyes and said nothing but hustled the children out as soon as they decently could. Earl raved on.

One night, exhausted by the ordeal he had imposed on himself, he returned to the mansion for another tortuous night of telephoning, drinking and semicoherent rambling. As he paced his rooms, his wife, herself forced to take sedatives to rest in the midst of the bedlam created by her husband, slept fitfully, waking often. From time to time she tried to soothe her distraught husband but he would have none of it. At times, glaring wildly at her, he accused her of conniving against him, of undermining his attempts at re-election, of failure to sympathize with his stand in the Legislature. Downstairs in the mansion office, a detail of state troopers, assigned to the governor's house on a more or less permanent basis, screened visitors and telephone calls, waited and watched uneasily as the sounds of angry shouting and excited conversations drifted down from the governor's quarters.

The next day, Thursday, May 28, drawn and haggard despite the freshly pressed light suit he wore, Earl appeared again before the legislative microphone. At the urging of his assistants and friendly lawmakers, the governor appeared ostensibly to apologize for his outbursts of the previous day, which had been seen and heard around the state on television. The assembled lawmakers sighed audibly as the governor began on a soft, conciliatory note. Their expectations, however, were short-lived. Within a few minutes Earl was off on a verbal sleigh ride of personal abuse and vilification that outstripped his performance of the previous day.

The first time Earl had ever stepped before a microphone in the state Legislature, he had picked up the singularly effective oratorical gimmick of addressing the body at large, then quickly singling out specific legislators by name and directing pertinent remarks or questions at them. Sometimes, Earl would cite a personality who was not even present to hammer home a point or evoke a laugh. Earl's most frequent target from the nonlegislative ranks was his old archenemy, Leander Perez, sometimes district attorney, sometimes district judge of Plaquemine Parish, a man who ruled that oil-, gas- and sulphur-rich province with all the iron-fisted tenacity of a feudal lord, much as Huey Long had ruled the entire state.

"Why," roared Earl, "he's the biggest thief in the state of Louisiana. Do you want me to say his name? I think you know who I mean." Then, shifting to individual legislators: "You know who I mean, don't you, Senator Sevier? You do too, Mr. Detessier." Perez refused to remain silent in the face of Earl's repeated attacks. His standard reply to Earl's charges: "He is a privileged liar." But the legislators, sighing resignedly, settled back in silence as another tirade impended.

Behind Earl, Lieutenant Governor Lether Frazar scribbled furiously on a scratchpad. House Speaker Robert Angelle dropped chin to chest and swung slowly in the swivel chair. Reporters and radio recording men (TV cameras had been barred for this meeting by the Legislature, which rightly feared a repetition of the previous day's outbursts) leaned forward, scribbled quickly and adjusted their equipment.

Clutching the microphone in one hand, setting his Coke bottle down with the other, Long pressed his mouth close to the speaker as his voice grated harshly. Singling out Representative Frank Fulco, he jeered at him for failing to support the voter bill, then stunned his listeners by shouting, "You got a little Dago in ya, but you're all right. You got as nice a little ole wife as God ever let live." Fulco, shocked, sat down, blinking back tears.

When Representative Wellborn Jack pleaded with the governor to sit down and open the bill for discussion, Earl took another gulp of his grape juice, swung his attention to one of Jack's friends and accused him of being "in league with the gin-heads." Before the legislator could reply Long swung to the other side of the chamber, accused another recalcitrant official of being a "Dillinger in disguise." Because he had purchased the time for a state-wide radio broadcast of his speech to the Legislature beforehand, thousands of Louisianians heard their governor screaming, ranting and abusing indiscriminately in a humiliating public spectacle that knew no precedent even in Louisiana's turbulent and colorful political history.

Brother Huey Long, in the Louisiana of long ago, had shown ready and frequent contempt for the state's lawmakers. "Hell," he was fond of saying, "I shuffle 'em like you would a deck of cards." But for Earl and Louisiana, Earl's performance on May 28 was a new and decisive low.

Even before Earl's repeated outbursts in the Legislature, Mrs. Long knew that the crack-up was at hand. In her *Life* article she wrote:

> About six weeks ago, I noticed that his condition was getting much worse. He began to abuse his closest friends. He was irritable all the time and his temper kept getting shorter. His friends knew he was not a well man and they began to avoid him. Hundreds came to me and told me what I already knew: that he needed medical attention.[1]

Sitting in a neighbor's house that week, a group of her friends and acquaintances with her, Louisiana's first lady heard her husband bulldoze and insult his legislators with his unbridled venom.

> I knew then that the end had come. My heart went out to him and I was so sick I wanted to cry. I wanted to go over there and get him, but I couldn't force myself to do it because I knew my heart would break if I saw him carrying on like that. His appearance on Wednesday only confirmed what we knew. Then we found out that he had scheduled a speaking campaign through the state for that weekend. We all realized that he would never live through it if we let him go.[2]

[1] *Life,* June 15, 1959.
[2] *Life,* June 15, 1959.

Blanche left the gathering hurriedly, sped back to the Governor's Mansion and prepared for action.

On Thursday, May 28, Blanche and others persuaded Earl to stay at the mansion. Although he insisted that he had to attend another meeting of the Legislature, that his desk was piled high with work, he was persuaded to stay put. Meantime, Blanche began to gather family and friends for the showdown.

The group that gathered in the east room of the executive mansion late that night was a solemn one. Upstairs, alone in his room, was Earl Long, the political master of Louisiana, dressed for the most part in his shorts, tears streaking his eyes as he sat on the edge of his bed, mumbling to himself, shouting at times.

That night, Russell Long had been in New Orleans to deliver a commencement address at Loyola University. A telephone call brought him to the mansion on the double. With him from New Orleans, Senator Long brought Dr. Robert Bernhard, an old friend and the personal physician to Senator Long's family. In addition, others who gathered at Blanche's request were Dr. Arthur Long, the governor's cousin; John Hunt, a nephew; and an added assortment of physicians. At one time, there were at least five doctors present to help determine what ailed Earl and what he needed.

Throughout the long night, the relatives discussed the governor's condition, argued back and forth. Doctor Long, the governor's cousin, argued most strongly for immediate commitment to an institution where the ailing Earl could get plenty of rest and quiet. At length, Senator Long, though mindful of the political reverberations that would attend the commitment of his uncle, agreed that commitment was the only alternative. A couple of Earl's sisters, contacted by Blanche, at first strongly opposed committing their brother. In the words of one doctor: "They [the sisters] didn't see anything wrong with him at first. They thought he was just 'good Ole Earl.' " Blanche, Russell and Doctor Long overrode their objections.

Now the decision to commit had been made, but problems still remained to be solved. Where would the governor be taken? Would he go willingly if his real condition was made known to him? Or would he resist? If he did resist, what action could be taken? (As Louisiana's chief executive, he was capable of wielding awesomely effective power.) Meantime, what steps should be taken to protect the obviously deranged governor from harming himself, his wife, or others with whom he came in contact?

Obviously, reasoned the family council, the governor needed treatment in a mental or hospital-type institution. But it was equally obvious that the institution had to be outside of Louisiana. As chief executive, Earl could not be held in a Louisiana institution against his will. And even if he could be, it would be unfair and risky to ask a state official, whose very job depended on the gubernatorial grace, to place himself on so delicate a spot. Earl, as the family well knew, could be harsh and tyrannical with underlings who opposed him, but effectively magnanimous with those who indulged and accommodated him.

There was yet another, and potentially serious, complication. If the governor were to be taken across a state line against his will, could he claim that he had been kidnaped? Any such charge would surely bring federal investigators into a case that the family wanted handled as discreetly as possible. The family solved this problem by telephoning both the Department of Justice and the FBI in Washington and explaining the situation to them. Back came the word from Washington: If the family acted in the best interests of a mentally ill person, a kidnap charge would largely be an academic exercise in legalistics. In effect, the family had a green light from the Department of Justice to carry out its plan.

By six o'clock on the morning of May 29, 1959—the hour at which the Long family council retired for a brief sleep—the job of finding a suitable institution to which to send the governor had been turned over to Dr. Bernhard. Earlier, the family had discussed a number of places—one in New York, another in Florida, one in the Midwest. Finally, the talk focused on the small but highly regarded psychiatric clinic operated by Dr. Titus Harris in conjunction with the University of Texas Medical Branch—usually referred to as John Sealy Hospital—at Galveston. There were several reasons for the choice.

First, the clinic lay outside of Louisiana, but close enough to Baton Rouge to allow frequent visiting and telephoning. In addition, Dr. Harris, a short, cheerful, chain-smoking psychiatrist, enjoyed an excellent reputation for dealing effectively with patients who suffered from acute manic depression—the tentative diagnosis Drs. Long, Bernhard and others had made after talking to Earl. Moreover, the clinic would have at its disposal the varied facilities of a great hospital. Finally, although the primary purpose of transporting Earl to this particular clinic would be to treat him for a mental disturbance, neither the clinic nor the hospital bore the stigma that might have been associated with a state asylum or "mental institution." Instead, for all practical purposes, Earl would be treated under normal "hospital-type" conditions. Dr. Bernhard moved to have Earl admitted.

In Galveston, Dr. Harris picked up the telephone and listened to Dr. Bernhard describe the governor's symptoms and condition. In his mind, there was little doubt that the earlier diagnosis—manic depression—was at least partially correct. He had one question, however. Would the governor be a voluntary or an involuntary patient? Told that at this stage of the game Earl would probably resist confinement and treatment, Dr. Harris bluntly rejected the proposal. Said he, in effect: We're not equipped to handle involuntary, intransigent or violent patients. Moreover, half the problem of treating such cases is in gaining their confidence and co-operation. Under these conditions, he added, he failed to see how he could be of much value. If, however, he told Dr. Bernhard, the governor could be persuaded to come to Galveston as a voluntary and co-operative patient, he would admit him. Dr. Bernhard promised to consult the family and the governor and call back.

Friday, May 29. Downstairs, in the east room of the mansion, Blanche, Russell and other members of the family held continuous council. Upstairs, his door locked, dangerous implements carefully removed from his presence, the governor alternately pleaded, cursed, threatened, reviled and shouted at his captors. Once, when he lifted a pocket knife (which he had always carried) from his trousers, there was a brief flurry of excitement as the family took it away from him. During the day, the governor demanded a shave and a barber was let into the mansion to attend to him. Midway through the shave, a rumor swept the family circle to the effect that the governor had tried to get the barber's razor.

There was nothing to it. Still dazed from his massive drinking and other exertions, the governor fell asleep in his chair as the barber cut a two-day growth from his face.

By five that evening, Dr. Bernhard called Titus Harris again. The governor, he said now, had agreed to enter the Harris Clinic as a voluntary patient. With Harris' permission, the family would deliver Earl to Galveston the following day. Naturally, Bernhard added, the famiy wished to avoid any and all publicity, so the matter should be kept strictly quiet. Dr. Harris agreed to co-operate.

By evening Earl was up and in a state of uncontrollable rage. For Mrs. Long, who tried to reason with him, he had accusations ranging from political intrigue to personal malevolence. For his nephew, Senator Long, he had only violent contempt, as he accused Huey's son of trying to put him out of the way so that he—Russell—could take over Louisiana. For his cousin, Dr. Long, he had another contempt-filled lecture in which he accused that practitioner of being a horse doctor. Earlier in the day, the subject of the governor's violent behavior had been discussed at length. Finally Russell Long decided that in order to minimize the chances of Earl hurting himself or a member of the family, some restraining equipment should be on hand and ready for use if needed.

From Russell at the executive mansion went a priority call to Jesse H. Bankston, director of Louisiana's state hospitals. Bankston was fishing in North Louisiana when aides finally reached him, but he hurried back to Baton Rouge. There, Russell Long told him of the governor's condition and asked him to find a strait jacket and have it brought to the Governor's Mansion. For a moment, Bankston was at a loss. He tried to explain to Senator Long that strait jackets were a thing of the past, that modern methods of treatment—notably the use of tranquilizers—had practically obviated the need for strait jackets. Senator Long was adamant. He explained that Earl was in such a state that he refused to allow doctors near him. Consequently it was a difficult, if not impossible, chore to administer tranquilizers. Moreover, the governor had a weak heart, and it was not known what effect tranquilizers would have on him. Finally, Earl had, in the past, shown a marked resistance to tranquilizing drugs, even to massive doses. It was possible that any tranquilizer administered would wear off quickly, and he would be up and dangerous again before anybody could get to him. The strait jacket, said Russell, seemed to be the answer. Bankston promised to try to find one.

Late that afternoon, after searching every mental ward in Louisiana, Bankston finally unearthed a strait jacket at the state mental hospital at Jackson. Rushed to the mansion, it was taken inside in a paper bag and kept on hand that night. As it turned out, it was never removed from the bag and the political boss of Louisiana was spared the humiliation of being trussed up like a calf ready for branding, But, regardless of whether Governor Long actually needed a restraint as harsh and mechanical as a strait jacket, his condition and his continued, disturbing conduct at least convinced the family and his doctors that he was a menace to himself or to others. They felt, in short, by this time that the governor was in a complete state of irresponsibility and that his very life was at stake.

It is interesting to speculate why Russell's appeal for a strait jacket has never appeared in print. It might very well have come out some months following the governor's resumption of his executive duties in Louisiana, at the time a state police sergeant petitioned the state civil service commission for reinstatement to the job from which Governor Long fired him. The sergeant was on duty at the executive mansion the night before Long was taken to Galveston and, like other policemen at the mansion, was ordered not to interfere with proceedings on the second floor of the mansion, where doctors and Long's family kept him locked up. Governor Long later fired him, charging that the sergeant had been assigned to him as a personal bodyguard, but that he had failed to perform his duty by allowing the family and doctors to take him to Galveston.

At the civil service hearing of the sergeant's petition, the sergeant, Doctor Long, Senator Long and Hospital Director Bankston all testified to the events that took place immediately prior to Long's trip to Galveston. The strait jacket incident was not injected into the evidence. Had it been, there is little doubt that Senator Long would have experienced some unfavorable political reaction. It must be remembered that Earl's later, repeated charges that Russell's part in the affair had been politically motivated—that is, that he wanted Earl out of the way in order to run for governor himself—found a ready audience in some quarters loyal to the governor. As it turned out, even without the disclosure that Russell had sought a straight jacket, Louisiana's voters quickly grouped themselves into two camps: those who believed that Earl's family had acted in his best interests and those who convinced themselves that Russell and Blanche had turned Earl's illness into a cheap grab for political power. Time and events, of course, have proved the latter view to be another of the fantastic concoctions that, at times, typify Louisiana's politics. Russell, with half of his six-year Senate term still remaining, had neither the intention nor the desire to run for governor at a time when Earl's friends could have smeared him as a cheap political opportunist. And Blanche—wise to the ways of politics through solid experience—must have known that Earl's backers, who represented a sizable chunk of Louisiana's voter strength, would be less than charitable in their opinions of her. Then, too, the entire Long family name would be smeared by the publicity that followed the governor's confinement. To say that Russell and Blanche welcomed this airing of dirty family linen on the public clothesline is stretching credulity to the breaking point.

As the drama surrounding the raving governor crept to a climax that Memorial Day eve, most of Louisiana had no idea that its governor was a prisoner in his own mansion, that the state, for all purposes, was drifting rudderless. Newsmen, who sensed that something was afoot, were either barred from the mansion or told that the governor was resting from his trying ordeal before the Legislature. Visitors to the mansion (the few that were allowed inside) found themselves being doubly screened. Downstairs, in the mansion office, State Police Captain John Vitale, who was in charge of the mansion police detail, stayed close to the telephone, relaying messages to the governor's family as they came in.

Early that evening, Senator Long conferred again with Hospital Director Bankston. The situation by now, he told Bankston, was acute. He asked the hospital boss to round up a couple of trusted hospital attendants who could be placed in the room with Governor Long to keep a constant watch on him. Bankston called the Southeast Louisiana Hospital (the mental institution to which Earl would eventually be taken). A short time later, two burly attendants appeared at the mansion, were led upstairs and took their positions near Earl's door. At one point, Earl made a mad dash for the mansion elevator and almost made it inside. The two attendants, Russell, Dr. Long, and Victor Bussie, president of the Louisiana State Labor Council, a close friend of the family who had appeared at the mansion a short time before, grabbed Earl and literally dragged him back to his room.

Later, testifying at the civil service hearing at which the entire mansion episode was rehashed, Bussie injected one of the understatements of the hearing into the record. Asked to testify whether, in his opinion, the governor resisted attempts to keep him inside his room, Bussie remarked dryly, "He was very much opposed [to the idea]. He wanted to get out and begin a stumping tour the next day."

Earl's wrath by this time knew no bounds. As any member of the family, or anyone else in the mansion, hove into sight, Earl would demand his release, then beg for it, then promise, threaten or abuse—according to his frame of mind of the moment. Getting help from no one, he took matters into his own hands.

With a mighty kick and a wrench, Earl turned his wrath on his bedstead, ripping the front end apart. Grabbing up an ashtray and a bottle of milk of magnesia, he hurled these through his bedroom window, then stood at the broken pane yelling "Help, murder!" for a few plaintive seconds until the attendants and the family rushed into the room. Once, when Mrs. Long called a police sergeant to come quickly and bring help, the governor appeared at the head of the stairs (the sergeant later testified) and snarled at the trooper, "Get back down there. I don't want no goddam policemen up here." The sergeant retreated before the gubernatorial fury. But when the doctors and the family finally got Earl back to his room this time, they made sure he wouldn't make another break. Instead of being posted outside the door, the attendants were ordered inside the room where they kept watch over the near-hysterical governor throughout the night.

There remained one additional detail to resolve before the governor could be taken from the mansion and flown to Galveston—the mode of transportation. That Friday night, Senator Long called in Major General Raymond Hufft, adjutant general of the Louisiana National Guard, and briefed him on what the family proposed to do. Russell asked Hufft to ready a plane for the flight. At first Hufft debated the wisdom of using an official National Guard airplane for the flight, thinking that a private plane would attract less notice and therefore diminish the chances for undue publicity. He finally decided to use a National Guard C-47, as he testified later, because it was outfitted with bunks which would be used by Earl during the trip. The family considered, also, the use of an ambulance to take the governor from the mansion to the airport, decided later that the ambulance, too, would stick out like a sore thumb. Instead, they settled for a white state-police station wagon.

Memorial Day dawned bright and clear. Members of the Legislature had scattered across the state. Newsmen, unable to confirm their suspicions that something was terribly amiss at the executive level, had to be content with terse state-police reports from the mansion, which described the governor as exhausted but resting comfortably. The strange proceedings of the past two nights were still, to all intents, pretty much of a close family secret. Now, the truth was at hand.

Shortly before 9 A.M., the station wagon drew up to the rear of the executive mansion. In front sat the driver and an attendant. From the rear they lifted a stretcher and disappeared inside the mansion.

In his room on the second floor, Earl Long argued with his family and doctors. Where would they take him? Why did they need to take him anywhere? What made them think he was sick? Why, declared Earl as he was to declare repeatedly later, he wasn't mentally ill. "If I'm crazy," he shouted, "I've always been crazy."

There was no mention of Galveston, nor was there any hint of taking him outside the state. For the moment, deemed the family, it was far better to minimize the truth than to bare the facts to the distraught Earl. Consequently, family and doctors alike assured him that he was exhausted, in need of immediate hospital treatment, and that he was to be taken to New Orleans for examinations and observation.

The news did not rest particularly well with the governor, who still had little on his mind except the coming political campaign and the absolute conviction that he was the victim of a huge political conspiracy. If he could only get before the people, said Earl, he would show them that he was the same "Ole Earl" who had swept the state in the gubernatorial elections a scant three years ago. He demanded, for the last time, to be released and allowed to continue his campaigning. The family ignored him.

There was now no doubt that if the governor was to be taken at all, he would have to be taken by force. As Dr. Harris later put it, "sufficient manpower had to be employed to persuade him to comply with the wishes of his family." While attendants pinned Earl to the bed, a doctor injected one sedative into his veins, then another. Still Earl resisted. His trousers were taken from him and he was lashed, hand and foot, to the stretcher that had been carried in by the station-wagon people. Still raging, alternately crying and pleading, he was carried from the mansion, hoisted into the station wagon and, in what must have been one of the most remarkable rides in Louisiana's history, driven directly to the parked, fueled and warmed-up National Guard C-47 at Ryan Airport in Baton Rouge. There, still strapped to the stretcher, the ailing governor was lifted into the airplane, let down on one of the bunks and strapped in for the take-off. Once, he twisted his head and looked pleadingly at General Hufft.

"Ray," he implored, "don't let them hurt me." Hufft, a Long appointee, put his arm around Earl's shoulder and said softly, "Governor, I promise you no one is going to hurt you. I am going with you wherever you go." As the big plane roared off the ground, Earl lay back resignedly, muttering to himself. It was the last time he would see Louisiana for seventeen days.

13

Exile

HIGH up in the C-47, the effects of the sedatives doctors had given to Earl began to wear off, and once again he became his uncontrollable self. He accused his family of double-crossing him as he demanded that the airplane be turned back. But his demands fell on deaf ears. The plane bore on toward Galveston. Later, there was talk that during the flight, after he had unsuccessfully ordered the plane to return to Baton Rouge, Earl had turned his wrath on General Hufft, breaking him to a private's rank. Meanwhile, in an attempt to influence the pilot, he had elevated him from lieutenant colonel to brigadier general.[1]

Once during the flight, Earl said he doubted that the plane was headed for New Orleans. The others quickly stilled his protests by explaining that bad weather had forced a rerouting to Galveston. But no one told him about the Harris Clinic.

Back in Baton Rouge, the inevitable leaked out to the capital newsmen, but first reports were full of contradictions and the usual rumors that accompany a big, breaking news story. At first, newsmen learned only that the governor had suffered a sort of breakdown and had been taken away for treatment. Where? No one seemed to know. In due time, of course, the reporters learned of the National Guard airplane and the station-wagon ride to the airport. But here, again, they were momentarily led up a blind alley; the officials, in an effort to shake newsmen off the trail, filed a phony flight plan which showed that the C-47 was bound for Corpus Christi. As usual, the officials who wanted to elude newsmen should have saved

1 This episode has never been fully confirmed, but neither Earl nor General Hufft have denied press reports about the alleged "demotion."

themselves the trouble; about the time the C-47 landed in Galveston, the reporters had already determined the destination and were en route to that point to cover the governor's arrival.

The governor's plane landed in Galveston at 4 P.M. on Memorial Day. Shortly after Earl took off, Mrs. Long had gathered some of the relatives, hopped into the governor's official Cadillac with two state troopers, and departed for Galveston. She got there just two hours after Earl landed and was taken to the hospital.

From the moment Earl Long stepped out of the National Guard airplane that brought him to Galveston, he was sealed off from the rest of the world except, part of the time, for doctors and members of his immediate family. Taken from the airplane in a wheel chair, the governor was driven to John Sealy Hospital, where he was hustled into the maximum-security section of the psychopathic ward. The building in which the governor's second-story suite was located turned out to be a drab, cement, gray-colored structure that doctors and medical students had long ago dubbed "Psycho Two." The hallway doors that separated the various sections of the building were kept locked. Across the windows stretched heavy, dark wire mesh screening that stayed in place winter and summer alike. (Dr. Harris was to explain later: "We think that bars have a bad psychological effect on the patients, so we use the screening." Earl Long was to roar later: "Why, if a man tried to escape through one of those screens he'd leave his brains hanging on it.")

Dr. Harris was not on hand to greet the governor when he arrived. Instead, the psychiatrist was at his summer home, just south of Houston, spending the day with his family. An ardent skeet-shooting champion, Dr. Harris had planned to spend the weekend shooting, but thought he should stay close to home in case the governor's arrival presented any special problems. However, he didn't think it necessary to be on hand at the hospital for Earl's arrival since, as he explained later, "the governor was coming as a voluntary patient and there was no need for me to be there."

Less than twenty-four hours later, however, Dr. Harris got the first jolt he was to experience during Earl's eighteen-day stay at the hospital. Said Harris later in his gruff, hoarse voice (he had recently undergone a successful operation for cancer of the throat), "I had no idea the governor was coming as an unco-operative patient. I had been assured that his arrival was entirely voluntary. I must say I think that on this score I was deceived."

As he drove around his place near Houston the following day (Sunday, May 31) Dr. Harris had his automobile radio turned on and "it seemed to me that all the radio talked about was the way the governor was behaving." It took only a few bulletins for Dr. Harris to understand that, far from being a docile, co-operative patient, the governor was a raving, ranting, near lunatic. He decided to cut short his weekend and get to the hospital immediately.

Earl was in no mood to listen to a lot of medical gibberish from doctors as he sat in his guarded "Psycho Two" suite. Instead, he denounced everything and everybody in sight, with particular emphasis on his family. And he proved once again that he believed in his self-imposed maxim, that if he ever shut his mouth he would need Divine help.

One doctor who saw the governor briefly shortly after his arrival at Galveston described Earl's reaction: "The way he acts most of the time is beyond belief. If you tried to write a script about it and sell it to a TV show they wouldn't believe you. They'd call it fantastic. The man just talks and raves incessantly. He sits there and runs a blue streak about anything that comes to his mind, and things keep coming. For example, he'll talk about the National Guard and how they deceived him into coming here. The National Guard will suggest national defense to him and he'll be off on that for a while. National defense suggests the amount of money we're spending on it and he'll talk about the defense budget. The defense budget will get him thinking about his own state budget and he'll start in on that. It's ramble, ramble, ramble, on and on. He never shuts up."

Blanche Long, on hand by this time with the governor's sister, Mrs. John Hunt, came in for particular treatment. As she sat next to Earl in his suite, Blanche talked softly, calmly, trying to convince her husband that the treatment he got would be for his own good, and that it would be a temporary thing. As she later told newsmen:

"I felt it was my duty as a wife to assure him of this chance of full recovery. I sincerely pray that when he is well, he will feel that the family has done the only thing possible under the circumstances. I felt it was absolutely necessary to heed the advice of five Louisiana doctors and three doctors with the John Sealy Hospital in Galveston . . . to see that Earl is given every opportunity to be restored to good health and a full and happy life. All were fully agreed in accord with the doctors' recommendations that Earl remain in the hospital for medical care and therapy. His condition . . . is caused by overwork, causing complete physical and mental exhaustion. They [the doctors] feel certain that with proper care Earl will return to good health in a short period of time. I felt it my duty as a wife to assure him of this chance of full recovery."

Neither Blanche's soothing words nor her continued presence quieted the upset governor. Indeed, if anything, they irritated him to a repetition of the outbursts that had marked his conduct at the mansion in Baton Rouge.

Dr. Harris described a typical scene between the governor and Blanche: "Blanche would come in to see Earl and he'd start off calmly enough, talking about why he was there and his need for rest and so on. After a few minutes he would begin to get excited again. He'd accuse Blanche of being in cahoots with his political enemies and before you knew it he was cursing and raging and screaming at her. Naturally, she'd have to leave. After a while, we decided her presence was doing more harm than good and she stopped seeing him."

To Dr. Harris, who arrived at the hospital on Sunday, the day after Earl got there, one look at the man, the history, the symptoms and the conduct were enough to tell him volumes. He decided almost immediately that Earl was suffering from a deep-seated psychosis with manic-depressive overtones, but he had no way of knowing, of course, what was causing the emotional upheaval in his important patient. Dr. Harris decided not to rush into any diagnosis or treatment of Earl. Instead, he set out to win the governor's confidence with easy talk, low-pressure questioning and completely casual visits.

Dr. Harris' appearance had an alarm-clock effect on the governor. Into Harris' sympathetic ear Earl poured out tales of being drugged and dragged to Galveston, of being kept a prisoner in his mansion, of being manhandled by "bone crushers" from a state asylum and, finally, of being used as a pincushion by injection-minded doctors in Louisiana. Dr. Harris nodded sympathetically, interjecting a question here and there, assuring the governor that nothing so dark would happen to him during his stay in Galveston. Earl brightened perceptibly, stuck out his hand and elicited from the doctor a solemn promise that no needles would be jabbed into him. Dr. Harris shook hands and agreed that no needle would be used until Earl gave explicit permission. Earl then settled back a bit more calmly, himself promised to co-operate with Dr. Harris and the staff. Dr. Harris knew exactly what to do.

For the first few days, the treatment devised for Earl was pretty routine. He was kept away from all friends and visitors, except certain members of the immediate family. Blanche came for a while, then returned to Baton Rouge, saying, "I sincerely pray that when he is well he will feel that the family has done the only thing possible, under the circumstances, to assure his return to a happy and full life. I ask all his friends throughout the state to join me in daily prayer for his speedy and full recovery."

Next, Dr. Harris prescribed complete rest. He particularly wanted Earl kept away from whisky (although, as it turned out, some whisky was smuggled in to the governor during his Galveston stay by loyal henchmen) and the telephone, over which the governor could work himself into a lather as he had done so often in the past. For rest, Dr. Harris prescribed tranquilizers, particularly thorazine.

Finally Dr. Harris, by now on an easy, friendly plane with the governor, induced Earl to allow some blood to be taken from him. At this point Dr. Harris strongly believed that Earl's behavior resulted basically from some deep-seated organic deficiency. More specifically, Dr. Harris suspected Earl might be suffering from syphilis or paresis. Earl reluctantly agreed to give the blood for the Wassermann and eventually submitted to a spinal tap. Both tests proved to be completely negative, showing that Earl had never been the victim of a venereal maladjustment. In the first comprehensive bulletin issued by Dr. Harris during the early stages of his observation, he appeared to be convinced, however, that Earl's underlying trouble was basically organic. In Dr. Harris' words: "All information available at this time indicates that he is suffering from an acute illness that well may be the outgrowth of some underlying physical condition that has brought about secondary changes in the central nervous system and that with adequate care and treatment the outlook for recovery is an excellent one. Acute disturbances of this general nature are not uncommon and ordinarily a favorable outcome can be expected."

It was at this point that Dr. Harris told newsmen that his patient was "co-operating reluctantly," but that he (Earl) still "doesn't think he is sick," a stand Earl was to continue to take even after Harris and his colleagues reluctantly agreed to let him leave the Harris Clinic without any really significant improvement in his basic condition.

While Earl fumed as a prisoner of the state of Texas, Louisiana's officialdom divided over the effect of the commitment on Earl's future. By and large, Long's close allies stoutly maintained that their chief's departure was a thing of the moment and that the Galveston incident would have no measurable effect on his political future. Long's enemies, on the other hand, seized the incident as an excuse to heap abuse and scorn on the sick governor, insisting that their perennial charge—that he was basically irresponsible—had now been completely justified. Most of the state's official body, however, steered a middle-of-the-road course, keeping one eye cocked on Galveston, the other on the maneuverings that had begun to take place in Baton Rouge.

The political intrigue that accompanied Long's departure, and his loud charges that Blanche and Russell had teamed up into a solid conspiracy to depose him, gained some momentum from an unwitting Russell Long. In probably the single most ill-advised gesture of the whole episode, he insisted on descending on the capitol to deliver an explanatory speech to a joint session of the Legislature.

On the Sunday following Earl's departure, Russell appeared in the House, speech in hand, and clambered to the rostrum before the microphones. Hardly had he spoken before hoots and catcalls drowned out what he was trying to say. At least six of the legislators present demanded that he leave the hall without delivering his speech. No invitation, they insisted, had been extended to the junior Senator from Louisiana to address the Legislature. By the rules of both Houses, the critics said, no one—not even the governor himself—could address a joint session without a specific invitation from both Houses.

Russell, in his haste to take his case for confinement before the Legislature and the people, now made one of the classic blunders of his political career. Instead of turning the other cheek to the incensed legislators and requesting their permission to speak, he turned into a small, pouting boy. As the catcalls and hooting died down, Russell gathered speech in hand. With a petulant expression on his face, he stepped from the rostrum and made his way to the door. His whole attitude said: "Well, if you won't let me play, the hell with you."

Several of his close friends stopped him, implored him to return to the rostrum to deliver his speech, pleading at the same time with the opposition legislators to let the senator have his say. Like an aggrieved guest who suddenly decides to leave a party in a huff, but is finally soothed and persuaded to stay, and amid grumbling from the dissident lawmakers, Russell went back to the microphones to tell again how he, Blanche and other members of the Long family had wrestled with their consciences but, in the end, had to perform the unpopular and unpleasant chore of sending the governor to a hospital for his own good.

Realistically speaking, Russell's speech in and of itself was a pretty tame announcement of the facts. Russell emphasized that neither he nor Blanche had any designs on the governor's office, but had acted in good faith to safeguard Earl's health.

But Russell's petulance and his disagreeable manner in insisting that he be allowed to speak, together with the arbitrary manner in which he presented himself, combined to work toward his political detriment. Long after Earl returned to Louisiana and reassumed his office, rank-and-file voters were denouncing Russell's poor showmanship and the part he played in Earl's confinement.

Meantime, the job of running Louisiana fell to easygoing, mild-mannered Lieutenant Governor Lether Frazar, who was himself in questionable health. Frazar assumed the temporary leadership of the state hesitantly. Said he to newsmen who pressed him for an answer about his status, "I don't know. There has been no official ruling on it, one way or the other." As to Governor Long's position, Frazar clucked sympathetically. "He has been working so hard recently that it would be enough to kill a man twenty years younger. We all hope that he will be able to return, but none of us is too hopeful. It is possible he has served his last day as governor. The main thing we all want is for him to recover his health. For now, we are kinda letting things ride for a few days."

In the House, Speaker Robert Angelle was more emphatic. A Long ally and supporter, Angelle had no doubt about who still bossed the state. Said he, "He'll be back. And what's more, he'll be re-elected by one hundred thousand votes when he runs again." Attorney General Jack Gremillion, caught between pro-Long and anti-Long forces, and mindful of his own plans to run for re-election, cagily withheld an official ruling as to who was governor. For all practical purposes, however, with the governor out of the state, Lether Frazar was the acting governor in fact and in name. But there was little doubt in his mind, or in the minds of Louisianians in general, that the mantle he had assumed in the governor's absence was merely a temporary one. Earl, everybody felt confidently, would be back. It might take time, but he would indeed be back. For some, the prospect was unnerving.

The legality of keeping Long in the Galveston hospital now had to be faced by Earl's family. Under Texas law, the patient could be kept in the hospital against his will for a period of ninety-six hours. After that, he either had to be set free or formally committed—that is, by a court order—for a period of not less than fourteen days. Following that, he had a right to a hearing, at which he could either ask for a jury trial to test his sanity, or agree to a voluntary commitment. In any case, the family had ninety-six hours from the time Earl arrived at the John Sealy Hospital to decide which course to take.

There was no doubt, at this point, that Long wanted to get out of the hospital and would use any means at his disposal to achieve this end. In summing up Earl's attitude about confinement, Dr. Harris told newsmen, "He is firmly, stubbornly convinced that he is not sick and that he shouldn't be here. He displays great animosity toward certain members of his family. He believes that certain members of his family are in cahoots with his political enemies, and that they wanted him out of the state and that that is why he was sent here. He is definitely opposed to being in the hospital."

This point of view, strangely enough, was shared by at least some of Earl's closest relatives. One John Sealy official put it this way: "Mrs. Long and Dr. Long, who have been with him most of the time and who have seen him in action firsthand, definitely favor commitment, at least on a temporary basis. Dr. Long is strongest in favor of this, while Mrs. Long, who really thinks he ought to be committed, still has some reluctance about it because he's her husband. But some of his sisters see no reason why he should be kept in a hospital. They say there's nothing wrong with him and that he's acting the way he always acted. To them, he's just 'good Ole Earl.' "

By this time, the hospital authorities were frankly getting fed up with Earl, his nonco-operation, the hemming and hawing of the family on the matter of commitment and the sudden white glare of publicity. Hospital Director John Truslow, Dr. Harris, and the hospital's attorney, Preston Shirley of Galveston, decided that the time had come for the family to act one way or the other. To speed the decision, they called a meeting of the group and explained that the hospital was in a delicate position on the matter of confinement. The family would have to act one way or the other if they wished the governor to receive further care.

The group met in a Galveston motel on the night of Monday, June 1. There Attorney Shirley carefully explained the legal aspects of commitment. Dr. Long, from the beginning, completely favored commitment. His own diagnosis of the governor's condition—manic-depressive psychosis—had convinced him that Earl needed extensive and prolonged treatment. Blanche Long, too, had no doubts about the necessity of further treatment for her sick husband. Understandably, however, she was reluctant to take the formal legal step toward commitment. What brought her around in the end, however, was the reassurance of hospital officials that Dr. Long's signature in itself was legally sufficient to commit the governor, but that public opinion would react more favorably if both she and Dr. Long signed the commitment papers. Blanche agreed to add her name to the document.

The commitment papers were signed the next day by Blanche, Dr. Long, and Galveston County Probate Judge Hugh Gibson, Jr. Finally, there it was in cold, hard, legal print for the world to see: Earl Long, the stellar member of a political dynasty that had ruled Louisiana for a quarter of a century, the governor of a sovereign state, was, in the opinion of his family, a "mentally ill person" in "immediate" need of medical care.

> To the Sheriff of Galveston County, Texas [read the stark, legal phraseology], Earl Long . . . a mentally ill person . . . has been examined . . .and the said examinations concur that . . . Earl Long is mentally ill and because of his mental illness is likely to cause immediate injury to himself or others if not immediately restrained. . . . It is therefore ordered that the said Earl Long be, and he hereby is detained in protective custody and that the John Sealy Hospital of Galveston, Texas, assume and maintain protective custody over the patient and there safely keep him pending further orders of this Court.

Earl Long, the garrulous leader of Louisiana politics, the successor to the late Kingfish's mantle, was now a prisoner in an alien state. And neither all his tears, nor the state police he commanded, nor the political influence he wielded could wash away a single word of the order signed and executed by an obscure probate judge in a city three hundred miles from his seat of power.

The curious chain of events that ended in Earl Long's release from Galveston's John Sealy Hospital began innocuously enough when Galveston County Deputy Sheriff Gerald Leslie presented himself in the governor's suite on June 2. In his hand Leslie carried a set of the formal commitment papers, signed by Mrs. Long, Dr. Long and Judge Gibson—the legal authority under which the state of Texas held Ole Earl a prisoner.

As Earl spotted the booted, Stetsoned deputy advancing on him, papers in hand, he beamed perceptibly, stuck out his hand and shook Leslie's warmly.

"Well," boomed the governor of Louisiana, "a Texas Ranger. Sit down, Ranger. I'm glad the law's on my side now."

Leslie, still standing and shifting uncomfortably, informed the governor that he was there to formally serve the notice of confinement on Earl. The papers, he explained, contained all the legal terminology that went with matters of that sort. Handing the papers to Dr. Truslow, who was also present, Leslie stood by while Truslow read them to Earl. The governor listened intently, interrupting occasionally, then took the papers that Truslow handed to him. Sipping a soft drink, Earl asked Leslie, "When am I going to court?" Leslie said he didn't know. "Would you," demanded Earl, "vote for a crazy man?" Replied Leslie diplomatically, "I'd vote for you, Governor." Said Earl, "Get Governor Daniel [2] on the phone for me." Leslie, his duty discharged, shook hands with the governor again, turned and left the room, as did Truslow. Earl sat in a chair next to his window, the soft drink in one hand, the commitment papers in the other.

For the next thirteen days Earl was in the hands of the doctors. For a while, he asked for no newspapers and got none. Occasionally attendants delivered a letter or a floral wreath from some well-wisher. Late in his stay at Galveston, Earl began to see Blanche once again.

This time the governor pursued one persistent theme, but he altered his tactics to gain his objective. In the beginning, he insisted that he had been committed illegally, that he was well and should be discharged and allowed to return to Louisiana. Blanche stoutly maintained that nothing had changed and that she intended to abide by her earlier decision to see that he received the treatment he needed.

Earl asked for and was granted a habeas corpus hearing at which he intended to show that he had been brought to Galveston illegally and that Texas had no jurisdiction over him. To represent him Judge Gibson appointed three local attorneys. The hearing was held on June 15—the day before Earl was scheduled to appear before Judge Gibson for a preliminary sanity hearing—before another district judge, L. D. Godard. Although it was far from a full-dress hearing and was held merely to sustain or rebut a delicate point of law, the hearing marked the first time Earl appeared in public since his incarceration in

[2] Governor Price Daniel of Texas.

the psycho ward. The courtroom, naturally, was filled to capacity with attorneys, Long's friends, newsmen and the curious.

Dressed in a blue suit, wearing a wide-brimmed, floppy straw hat, a thin and haggard Earl entered the courtroom and took his seat at the attorneys' table. Accompanying him were a nurse, a male attendant and a young intern, who sat directly behind the governor. As the lawyers droned on, Earl busied himself writing notes which he passed to friends, taking gulps from a paper container filled with grape juice, from time to time snatching out a paper napkin to wipe dust from the table top. At other times, as he spied a friend in the audience, he smiled slightly, raised a hand and waved. Once, in a pointed gesture at Nephew Russell, who sat in the courtroom, he had a container of juice sent to a friend sitting next to Russell, waited until the man got the container, then raised his own container in a toast.

It was too much to expect that the spirited Earl could contain himself throughout an essentially dull courtroom proceeding. At one point he jumped from his seat and strode to the jury box to listen to the hearing from that vantage point. Once, he leaned over and asked Nephew Russell, "How much will you charge to run?" When a witness described how one doctor had administered to Long at the mansion in Baton Rouge, Earl said loudly, "He's nothing but a horse doctor." When Dr. Long's name was introduced into the hearing, Earl interjected, "He's another horse doctor. And a loan shark, too." When a witness described how hospital attendants had put Earl on the stretcher for the flight to Galveston, Earl exclaimed, "They were bone crushers." Once, Earl picked up an ash tray and spat into it. When a courtroom attendant handed him a paper cup, Earl looked at it blankly for a moment, put it down and spat into the ash tray again. At one point an exasperated Judge Godard ordered Earl to "shut up."

At another point in the hearing, Earl passed an almost prophetical note to Senator Long. *Russell,* read Earl's note, *I will be in Ochsner Clinic no later than Wednesday. Earl K. Long.* As events turned out, Earl hit the nail on the head.

For all its importance, the habeas corpus hearing might as well have been canceled. The hearing on Earl's sanity, due the following day, was postponed when Judge Godard announced that he would need a week to come to a decision on the legality of

Earl's commitment. Meantime, Earl began the out-of-court maneuvering that was to win him temporary freedom and get him back to Louisiana and in position to exercise his extensive powers as the state's chief executive.

For several days Earl continued to persuade Blanche to withdraw the commitment order, but when he saw that this plea had little effect on his wife, Earl tried another tack. In a complete reversal, Earl admitted to Blanche that he now realized that he was sick and that he needed care. But, he persisted, Galveston was not the place for him to get it. He wanted to return to Louisiana, to his own state, where the care was just as good. Moreover, he told Blanche, if he were in a secure, familiar atmosphere, away from the shadow of a foreign institution, he was convinced that he could recover more quickly. He vowed to Blanche that if she relented and withdrew her commitment order, he would voluntarily enter the famed Ochsner Clinic at New Orleans for treatment.

Under the weight of his pleas, a distraught and bewildered Blanche wilted. Finally she agreed to his proposal, but insisted on two conditions. The first, she said, was that the governor would sign a paper releasing Blanche, Doctor Long and all the others who took part in his confinement and commitment from any liability for their actions. The second condition Blanche imposed was that the governor sign an affidavit agreeing to enter Ochsner's Clinic on a voluntary basis. Earl readily agreed to meet both conditions. The stage was set for his release and Earl settled back to wait for the legalistics to be cleared away.

Blanche's first move was to inform Dr. Harris that she had decided to allow Earl to return to Louisiana. She told Harris of Earl's agreement to enter Ochsner.

Blanche's announcement threw Dr. Harris into something of a temporary conflict. Although he had wanted to be rid of the rambunctious Earl since the first day he appeared as an involuntary patient, Dr. Harris' sense of medical and personal ethics played strongly on him. He felt honestly that Governor Long required further treatment and that he was far from cured or adjusted. He told Mrs. Long of his misgivings about releasing Earl. Mrs. Long, however, was adamant. When Dr. Harris saw that he could not change Blanche's mind, he heaved the sigh of relief one feels when he has done his duty to the best of his ability. In accordance with Blanche's wishes, Dr. Harris drafted and sent to Judge Gibson the following letter dated June 17:

> Under the circumstances existing at the moment, I think that it is very advisable from the standpoint of Governor Long's health that he be dismissed from the hospital today to return to Louisiana to enter the Ochsner Memorial Hospital. Governor Long has agreed to do this and to place himself under physicians at that hospital. I have been in communication with doctors at that hospital who will have charge of him and they are prepared to carry on the treatment that has been instituted here.
>
> Governor Long was assured by his family yesterday that this would be done. He has been anticipating leaving the hospital and I, too, on the advice of his family, assured him that he would be released today. For him to be restrained here longer would cause a reaction in him that would be bad for him from a health standpoint.

Dr. Harris' letter to Judge Gibson was followed by two documents from Earl himself. Both documents were dated June 17, the day he got out of "Psycho Two." The first took Blanche, Dr. Long, Russell and others off the hook for taking Earl to Galveston in the first place.

> I, the undersigned Earl K. Long [read the paper], for valuable consideration, do hereby fully RELEASE Blanche R. Long, Arthur D. Long and all other persons (whether named herein or not) having anything whatsoever to do with my custody, transportation, detention, examination, certification, apprehension, treatment and discharge, and all other acts, matters and things, events, words and deeds, wherever occurring, in connection with, arising out of or leading up to my hospitalization at John Sealy Hospital . . . and the proceedings in Probate Cause No. 25,828 on the docket of the Probate Court . . . of and from all liability of any and every kind whatsoever by reason of said matters, this being a full, complete and general release covering all persons and the entire matter from beginning to end.

Earl's second document was as much to the point as the first. Wrote the governor:

> June 17, 1959—I, the undersigned Earl K. Long, do hereby solemnly promise and do hereby bind and obligate myself,

> immediately upon release from the protective custody heretofore ordered by the Probate Court of Galveston County, to proceed directly to the Ochsner Foundation Hospital at New Orleans, Louisiana, and to enter said hospital voluntarily as a patient. I make this promise and obligation of my own free will.

After a forty-five-minute conference wtih Mrs. Long, both Judge Godard and Judge Gibson complied with the handwriting on the wall. Judge Godard dismissed the commitment application originally signed by Blanche and Dr. Long. By five o'clock that afternoon, with a Louisiana National Guard C-47 waiting to take him to New Orleans, Earl Long, having nervously packed and unpacked for the third time, walked out of "Psycho Two" a reasonably free man. Mrs. Long, Margaret Dixon, managing editor of the Baton Rouge *Morning Advocate* (and a close friend of Earl's) and two attorneys came to escort Earl to the airport. But as soon as he was set free, Earl hopped into a deputy sheriff's car and headed for the waiting plane without escort.

At the airport, a crowd of well-wishers, newsmen, cameramen and Louisiana officials crowded around a triumphant Earl, who willingly posed for photographers, smiled thinly, limped slightly as he walked with the aid of a cane.

"How do you feel, Governor?" asked one newsman.

Earl considered for a moment, then said, "I feel better. I've rested some." Then, as he headed for the waiting C-47, another newsman popped what was to be the sixty-four-dollar question.

"Are you still governor?" he asked Earl as they reached the airplane.

Earl swung slowly, faced the crowd. Then, pursing his lips, he said hoarsely, "The minute I hit the [state] line." Then, while Blanche steadied him from behind, Earl slowly clambered into the plane. Five minutes later, he roared off toward a waiting Louisiana.

14

Mandeville

THE news that Governor Long had succeeded in extricating himself from the Texas hospital hit official Louisiana like a bombshell. One veteran newsman, waiting at New Orleans' Moissant Airport for the C-47 that bore Earl Long toward his political happy hunting grounds, remarked wryly, "That tremor you feel is everybody shaking in their boots. When the old man gets back so many heads will roll you'll think it's the French Revolution all over again."

Even as Earl winged his way homeward, political lights from around the state converged on New Orleans to pledge their loyalty to the returning governor. From Opelousas, Long's Senate floor leader B. B. ("Sixty") Rayburn arrived on the run, as did House Speaker Angelle. Lieutenant Governor Frazar, whose timidity in grasping the state reins during Long's absence had allowed Louisiana to drift aimlessly, arrived at New Orleans to greet his returning chief. Exuding visible relief, Louisiana's second-in-command confided to waiting newsmen, "I'm just glad to be lieutenant governor again." His relief was destined to be short-lived.

Aboard the airplane bearing Long, his wife and the returning party, Earl, dressed in tan trousers, zippered jacket, flowered tie, and carrying a soft-felt, wide-brimmed hat in his hand, sat on one of the plane's bunks, saying little. As he sat there, Blanche sat down beside him, took one of his hands in her own and leaned back. One of the passengers reported: "They sat there like that during most of the trip. They didn't say much. But Blanche looked somewhat content. I think she was convinced she had done the right thing in bringing him to New

Orleans. I know she was afraid that if she had left him in Galveston he might have died there."

Shortly after seven on the evening of June 17, Earl's plane landed at Moissant, taxiing far out from the terminal in order to avoid the waiting cluster of cameramen and reporters. From the terminal ramp sped a black limousine which pulled up to the plane just as it rolled to a halt. Quickly Earl and Blanche stepped from the plane, disappeared into the limousine and roared off toward Ochsner Foundation Hospital. There, unlike the man that had been dragged kicking and screaming to John Sealy, a calm, straight-faced Earl walked unhesitatingly into the building, into an elevator that whisked him to a turquoise and gray fifth-floor suite overlooking the Mississippi River. A few minutes later, as he stood at the window gazing at the storied river, the city, and the Huey P. Long Bridge that his late brother had built, Earl spied the first of the group of newsmen who had followed him to Ochsner's. Hands on hips, he grinned in recognition. Then slowly, deliberately, he raised both arms, V-fashion, in a signal of triumph. It was an eloquent gesture that could not be mistaken. It said simply: I'm back. I'm the boss and I'm back. I've won.

Long's apparent docility and his willingness to co-operate with family and doctors temporarily succeeded in masking his real plans. But a series of events that took place immediately after he entered Ochsner's revealed his real purpose—and his unquieted taste for power.

Shortly after he signed in, the doctors suggested a complete physical examination. Earl readily agreed. By the time he retired for that evening, doctors had taken X-rays of his chest and throat, an internist had conducted a rather complete examination of him, and he had submitted to a cardiogram. His whole attitude bespoke co-operation.

Speaker Angelle and Senate Leader Rayburn attempted to see the governor but Blanche took charge, saying that Long was asleep and could not be disturbed. Later, when Rayburn told reporters he thought the governor was so well he would be out in a few days, Blanche tartly corrected that impression by telling the reporters that Earl would be at Ochsner's "two weeks or longer." Earl, she added, would not attempt to take up the duties of his office and turn his fifth-floor suite into a "little capitol." Instead, she announced, the "routine" duties of running the state would be handled by the governor's executive secretary, Mrs. Wilma Lockhart. At this point Blanche appeared to be very much in charge.

Nor did there appear to be anything devious in the governor's conduct toward Ochsner's doctors. In statements issued by hospital spokesmen, it was apparent that they were proceeding almost leisurely, taking things in order, acting on the presumption that Long would be their patient for some time to come. In a statement issued by the hospital (which Blanche approved) a spokesman said Ochsner's doctors were "concentrating presently on his general condition. He was given a thorough physical examination last night by a specialist in internal medicine." The spokesman added that for the present the doctors would delay any psychiatric examinations until after the physical investigations had taken place. Moreover, they said, they would not take into account any previous psychiatric findings, but would "start from scratch."

Hospital statements about the change that had come over the governor were so confident in tone that Earl appeared to be, indeed, in complete possession of his good senses. The statements emphasized that Long was "an entirely voluntary patient," who could "leave the hospital any time he wishes to." But the implication of the statements was that this was an unlikely possibility. One spokesman even went so far as to suggest that Long was a completely changed man from the rebellious, ranting patient of three weeks ago. In appearance, said the spokesman, Long was "a very far cry from being governor. I think," he added, "he is now a scared man."

So it was, in this atmosphere of sweet reason and complete co-operation, that Earl Long, the arrant son, had returned to his native state and to the forgiving bosom of his family. If anything, the episode served to highlight one significant fact. For all their exposure to it, neither Earl's family nor his friends had ever completely comprehended the deviousness of the turbulent mind that functioned behind the broad forehead—at times with a Rasputin-like fury, again with disguised Machiavellian subtlety. They were to learn, to their great dismay, within twenty-four hours.

On Thursday, June 18, Earl Long, as usual, rose early to read the newspapers and breakfast with Blanche, who had stayed with him overnight in his hospital suite. Disarmingly, almost casually, Earl gave the first hint of what really ate at his mind. Hospitals, he informed Blanche, were all right for some peope. But not for a gregarious, grass-roots country boy like himself. He was pretty well convinced—and didn't she think so, too?—that his quickest recovery would come when he was out of the hospital and back in the bucolic peace of his pea patch at Winnfield. For the moment, Blanche let this danger signal pass. That, she said, was probably right. However, time enough for that when the doctors at Ochsner's finished with him. That had to come first.

Earl hedged. The sooner out of Ochsner's the better for him and everybody else, he told Blanche. After all, there was a state to run and his political enemies were taking advantage of his absence. Once more, he reiterated his intention to run for a fourth term. Blanche hesitated, argued, remonstrated. Finally, she pointedly reminded the governor of his written promise to enter Ochsner's for the treatment everybody agreed he needed so badly.

By this time Earl had dropped most of the pretense about staying at the hospital. Just as pointedly, he reminded Blanche of one salient fact nobody had seemed to notice. He had promised to enter Ochsner's and he had kept his promise. Nowhere had he said in writing just how long he would stay. That, he continued, was entirely up to him and he wasn't at all sure he wanted to stay any longer. Even more pointedly, Earl reminded Blanche that now he was on much firmer ground than he had been at Galveston. In words of one syllable, he told his wife that in Louisiana he was still boss and could do as he pleased. And what pleased him now was release from Ochsner's.

Blanche got the message. Without ado, she called in an Ochsner's doctor and Earl's great and good friend, New Orleans physician Martin O. Miller, a wealthy oilman on the side and a participant in the mansion nightmare. From eleven o'clock that morning until past three that afternoon, the two doctors discussed, reasoned and pleaded with the adamant governor, assuring him that the worst possible move he could make now would be to leave the hospital. They pointed out to him that his situation had changed vastly, that he was no longer a prisoner and that he was free to leave at any time. But, they added, he was a sick man. They implored him to stay on, at least for the time being, for continued examinations and treatment. Earl gave them one final word: No. He had been kept a prisoner for seventeen days at Galveston while all sorts of news stories filled the papers and the air waves about his condition. He would leave the hospital, rest up at his Winnfield farm, then take to the stump to show Louisiana's voters that he was as sane and hearty as he had always been.

There was one legal technicality to resolve and Ochsner's director telephoned the hospital's attorney to find out. If Mrs. Long wanted her husband kept at the clinic, could he legally be kept there? Back came the attorney's ruling: Absolutely not. Since Earl had entered as an "entirely voluntary" patient, he was free to leave at any time. The clinic had no legal hold on him and neither did Mrs. Long. Indeed, said the attorney, if the clinic attempted to prevent the governor from leaving, it was inviting a lawsuit. Hospital officials called in Blanche, told her the sad news, then prepared to discharge their famous patient.

Blanche didn't need telling. By early afternoon she knew full well that Earl had once again made up his mind and that no amount of urging would change it. Even as the doctors reasoned with Earl, Blanche acted.

Shortly after two that afternoon, while he waited to testify in a routine court case in Baton Rouge, Dr. Chester Williams, the young coroner for East Baton Rouge Parish, looked up to see a messenger signaling for him. Mrs. Blanche Long, said the courier, was trying desperately to reach him. Would he telephone her at New Orleans?

Ten minutes later Dr. Williams was talking to Blanche, who spoke from Brent House at Ochsner Foundation. Quickly she described the events of the morning, adding that even now doctors were trying, without success, to persuade Earl to stay on at the hospital. Mrs. Long told Dr. Williams that Earl needed treatment and hospitalization, that if he were set free he would be his own undoing. She asked Dr. Williams to have the legal papers necessary for commitment in a Louisiana mental institution drawn up at once. Hesitantly Dr. Williams suggested that Mrs. Long could pursue the same legal remedy through the

Orleans Parish (New Orleans) coroner. Mrs. Long, however, insisted that the matter be handled in Baton Rouge, since she was sure Governor Long would head that way as soon as he left Ochsner's. Dr. Williams told Mrs. Long he would take the necessary legal steps, but that he would need Mrs. Long, as a next of kin, to sign the papers that under Louisiana law would be necessary to commit the governor. Mrs. Long promised to start for Baton Rouge immediately.

Now was to begin a drama without parallel in modern American political history, involving a governor in flight, the unsuspecting object of a police surveillance; an averted clash between the state police, answerable only to the governor, and a set of parish deputy sheriffs, answerable to the legal dicta of a court of record; the introduction of curbstone psychiatry; the forcible incarceration of a chief of state; and, finally, the coldly calculated political gimmickry employed to release him. If, at times, the action reached soap-opera levels in which the actors resembled Keystone Kops, it was kept from reaching that ludicrous level by two compelling facts. The leading characters in this drama were not playing games. And, to a large extent, more than three million residents of the state which their governor ruled, acting at all times as completely detached witnesses, were unwitting pawns in the proceedings.

In New Orleans, satisfied that the legal machinery for Earl's second commitment had been put into gear, Blanche Long lost little time in carrying out her role as the heavy in the plot. With two state policemen, she climbed into a black Oldsmobile, headed north on Highway 61 and, at speeds of up to eighty miles per hour, roared in the direction of Baton Rouge, seventy-nine miles away. She had left Ochsner's at 4:20 P.M. without tipping her hand to anyone except Dr. Williams.

At 4:40, hat planted firmly on his head, flanked by Dr. Miller and a state police sergeant, Earl Long left Ochsner's. The dramatic departure was chronicled, minutes later, in a bulletin over the wires of United Press International, which read:

> Gov. Earl Long stalked grimly out of the hospital he agreed to enter for mental and physical treatment today and apparently set out for the capital with state police troopers around him.

As he left the hospital, reporters asked Long if he intended to head for Baton Rouge to actively take over the gubernatorial office once again. Smiling, Long sought to throw reporters off his trail. No, he told them, he would stay in New Orleans for a while and rest at the home of his friend Dr. Miller. With that, Louisiana's political ruler clambered into a white, unmarked state-police sedan and drove off. With him were Dr. Miller and two troopers.

As Blanche Long raced toward Baton Rouge in one car, and as Earl Long, proceeding at a more leisurely pace, followed without knowing what lay ahead for him, Dr. Williams moved quickly in Baton Rouge.

Long's erratic behavior came as no surprise to Williams. As far back as the 1956 session of the Legislature, when Earl harangued his legislators and publicly scuffled for control of the chamber microphone with Secretary of State Wade O. Martin, Jr., Williams had had gnawing doubts about the governor's condition. During the session in May, Dr. Williams had gone to the legislative chambers to hear portions of Earl's celebrated monologues. He had been appalled at Earl's behavior and condition. Once, he had half-jokingly remarked to a medical friend that one day as coroner he might have to face up to the question of passing on Long's mental condition. Now the question was at hand and Dr. Williams acted.

To District Judge Fred S. LeBlanc, Dr. Williams related the essentials of the story he had heard from Blanche Long. If the facts warranted, he told the judge, it would be necessary to have commitment papers on hand and signed by the time the governor reached the city. Judge LeBlanc ordered the papers.

As the East Baton Rouge coroner, Dr. Williams had interviewed more than two thousand individuals to determine their mental condition. Nevertheless he now called in Dr. Sparkman Wyatt, a friend and a practicing Baton Rouge psychiatrist. Dr. Wyatt agreed to help with the examination of Earl Long. The two met in the basement of the East Baton Rouge courthouse—a few feet from the room in which Dr. Williams normally performed his autopsies—and waited for their unsuspecting patient.

Meantime Judge LeBlanc had called East Baton Rouge Sheriff Bryan Clemmons to fill him in. Sheriff Clemmons, in something of a delicate position, ordered his two top aides—Assistant Chief Deputy George LeBlanc (no kin to the judge) and Chief of Detectives Herman Thompson—to ride to the parish line, seventeen miles from the courthouse, to await Long's coming. He gave explicit orders to the two. Since no commitment papers had yet been signed, they had no legal jurisdiction over the governor. In no case were they to interfere with his progress until Sheriff Clemmons specifically notified them to act. The two deputies departed to take up their parish line stations.

As they sat there waiting, Blanche's black Oldsmobile flashed by. The deputies radioed the sheriff's office that the First Lady was at hand.

Ten minutes dragged by, then fifteen, then twenty. After a half hour, Earl's white car hove into sight. The waiting deputies radioed the news to the sheriff, then waited for instructions. Back came the message. In effect, it told them to fall in behind the governor's car, follow it, but keep hands off it. The deputies complied.

LeBlanc and Thompson followed Earl's car for eight miles. They could see the governor clearly, sitting in the front seat, chatting amiably with the trooper who drove and with Dr. Miller and the other trooper in the rear. If he had any inkling that something was amiss, he didn't show it.

Suddenly the deputies' radio came alive. "The papers have been signed," crackled the receiver. "Put your plan into effect." The deputies swung to the left, came abreast of the police car and signaled the driver to pull over.

It was a calm but uncertain Earl Long who looked up to see the deputies advancing on him. "Howdy, Governor," said Deputy Thompson. "We've been ordered to escort you into town."

"Well," beamed a relieved Earl Long. "Glad to see you." Thompson said later, "At this point, I'm sure he believed that we were there to escort him into the city as a sort of guard of honor. I don't think he knew a thing about the papers being signed."

For a moment there was an abrupt tenseness between the deputies and the state troopers, who divined what was happening. Technically, the troopers at this point could have forced the deputies' hand and protected their chief. As it turned out,

Thompson and LeBlanc moved quickly and firmly to forestall such a situation.

As the governor continued to beam and chat, Thompson moved quickly to the driver's door, opened it and motioned the trooper out. As the trooper hesitated Thompson said softly, "Get out. I'll explain everything later." The trooper climbed out and Thompson slid behind the wheel, next to the governor.

The ride to the courthouse was a mixture of suspense and unreal ease. In the front seat, Governor Long rambled on, asking the deputies about themselves, chatting about mutual friends, learning that LeBlanc's father held a state job with the Department of Corrections. In the back seat Dr. Miller, not nearly as much in the dark as Earl, maintained a stony silence. Threading his way through the last remaining lines of evening rush-hour traffic, Deputy Thompson maneuvered the car down the basement ramp of the courthouse, rolled to a stop at the entrance and sat waiting for Earl to debark.

Now the awful truth began to dawn on Earl, as Miller and LeBlanc stepped from the rear of the automobile. As he looked up, Earl could see deputies holding back the crowds, drawn by a deluge of radio and televsion news bulletins, that had gathered to witness the governor's arrival. For a moment Earl stared at the crowds, then swung his head to glare at Thompson. "What," he demanded, "is going on?"

Carefully Thompson explained that Earl's wife had preceded him, had signed new commitment papers, and that Earl was to be examined again. Earl's face clouded with disbelief.

"Goddam, goddam," shouted Earl at deputies and crowd alike. "You all are doing it again." Livid with rage, Earl turned to face Thompson squarely. "Goddam you," he screamed, "I'll get you for this. I'll get all of you." At Deputy LeBlanc he shouted, "Your old man just lost his job." As the crowd pressed forward to see the governor, Earl raged. "You all look here. You all look. See?" he implored the crowd. The crowd murmured uneasily, setting off a ripple of oh's and ah's, as flash bulbs popped and television cameras whirred.

Deputies and doctors alike, at this point, were in perhaps one of the most ticklish moments of the whole situation. They had to make the governor co-operate, to an extent, to get the medical examination into the record. But here, in full view of a healthy slice of the Louisiana public, they had to act cautiously. Deputy Thompson asked Long to leave the car and come into the courthouse where the doctors awaited him. Long refused and Thompson sent a deputy to tell Williams and Wyatt. Presently the two doctors came out, walked to the car, asked the deputies to leave, and got inside with Earl.

Dr. Williams was not entirely unacquainted with the recent developments in Long's physical and mental condition. Because he had sensed earlier that he might eventually have to deal with the truculent politician, Williams had driven to Galveston to watch Long at the habeas corpus hearing. Moreover, while Blanche and Earl sped from New Orleans to Baton Rouge, Williams had used that time to call both Dr. Harris at Galveston and Dr. Ted Soniat at Ochsner's. From both, he got a rundown on Earl's condition. Now he pumped Long with his own questions and, from the back seat of the auto, Dr. Wyatt interjected questions at regular intervals.

For upwards of forty-five minutes the two doctors—mainly Williams—plied the governor with questions. Did he remember his conduct before the last session of the Legislature? Yes, said Earl, he did. Why, asked Williams, would Ole Earl want to tell as repulsive a story as he told about his "pore ole uncle" being shot by a colored man, whose wife the uncle tried to seduce? Earl replied that he had told the story because it was true. Looking over the crowd, he spied a cousin, Dr. Roy Wright. "Ain't that right?" he shouted to Dr. Wright, who lowered his eyes in embarrassment.

At times it was unnecessary for Williams and Wyatt to question the governor, since he divulged, unprompted, revelations so personal in nature that even the doctors were discomfited. He talked about his oil deals and he made no bones about his consuming dislike of Nephew Russell, whom he characterized as a double-crosser. He blamed Blanche for a big share of his troubles and volunteered that he and his wife had been having marital difficulties long before she whisked him off to Galveston. In the end, there was no doubt in the minds of both doctors that Louisiana's governor needed medical care. They delivered their recommendations to Judge LeBlanc, who swiftly signed the legal commitment papers. Wrote Dr. Williams on the commitment report:

> I have observed Earl K. Long in the legislature, at a hearing on a writ of habeas corpus in Galveston, Texas and today, 6-18-59, and I am of the opinion that he is a paranoid schizophrenic in need of hospitalization both for mental and physical care.

Dr. Wyatt's message almost duplicated Dr. Williams'. Wrote Wyatt:

> In my examination at the court house today with Dr. Chester Williams I formed the opinion that Gov. Long is suffering from delusions of persecution which are "fixed." He would fit into the diagnostic category of paranoid schizophrenia with cycles of manic-depressive activity.

The rest became a matter of mechanics. Once again Deputy Thompson took over the wheel of a car and once again Earl was whisked off to a mental asylum. Even now, however, Earl had little or no idea that he was to be committed to another hospital. Proof of this was the amiability he displayed as deputies drove him away from the courthouse, amidst cries from the crowd of "So long, Earl," and "Good-by, Governor." Only toward Deputy LeBlanc did he show some resentment. When LeBlanc offered him a cigarette Earl refused, saying, "You tricked me."

To all intents, however, Governor Long was under the impression that he was being returned to Ochsner's at New Orleans. As he drove along, he reminisced about people he knew in Louisiana, about events that had taken place during his political career. Moreover, he got a big kick out of the crowds (alerted again by radio and TV bulletins) that lined his route as he headed toward the hospital. As they waved and shouted to him, Earl waved and shouted back.

It is approximately seventy miles from Baton Rouge to Mandeville, the site of Louisiana's primary mental institution, the Southeast Louisiana Hospital. But it was not until Earl almost reached there that he tumbled to what was taking place.

As Deputy Thompson drove the car through Madisonville, Earl looked up to see a highway sign which read: MANDEVILLE,

LA., 8 MILES. It was only then that Earl looked at the deputies and said, "Why, that's an asylum. I hope y'all aren't bringing me there." When the deputies told him the truth, Long lapsed into silence.

By the time the car rolled through the asylum gates, however, Earl had become vocal again. At first, he refused to leave the car. Then he changed his mind and got out. Dr. Charles Belcher, the acting superintendent of the hospital, approached, stuck out his hand and said, "I'm Dr. Belcher, Governor." Earl glared and snapped, "The hell you are. You were Dr. Belcher."

By nine that night Earl Long was, for the second time in the space of three weeks, a prisoner in a mental ward. This time he occupied an uninhabited, pea-green-colored wing of the hospital where he roamed about in solitary preoccupation, like a twentieth-century Napoleon in his modern Elba.

Huey had been threatened, hailed before courts and legislative committees and finally shot down in the corridors of the capitol he had built and ruled with an iron fist. In death, however, he had become a martyr whose shadow fell across Louisiana and its political life for a quarter of a century. In death, he lived on. Clapped in a lunatic asylum, however, Earl Long, the heir to the Long mantle, was more pathetic than powerful. A gaunt, stooped, haggard figure stripped of his official trappings, the prisoner-governor could only stand at his window and bay at the Louisiana moon. At first, only a few heard him.

15

Bloody But Unbowed

HUEY LONG had been an ardent advocate of the maxim that publicity—any publicity—was better than no notice at all. In his heyday, he capitalized on editorials that denounced him, converting potentially damaging news stories into vote-getting coups. When he decided that pure blurbs were needed to offset adverse publicity, he founded the *Louisiana Progress*. There is no doubt that he grasped quickly and exploited expertly that newest communication medium, radio, in his political escapades. He became, of course, the darling of pundits and high-brow intellectualizers in the sobersided magazines, the object of free lancers bent on hammering out "quickie" portraits and even the constant profile in the big, slick national magazines.

From the moment he arrived in Galveston, Earl too became the target of every journalistic device, including television. But now that he was locked up in one of his own mental wards, the coverage and comment intensified.

In Paris, a French magazine carried his picture on its cover and labeled him the *Louisiana Clown*. *The New York Times, American Weekly, Time, Life, Newsweek, Look,* and most of the other magazines reported his progress. He became prime copy in every newspaper from Los Angeles to Liverpool. In his home state, the papers reported his every word and, when they could, what he ate, when he slept, whom he saw. Augmenting the straight news were features, personality sketches, favorite quote pieces and editorials that, for the most part, cluck-clucked about the sad state of affairs in Louisiana.

More than one paper took a decidedly Christian-humanitarian view of Earl's troubles, while editorializing that the "poor Governor" had been subjected to inhuman and indecent treatment. The Shreveport *Journal* raised the "resignation issue," and harked back to the Dick Leche regime when Leche blithely announced that if his "resignation" was not accepted by a certain hour he would simply "walk out" of his office.

There was even a psychiatric diagnosis from afar, as the *North Carolina Medical Journal* soberly editorialized about the "four lessons to be learned from the tragicomedy" of Earl's plight. Said the editorial, "Certainly few would agree with Gov. Long's diagnosis of himself as 'the best damn governor Louisiana ever had.' " Earl became fair game for psychiatrists at home and in other sections of the country. Indeed, one doctor, who refused to be quoted by name, solemnly told reporters that, as he saw it, Earl suffered from a subconscious, deeply rooted desire to be shot down, as Huey had been before him. When other medics scoffed at the diagnosis, the doctor exercised the time-honored prerogative of declaring he had been misquoted.

From all this journalistic enterprise, Earl Long was almost completely isolated. Sealed off in an otherwise uninhabited wing of the hospital, Earl at first had no visitors, saw no newspapers, got no telephone calls, watched no television. Tough state troopers, under strict orders to keep reporters away, patrolled the hallways leading to Earl's suite, the entrance to the hospital building and the gates leading to the hospital gates themselves. Cameramen were not allowed within fifty feet of the entrance gates.

The doctors meantime got down to the business of prescribing for their turbulent patient, while Earl co-operated in a half-hearted manner. The doctors knew exactly what they wanted to do. First, they would let the governor rest and calm down for the usual fourteen days. During this period he would be kept on tranquilizers. Finally, he would be subjected to electroshock treatments that would be designed to jar him out of his hypertense condition. So, at any rate, went the plan.

Earl, of course, had his own plans. Roughly summed up, they covered four main points: a) get out of the asylum; b) take over as governor again; c) get even with—that is, fire—those whose acts of omission or commission had got him in this fix; d) get rid of Blanche so that she couldn't have him slapped in the hospital again. In putting his plans into operation, Earl lost little time as a fascinated America—and a frightened official Louisiana—watched and waited.

To lay the groundwork for the legal strategy by which he would spring himself from the Mandeville hospital, Governor Long called on his old friend and political ally, Baton Rouge Attorney Theo Cangelosi, wealthy head of the Louisiana State University Board of Supervisors. Cangelosi had long been identified as a close supporter of Long's but he had been identified, too, as a close friend of Blanche. The question now was: With whom was he more friendly? The question remained moot because, in the end, Long turned to another, perhaps friendlier ally—Hammond Attorney Joe Arthur Sims. Here, at last, Earl found a man in whom he could place his complete confidence. Sims immediately became Long's official outside-the-walls spokesman. And he lost no precious time in equivocating. Said he bluntly after his first encounters with Earl inside Mandeville's gates, "Long should come free and he will."

In the capital city of Baton Rouge, word that Long planned to fight actively for release was met with some consternation. Although Attorney General Gremillion had ruled that Lieutenant Governor Lether Frazar was the acting governor, few took this ruling seriously. Earl, they reasoned, either was governor or there was, in fact, no governor for the time being.

As tension over Earl's coming fight to free himself increased, the newspapers and wire services carried daily accounts, in which they quoted "reliable sources" who described state house employees as "scared as hell" over what might happen if an irate Earl were let loose. Weight was lent to this feeling when word leaked out that Senator Long had washed his hands of any further attempts to hospitalize his uncle, and that Blanche herself had fled the state. First reports had her listed, variously, in the Bahamas, in Mexico City, in Cuba and in various states. In fact, however, Blanche merely secluded herself in the Long's new home and kept to herself.

Earl stayed inside the hospital at Mandeville for eight days, but even from inside those forbidding walls he made his voice felt and his intentions known through his attorney. When Attorney Sims arrived at the hospital to see Long on Wednesday, June 24, he had with him a tape recorder. Hospital authorities permitted him to take it inside on the promise that it would be used by him merely to record Long's instructions about carrying through a habeas corpus proceeding which had been scheduled for the following Friday before District Judge Robert Jones at Covington. The purpose of the hearing was to decide whether Long was being held illegally. Attorney Sims no sooner got inside with the recorder than Earl made a full "statement to the people"—in effect a political talk. Sims no sooner got outside with the tape than he released it to the newspapers, radio and television. Said the tape:

> This is Governor Earl K. Long talking from Mandeville hospital. I'm glad to tell you good people that as far as mentally, I never was in better health than I am today. In my whole life, I've never been unconcious except when I was asleep.
>
> 'Course you know I've gone through quite a bit in the last three or four weeks. I've been undermined by my nephew, by my wife, and my supposed-to-be cousin, Arthur Long in Baton Rouge, who means no more to me than the moon.
>
> These people who wanted to kill the loan shark bill and Russell Long, wanting to be governor, have conspired with my wife, who is one of the most jealous women that God ever let live on this earth and really and truly she has very little to be jealous about. I've never told the people of this state that I was a saint or fit to belong to the Baptist Church. That's why I was so long joining it. I am a Christian and honor everybody else that is a Christian and I honor everybody's religion having the right except snake chunking to do anything they want.
>
> Now as far as the state, it is in safe hands. Lieutenant Governor Lether Frazar and president pro tem Bill Cleveland are both honorable men, intelligent men and they're middle-aged men and know what it's all about from all directions. And I assure you that although I may not be middle-aged, 'cause I'll be sixty-four in August, but mentally I'm as good or probably better than I've ever been in my life.
>
> I'm sorry that I can't tell you about myself physically. Some of you don't know it, but I started reducing last September. I was down from 203 pounds to 173 pounds which they said was the perfect weight. After they got through shoving me from one street corner to another, and putting me on stretchers and tying me and shooting me with hypodermics that I can't tell you seriously that I'm as well off as I was.
>
> I weigh 162 pounds, which is 11 pounds less than when I entered the hospital in Galveston. I've satisfactorily recovered

mentally. I have always worked best under pressure. And people that know me well know this to be true.

If I thought for one second that my mentality wasn't equal to the occasion of the governor's office, I would resign in a minute, because I know that with Mr. Cleveland and Mr. Frazar, the government would be in safe and capable hands.

We have worked together for the last three years, and I don't think we've had as much as a minor spat. I have never enjoyed working more with anybody than with Mr. Cleveland and Mr. Frazar, who have at all times taken their work seriously and gone about it in an honorable, decent, fair way.

You know I have a lot of political enemies in this state. I have never yet tried to take advantage of them politically or tried to hurt them in any way because they didn't vote for me, because I think voting is a man's privilege and maybe he can see something in a governor that he appreciated and could see it in every fellow.

I have never believed in reprisals. In fact, I believe the difference between a big man and a little man is the big man can give and take and let his enemies and his friends and everybody live happily together. Because after a man's governor he is governor of all the people and not just a handful. That's the way I try to operate. I want to thank Mr. Sims and all the other fine attorneys who so nobly and so courageously have gone about helping me.

They need a little bread money, a little get-around money, and Uncle Earl will some way, or some of his friends will, make it up. I want to thank you again for this opportunity to visit with you and talk with you and I feel certain that having a man like the Honorable Robert D. Jones of this district deciding my case that I'll be a free man Friday. And I want to say this. I have no idea of impeaching anybody, taking advantage of anybody. Anything that I do after I get to be governor again will be done deliberately with the advice of friends and people which are well informed on the subject.

I think the special session of the Legislature erred in two or three ways. I think the loan shark bill should have been a law. I think they went a little too strong in giving the teachers 75 per cent because I'm afraid that's gonna close hospitals and close other institutions that have just as much right to live as the schoolteachers. I'm the schoolteachers' friend. I'm perfectly willing for them to have 75 per cent, but I want the last 12½ per cent put on the tail end.

And I don't believe there's a governor who would appropriate it that won't be able to reach the people. But in some cases, if you put the teachers and a few people too far up, you're gonna put the others back to where it's too late to recuperate enough to keep them active during the one month they may be needed.

I want to say this. You have the best hospital system in Louisiana of any place not only in the United States but in the civilized world. The Charity Hospital in New Orleans takes care of more people for less money and less assistance than any other hospital that tries to.

Thank you very much and I wish you all good luck and I hope you'll stand by and pray for me, and continue to pray for me to get a square deal. Thank you and good luck to all of you.

In the midst of his maneuvering to get out of Mandeville, Earl moved to see that Blanche, who had played the leading role in twice having him committed, could not interfere again. Through his attorney, Sims, he filed a suit for separation from Blanche—the first legal step toward divorce in Louisiana—charging that she had publicly "defamed" him in the Mandeville commitment episode, that she had fled the state and, thereby, his bed and board, and that she had, in effect, abandoned him. He asked for a court-supervised inventory of the couple's community property as a prelude to the divorce. Later, he was to tell newsmen, "I'd have divorced her long ago if I hadn't been in politics."

Now the stage was set for Earl's second release. But this time he found it unnecessary to deliver impassioned pleas (as he had to Blanche at Galveston) or to make promises he had no intention of keeping. Technically speaking, the state's attorney general, Jack Gremillion, would be the chief legal obstacle to his freedom, and in Baton Rouge Gremillion made it abundantly clear that while he would go through the motions of representing the state hospital authorities as the state constitution required him to, he had little appetite for the task of opposing—and possibly offending—Louisiana's most powerful politician. From Baton Rouge, Gremillion issued a hasty statement in which he said he wanted to make it "crystal clear" that he in no way opposed the governor's release.

"My office," said Gremillion, "will represent the aforesaid

agency [the hospital department] and personnel and present their legal positions in this matter to the twenty-second judicial court not in the spirit of opposing Governor Long's release if warranted, but in seeing that the court has all the law and facts of issues. If, in the opinion of the court, Governor Long should be released, I can only reiterate what I have said all along that my only concern is to perform our duties to the best of our ability fairly and impartially and that whatever decision is made that it will be in the best interest of Governor Long's health and welfare." Significantly, Gremillion said nothing about the "best interest" or "welfare" of the state. At this juncture, it was clear, the governor's welfare played heavily on him.

Attorney Sims himself tipped reporters to the strategy he would employ in seeking release for his client. First, he would contend that his client was confined illegally. Failing that, he would show that if Long had been mentally ill, he had now recovered. Finally, if these two attempts failed, Attorney Sims was prepared to press for a full-scale sanity hearing.

Such were the legal minutiae in the Long case as tensions mounted and the red-letter day approached. Louisianians should have known Earl Long better. Brushing aside the legal verbiage, ignoring motions, subpoenas and docket arrangements, Long chose not to skirt the law but to bludgeon it into submission. Like Huey, Earl preferred to "stomp" his enemies rather than beat them.

The hearing on the legality of Earl's commitment was scheduled before Judge Jones for ten o'clock on Friday morning, June 26, but Earl moved rapidly the day before. Through Attorney Sims, who appealed to news media for help in relaying the news, Earl called a special meeting of the seven-man state hospital board, whose members are appointed by the governor. Brazenly, Earl called the meeting for nine o'clock Friday morning in the very courtroom in which he himself would face the judgment of the court.

Covington sits in southeastern Louisiana, sixty miles east of Baton Rouge, and for one day it became Louisiana's mecca. In the old days, as Huey had faced a recalcitrant Legislature, an investigating U. S. Senate committee, or when he needed votes, the rednecks and backwoods freeholders had streamed to his aid, arriving on bus and on train, aboard steaming Model-T's and, in some cases, in horse-drawn buggies. Now the backwoods came alive once more, as overall-clad farmers and their print-dressed, sunbonneted wives arrived in force. With them came squads of sweating deputies and state troopers, newsmen, lawyers in uncomfortable business suits and politicians from the state capital.

Before dawn, and as early as two A.M., the populace converged on the spacious gymnasium of Covington's Junior High School, where Judge Jones, who would be sitting beneath a folded-up basketball backboard, would hold court while the regular courthouse underwent badly needed and extensive repairs. By dawn the area resembled a circus grounds, as redneck and politician rubbed elbows with lawyer and businessman. Newsboys shouted headlines and television camera crews strung their miles of wire. Radio mobile units stood by and the enterprising ladies of the Covington Junior High P.T.A.—anticipating both the crowd and the steaming, ninety-degree weather—sold soft drinks from hastily erected stands near the main entrance to the court. Inside the gymnasium-court, deputies guarded every entrance as the inpouring crowd took seats on the folding chairs that had been set up, or stood along the walls and in the aisles.

At the rear of the courtroom stood a temporary plywood office whose interior was hidden from the crowd's view. Into this office, shortly after nine, stepped Earl Long, his attorney, Sims, Attorney General Gremillion, and members of the hospital board. Sighting the gaunt, perspiring governor, the crowd let out a whoop.

Inside the temporary office Attorney Sims, speaking for Earl Long, outlined the governor's desires. Long, said Sims, had been committed by a jealous wife and an ambitious nephew. Moreover, the legality of the commitment was questionable, coming as it did at the end of a forty-five-minute curbside interview. At the moment, said Sims, only two people stood in the way of the governor's release—State Hospital Director Jesse Bankston and Dr. Charles Belcher, acting superintendent of the hospital at Mandeville. Attorney General Gremillion presented no problem, said Sims, because he was acting merely as the legal representative of the state hospital officials. What the governor wanted now was to remove Bankston and Belcher, who opposed his release. In their places, he wanted two other men who would have no reason to keep him locked up. If the hospital board concurred that the governor was in satisfactory mental condition, it was their duty to follow the governor's recommendations, fire the first two officials, and replace them with others. The hospital board needed no further prompting. Nodding sympathetically as Earl poured out a tale of hypodermics and bone crushers, the board acted with unusual dispatch. In the short space of ninety minutes, Earl Long had exactly what he wanted. As he walked from the temporary office at the rear of the courtroom to the witness stand that sat alongside Judge Jones' chair, Earl, smiling and waving to the cheering crowd, knew that he held every ace in the deck.

Earlier that morning Judge Jones had sentenced two felons, and earlier that week he had passed the death sentence on two murderers. Now, as the crowd cheered Earl, Judge Jones' patience snapped. Banging his gavel, he rasped, "This is a court of justice and you keep quiet in this courtroom. If there are any more outbursts I'll clear this place." Leaning back, Judge Jones motioned for Attorney Sims to proceed as the crowd fell silent.

What followed has been described as a legal travesty. It was, in fact, a calculated farce, rigged from beginning to end, and leaving Judge Jones no alternatives. In the end, he had to face and accept the inevitable.

The entire proceeding took just eight minutes, with Attorney Sims monopolizing almost every second of that time. First, he read a letter from the hospital board to Hospital Director Bankston. Its effect: Bankston was fired as of that morning. The letter was signed by Long, Lieutenant Governor Frazar and Senate President Cleveland. Next, Sims read a second letter which fired Dr. Belcher. This, too, was signed by the state's three top elected officials. Finally, Sims read two additional letters, the first appointing Charles Rosenblum, a member of the Long-appointed board, to Bankston's job, the second from Dr. Jesse McClendon, appointed to Belcher's job.

Said Dr. McClendon's letter to newly-appointed Hospital Director Rosenblum:

> I have had a lifetime acquaintance with Governor Earl K. Long and have had opportunities to consult with him and advise with him prior to the time he was taken to Galveston, Texas, and have seen him this morning, consulted with him, and

in my opinion there is nothing wrong with him and he should be released from this institution immediately and I intend to do so.

Sims, having read the letters, now turned to Attorney General Gremillion, seated at the far end of the attorneys' table. "Your honor," he said, "I believe that Mr. Gremillion now has something to say to the court."

On cue, Gremillion leaped forward. He said simply, "Your honor, there is no one now with authority to hold Earl K. Long at the hospital. The state joins in a motion to discontinue."

Judge Jones hesitated just thirty seconds. Then, with a bang of the gavel, he announced, "Since there is no opposition the motion is granted and the suit is dismissed." Then Jones, who had announced earlier that he was "tired" as a result of the murder cases, leaned back, his work done.

The rap of the judge's gavel was the signal for the crowd to react. From the audience came a deafening roar of applause, followed by a sustained cheer. On the stand, a haggard Earl grinned feebly, accepted the back-slapping and the outstretched hands, once raising his arms above his head in a V-for-Victory salute. Then, flanked by deputies, state troopers, attorneys and well-wishers, he started slowly for the door and his waiting automobile. As he pushed toward the door, a reporter shouted, "What are you going to do now, Earl?" Said Long shakily, "I'm gonna be governor."

As he walked away from the Covington courthouse that day with the cheers of the "great unwashed"—as brother Huey had called the state's masses—resounding in his ears, there was no doubt that Earl had one thing uppermost in his mind: revenge. It is about a three-minute drive from the junior high school to the old two-story, pink brick Southern Hotel in downtown Covington. There Long established his temporary headquarters. But even before he reached the hostelry, word seeped out from his official party. Long's first act under his new gubernatorial lease had been to fire State Police Superintendent John Nick Brown, the head policeman who had woefully failed to protect Earl from both Galveston and Mandeville. Into Brown's job went former State Police Superintendent E. P. Roy, who had first been appointed to the post by Brother Huey, and whose complete loyalty to the Long name had never been questioned. That chore disposed of, Earl settled into an air-conditioned room to map the strategy for his blazing re-entry into state politics, and for his campaign for an announced—and unprecedented—fourth term as governor.

Huey had always believed that if he talked loud enough and hard enough to enough people he could get the people to believe anything he said. Earl followed the pattern Huey had set. Propped up in a bed in Covington's Southern Hotel, a Baptist preacher having delivered a short prayer of thanks (which Earl had requested), his well-wishers crowded about him, Earl—between spoonfuls of hot tamales and swigs of ice water—turned expansively political.

"I have never," he declared solemnly, "been insane one second in my life." Then, warming to his old role as a stentorian crowd pleaser, Earl plunged ahead. "I am very happy to have won release this morning. I would trust my life with Judge Robert D. Jones because I know he would always do the right thing and give me a square deal.

"When I found out my case would be tried in his court, I didn't have a minute's worry. I am sorry I cannot say the same, had my case come before Judge Fred LeBlanc. We have had political differences that may have prejudiced my case.

"I am grateful to everyone who helped me gain my freedom. I especially appreciate the prayers that were said for me by the Catholics, Baptists, Methodists, the Church of God, and, in fact, by those of all faiths.

"I have never been insane one second in my life. I love Louisiana; I love its people, its institutions, its schools. Through its fine people, I have been highly honored many times far more than any man deserves. I would never let those fine people down.

"As I have stated on many occasions, I am a good friend of the poor white man, the poor colored man, as well as those among the rich who want to do right. When I cease to be, I hope the almighty God, by means best known to Him, will relieve me from doing wrong or harm to our state and its fine people.

"From the bottom of my heart, I want to thank everyone for

their thoughtfulness, for the help they have given me, and again, above all, for their prayers."

Earl issued the message in the form of a press release, appended his signature with a flourish—*Earl K. Long, Governor*—and asked that the statement be sent to newsmen. To a beaming race-track tout who, heartened to see the old bettor on the loose again, rushed up to him, Long said, "If ya got any tips, keep 'em." Then he laid his plans for the next few days.

For a starter, Earl decided that he wanted to move to new quarters. That afternoon, while state troopers decoyed newsmen to the front entrance of the hotel, Long and his aides slipped out a side door and raced off to the Pine Manor Motel on the edge of Covington. There Long set up a command post.

Stretched out on a cot, his false teeth removed, a bed sheet wrapped around him, a disheveled Earl received the press and issued some previews of things to come.

One of his first acts, on returning to Baton Rouge, said Long, would be to fire about forty of the state's employees. Musing about this, Earl rationalized: "Forty out of five hundred—that's not so bad."

Next, announced the governor, he had asked three psychiatrists to stay with him to supervise his mental and physical condition. Earlier, four doctors—including the three Earl asked to join his entourage—had written a letter to fired Hospital Director Bankston, in which they expressed "regret" that the "hospital board has taken the action revealed today" (that is, to free Long). Now Earl announced that he wanted the doctors along with him and he told newsmen, "My intention now is to do what the doctors say." Cannily, however, he left himself an opening. Added Long: "But if I think they might be erroneous, I'd reserve my rights to do otherwise."

Finally, Earl turned to a sister, Mrs. John Hunt, who hovered over him, and asked her to read a poem from the small volume she held in her hand. The sister read slowly, glancing from time to time at the bed-sheeted Earl, who sat nodding at intervals:

" 'Out of the night that covers me, Black as the pit from pole to pole, I thank whatever gods may be For my unconquerable soul' " . . .

Interjected Earl: " ' unconquerable and indestructible soul'—

put indestructible in there." Then he commanded his sister to read further.

" 'In the fell clutch of circumstance, I have not winced nor cried aloud, Under the bludgeonings of chance My head is bloody but unbowed.' "

Glancing up with an expression of complete satisfaction, Ole Earl appended a footnote. "This," said he, "is what I base my politics on. This was always a favorite of my deceased brother, Huey P. Long, and mine." Then the governor, safe now under the watchful eye of the properly chastised state troopers (Said newly appointed Police Superintendent Roy, "Nobody is going to molest him."), dismissed the press and most of his followers, drew his window shades, and turned to enjoy his first day of complete freedom in five weeks.

Doctors warned that he was still a sick man, with impediments ranging from small strokes and nervous exhaustion to possible coronary difficulties. They urged him to rest.

But the ebullient Earl was already thinking of hitting the stump. Asked by reporters if he still intended to run for another term, Earl smiled and said simply, "I know I am."

But what, asked reporters, about the effects of all this publicity about his mental condition? Chuckled a happy Earl: "Before all this I figured I'd have to make three hundred speeches to win. Now, it'll take only a hundred."

16

Westward Ho!

NO ONE knew better than Earl Long that his work was cut out for him in his bid for a fourth term. Chiefly, he had to convince Louisiana's voters that he had been manhandled and mistreated, and that his "shoving around" lay at the root of his physical and mental difficulties. Time after time, as he later stumped the state, Earl declared, "You have no idea of what I've been through." To make sure that no one else ever had to face the stresses and strains to which he had been subjected, he said, he would see to it that the state's mental health laws regarding commitment were changed. "I don't want a dog, a poor man or any man—white or black—to be subjected to the abuse I've gone through," Earl told the crowds.

In justice to Earl, it must be said that he had his points. He had been through an ordeal that might have felled a lesser man. His domestic life had been shattered. He had been embarrassed repeatedly by the publication of his personal, physical and mental difficulties. The Legislature, which Huey had contemptuously labeled a "pack of cards" that could be shuffled at will, had proved to be unusually resistant in considering Earl's demands, driving him more than once to the brink of frustration. Meantime, as his political machine showed signs of crumbling in key places, the "succession issue" seemed surely to be destined for the courts and Earl himself for another court battle, a prospect he loathed. These considerations and others aggravated Earl's outlook and played a prominent part in his mental and physical deterioration.

As usual, however, events were to prove that he was still his own worst enemy, that the abuse he inflicted on himself reached the proportions of a compulsion that plagued him even after he left Mandeville. To the external pressures that beset him, Earl added the burdens of his own lust for power in the face of a growing anti-Long skepticism.

Earl had promised to co-operate with doctors of his own choosing when he left Mandeville. Less than two weeks later, however, the doctors were sent packing after repeatedly admonishing—and irritating—Earl about his stump speaking. When Earl saw that the doctors had their own ideas about how he should conduct himself, and when the medics saw that their warnings were just so much verbal confetti (as far as Earl was concerned), the politico-medical alliance came to an abrupt conclusion. In Earl's words, he simply "dishired" the medics.

Earl had announced during his Covington motel stay that his fondest desire was to get to his backwoods pea patch where he could regain his strength amid rustic and familiar surroundings. But no sooner had he reached his farm at Winnfield than he was off again, crisscrossing the state in his official limousine, breaking speed limits as he took his case to the people. Speaking in upper ninety-degree temperatures, the Louisiana sun blazing down on him, Earl would harangue a crowd until his natural hoarseness dimmed to a frustrated whisper. Then he would sag limply into a chair, rest a few moments, rise and shufflle off to his waiting car. As his stump crowds applauded his antics, Earl drove home one persistent theme: "If I'm crazy now, I've always been crazy." There were some who took him at his word.

In the midst of his meanderings, Earl's political prestige sagged under a series of blows that, until now, had been overshadowed by his asylum visits and by his personal antics on the stump.

In Baton Rouge, Blanche moved to dissolve the twenty-seven-year marriage on her terms by filing a countersuit to the one Earl had filed three weeks before. Denying the governor's charges that she had publicly defamed him or that she had abandoned him, Blanche charged that she had committed him partly to save himself from injury, partly to save herself from bodily harm. In a sensational indictment of Earl's behavior, Blanche asserted that Earl had tried to kill her less than forty-eight hours before she had him moved to Galveston. In responding to the divorce action instituted by Earl, Blanche asked for an accounting of community property. Meantime, she asked for temporary alimony of $2,500 monthly, a figure Earl branded as "ridiculous," pointing out that the sum exceeded by $10,000 his yearly $20,000 salary as governor.

In Baton Rouge, also, word leaked out that if Earl pressed his bid for a fourth term, his opposition would be formidable, with former Governor Jimmie Davis, the "peace and harmony" advocate, leading the parade. Moreover, New Orleans Mayor deLesseps Morrison was already stumping the state on behalf of his own candidacy, turning the governor's race into an early Donnybrook. With opposition of this caliber, Earl was in for the toughest fight of his stormy political career.

But additional revelations came almost daily, bringing with them an odor of personal and official scandal in the Long camp.

In New Orleans, millionaire oilman Louis J. Roussel, confirming a report by Washington Columnist Drew Pearson, blandly admitted that he had delivered $5,000 in cash to Earl during the 1956 session of the Legislature. The cash, Roussel said, had been given to him by New Orleans steamship interests shortly after the Legislature had passed a bill that increased the fees Mississippi River pilots could charge the shipping companies. Only the governor's signature was needed to put the bill into law. Significantly, Earl vetoed the bill after getting the money, Roussel said. Roussel added another interesting detail: Special agents of the Internal Revenue Service, still digging away at Governor Long's income tax returns for 1956, 1957 and 1958, had ordered him in for questioning. Roussel admitted that he had supplied the agents with an affidavit covering the transaction. In fact, he was so explicit about the delivery that he even recalled, for the benefit of inquiring newsmen, what the governor was doing when he gave him the money.

Said Roussel, "The governor was at his desk, eating catfish for lunch, when I walked in. I handed him an envelope, but he didn't even look inside. He just threw it into a drawer and said, 'Sit down and have some catfish.'" Earl later denied receiving any money from Roussel.

On the heels of the Roussel incident came a disclosure that the revenue agents were investigating an entire series of transactions involving money allegedly turned over to the governor as "campaign contributions." To all the allegations, Earl responded by saying he had no idea how much he had received in the way of campaign money. "I just reach down for money, and when there isn't any I go out and get some more," he explained.

Hailed before the same revenue agents who had quizzed Roussel, Claude Duke of New Orleans, a former legislator-turned-lobbyist for New Orleans steamship interests, denied that he had given Earl $10,000 at the time the governor received the pilots' bill for signature or veto. Revenue agents who questioned Duke strongly implied that he had transmitted the money to Earl as a "campaign contribution." But Duke steadfastly maintained that the money had gone to other quarters, some of it at the governor's request.

Earl, Duke explained to the agents, had asked him to round up some campaign money for a few members of the Legislature whom Earl wanted to see re-elected. Duke disclosed that he had obtained not $10,000 but $15,000—but that none of it had gone to Earl. Instead, he told the agents, he had made campaign contributions to a district attorney and to a state legislator with the first $5,000. From the remaining $10,000, he had contributed $1,000 to another legislator, had used $5,000 in his own campaign for mayor of New Orleans (he was defeated) and still had $4,000 of the money in a bank box. The $15,000, he told agents, had nothing to do with Governor Long, nor with Earl's subsequent veto of the pilots' bill. The fact was, said Duke, that he had no intention of contributing to the governor, since Earl had already assured him that the bill would be vetoed. Explained Duke: The governor considered the pilots' bill to have been lobbied through the Legislature by Plaquemines Parish District Attorney Leander Perez, Earl's archenemy. Under no circumstances, said Duke, would the governor sign into law a bill that would benefit a Perez client.

But Roussel and Duke were not the only people who had been contacted by the revenue agents. Suddenly, in the midst of the revelations about Earl's taxes, a new name bobbed to the surface.

In Alexandria, a bespectacled, moonfaced housewife named Cora Russell Schley admitted that the agents had questioned her, and that she had told them she had $7,000 of Earl's campaign money in a lock box in an Alexandria bank. Mrs. Schley, who identified herself as a part-time newspaper reporter and a public relations aide to the governor, said the money had been left over from Earl's 1956 campaign. Earl, she said, had instructed her to leave it in the bank box until he called for it. No sooner had the disclosure been made than Earl sent a state police captain scurrying to Alexandria to recover the money. The trooper collected the loot, returned it to the governor at Baton Rouge, and that should have closed the Mrs. Schley incident. Later, however, her name was to appear in connection with Earl's, and with more ominous overtones.

It was at this juncture that Earl began the gallivanting and cavorting that was to supply newspapers with a more lurid brand of copy than even Earl had heretofore provided. It was to mark, moreover, another chapter in Earl's compulsive conduct—deportment so unbecoming that some who vowed that Earl had recuperated began to doubt him again. The first episode occurred at the Roosevelt Hotel in New Orleans, the hostelry whose name has been inextricably woven into the fabric of the Long chronicle.

Arriving in New Orleans with his political entourage and trooper bodyguard, Earl took up quarters in the Roosevelt, giving off the air of a man in town on important business. At the hotel, Earl rode to his third-floor suite. As reporters crowded around him, as flash bulbs popped and TV cameras rolled, Earl calmly unzipped his trousers and relieved himself in the carpeted hallway. Then, just as calmly, he strolled to his suite and slammed the door behind him. From this point, newsmen who trailed Earl could expect anything.

In that gaudy labyrinth called the Vieux Carré, along Bourbon Street's show row, exotic dancer Blaze Starr performed nightly in a bistro called the Sho-Bar. Blaze, the amply rounded redhead who had entertained the governor in the past, now reaped a harvest of publicity. Describing her relationship with Earl as "platonic," Blaze shed tears as she explained, "He is one of the finest men I have ever known."

Late the evening of Earl's arrival in New Orleans, Blaze, draped on the arm of the governor's companion and cousin, Dave Bell, arrived at the Roosevelt to renew her friendship with

Louisiana's political boss. How long she stayed that evening only Earl and Blaze know. But from that point, she became singularly uncommunicative with the press.

The disclosures about Blaze Starr could not have come at a worse time for the harassed governor. In Alexandria, National Democratic Committeeman Camille Gravel, Jr., a former Long ally but now a supporter of New Orleans Mayor Morrison, called on the governor to submit himself to an out-of-state psychiatric examination. Never before, declared Gravel, had Louisiana faced a political crisis of such dimensions, what with Earl traveling and, to all intents, a governor-in-absentia. In Alexandria also, Representative Jasper Smith introduced, for the first time, the dreaded word "impeachment" by disclosing that he might begin an impeachment or recall movement. Smith let the trial balloon fall to earth when no one picked up the cue. Hearing of Smith's statement, Earl retorted, "He has about as much chance as a snowball in hell."

Back at the Roosevelt, Earl Long tended to the primary business at hand—that of seeing whether he could count on the support of the city's strongest political faction, the Regular Democratic Organization, in his fight for re-election. For a report on the drift of the political winds, Earl closeted himself with former Mayor Maestri, an old ally. When the conference ended Earl could see some of the handwriting on the wall. Emerging from the meeting, his face drawn, he headed back to Baton Rouge, reporters trailing behind him.

If the Blaze Starr episode gave Louisianians a mild case of surprise, spiced with ribald amusement, the disclosures that came next—some printed, others bandied about verbally—sent a ripple of incredulous shock and indignation down the state.

In Alexandria, Camille Gravel announced that Governor Long had called him at five one morning to threaten him about Cora Schley. The Gravel call came after Earl had placed a call to Mrs. Schley herself.

In his calls to both Mrs. Schley and Gravel, Earl had cursed and roared in his customary fashion. Moreover, he had threatened Mrs. Schley by promising that he, as governor and, therefore, head of the state's welfare department, would see to it that Mrs. Schley's attempt to adopt a two-year-old baby would be blocked. Mrs. Schley promptly reported the conversation to

Gravel, retained him as her attorney, and promised that she would fight to keep the baby.

Political buffs and the populace at large could perhaps understand, if not approve, Earl's bulldozing tactics in denouncing and embarrassing his political opponents, his family and public officials who refused to do his bidding. No one, however, could understand Earl's interest in blocking the adoption of a harmless child by the woman who had, by all accounts, served him faithfully in the past and who now presented no obstacle to his political future. Slowly, in bits and dribbles, the story came out. Although it found precious little space in the state's dailies, the reports and rumors sped from ear to ear until the Schley affair became the most talked-about secret in Louisiana.

Earl, Cora told her closest friends, had been hounding her unmercifully for some time while she carried out her role as a campaign public relations adviser. When she wearied of his tactics, she learned that her husband, a railroad engineer, was being harassed by state police. This in itself was unusual since the husband had neither political connections nor ambitions.

Far from knuckling down to Earl's threats, Cora related later, she and her husband resolved to complete the adoption procedure. At this point the affair took on an added twist.

To Alexandria to see the natural mother of the illegitimate child—a roadside restaurant waitress—came a state trooper and others. They asked the waitress to withdraw her adoption consent and reclaim the child. When the waitress refused, she was offered $1,250 to reconsider. Meantime she was reminded of certain legal difficulties of her father—troubles, it was hinted, that could be warmed up again. The waitress capitulated to the combination threat and reward and moved, through an Alexandria attorney, to have her adoption consent withdrawn. Part of the money was delivered to her in an Alexandria motel room.

In the midst of all this, Cora, her husband and the baby fled Louisiana and went into hiding in Mississippi. In Alexandria, Cora's attorney, Gravel, announced that he would fight for Cora's rights with every legal weapon at his command. Immediately Gravel drew up a list of sixty-two witnesses, including Earl, state troopers, the waitress, the Schleys, a district judge, newspapermen and others, to throw the entire case before the public.

As this was taking place Earl, by this time back at his pea

patch, announced that he would make a vacation tour of the western United States before returning to Louisiana to call a special session of the Legislature. Heretofore, except for the Galveston trip, Earl's antics had been confined to Louisiana. Now he was to make the country his stage.

Before he "dishired" them, Long's doctors pleaded with him to rest, lest he die of heart failure brought on by his exertions. But in mid-July Long turned his back on the doctors. With an entourage of friends and political allies, he roared out of Louisiana en route to Fort Worth, Texas, the first stop on his itinerary. There, he said, he would inspect cattle and "just visit." Before leaving, however, Earl leveled a characteristic blast at the press and its coverage of his activities. Moreover, he said, he planned to "buy newspapers in New Orleans and Alexandria," call them the "people's papers" and present "facts" to Louisiana's voters, which, he claimed, well-established organs like the New Orleans *Times-Picayune* and the Alexandria *Town Talk* refused to carry. Like Huey, who relied on his house organs, the *Louisiana* and *American Progress,* to take the "facts" to the people, Earl now decided he needed his own press to present his case.

Five minutes after Earl landed in Dallas en route to Fort Worth, everybody knew that the reports issued by his camp about the vast improvement in his physical and mental health were worthless.

Landing in Dallas, Earl found the press primed and waiting for him. As they converged on him in the airliner, Earl became once again the wildly gesticulating, screaming, incoherent and profane Earl who had blasted the Legislature.

"Get out of here," roared Earl to the newsmen, "get out of here and leave me alone."

Seeing that the newsmen planned to stay, Earl snatched the white cloth from the headrest of his seat and called for a knife. Shouting epithets at the newsmen, almost stabbing himself once, Earl gouged eye and ear holes out of the cloth, took off his floppy straw hat, lowered the cloth over his head and face like a Ku Klux Klan mask, then jammed his hat down on top. That way, resembling a Halloween apparition, he rode into Fort Worth.

Debarking there, the headpiece still in place, a rubbery-legged Earl almost fell from the plane ladder, but reached ground safely to wander aimlessly in search of the limousine that had been ordered to meet him. A newsman approached to ask a question, but Earl exploded again: "Get out of here, you reporter bastard."

As Long's Senate floor leader, B. B. Rayburn, led him toward the passenger terminal to wait for the limousine, as newsmen dogged his trail, Earl's wrath was heard in the night air.

"Give me that pistol in your pocket," he ordered Rayburn, "and I'll clear the damn hall."

Pleaded Rayburn to the reporters, "Give the governor a chance. He was planning to give you a press-conference audience tomorrow."

"Like hell," roared Earl. "Hell, no, I won't give a news conference." As the cloth slipped over his eyes, obscuring his vision, Earl cried, "Get the damn thing out of my eyes. Help me get my damn hat on." He was a movingly pathetic figure, a clown trapped in his own costume.

Only once during his airport stay did Earl simmer down. When a twelve-year-old boy asked for his autograph, Earl's natural affection for children broke through. Smiling as he patted the youngster's head, Earl autographed a five-dollar bill, handed it to the boy and patted him again. The boy promptly took up the governor's battle, hauled out a rubber band and shot it at newsmen.

Earl arrived at his Fort Worth hotel at the same time a television station presented an hour-long showing of the governor's remarkable appearance before the Louisiana Legislature. The showing was advertised in advance as "not recommended for children." But Earl was in no mood for TV.

At the hotel, the mask still hiding his face, he was whisked to his thirteenth-floor hotel suite. A Texas newsman who sought to ride in the governor's elevator was brusquely knocked down by a Louisiana state trooper, and Earl himself added insult to injury by announcing that Texas Governor Price Daniel had even more trouble than he did. "After all," observed Earl, "he's got that Texas Legislature to contend with." With that, Earl disappeared behind hotel doors. But newsmen who kept their hallway vigil through the night heard shouts and curses from behind the closed doors until the wee hours.

By morning, Earl had thawed. In an unusual gesture, he sent a written apology to waiting newsmen.

> I want to apologize for the episode in the . . . elevator last night [he wrote] . . . but that man did try to force his way in where he wasn't wanted. But I'll forget it and hope he can. If the press will leave me alone and let me rest and relax, I'll try to have a very short press conference . . . tomorrow and answer any reasonable questions. Photographers can take all the pictures they want. I'm still a sick man. I need rest.
>
> Reporters and photographers have been chasing me like a wild animal and they could drive me insane. I'm human and I make a lot of mistakes. If the press keeps after me as it has, then the only way I can stay alive is to escape from the press. As for my remarks at the airport about getting a pistol, that shows how a man can get whipped up—I've taken about all the abuse I can.
>
> I was getting along fine in Louisiana. And I hasten to apologize for any mistakes I've made in Texas. I probably got nutty and said some things I shouldn't have. When a man loses his temper, sometimes he loses his equilibrium.

Earl regained his good humor during the day. Noting that he was in oil country, he chuckled as he described himself as an oilman too. But he had only brickbats for some Texans. Said he, "Some of these Texas oilmen are good men, but a lot of them wouldn't pay a dime to get Christ off the cross."

Only a few days before, in reading Blanche's countersuit for divorce, Earl had termed her request for $2,500 monthly alimony as "ridiculous." Now, expansively, he told newsmen that a "long-shot wildcat oil well" had come in, handing him a $300,000 fortune.

"This," said Earl, "is enough to let me live like a gentleman at Winnfield, among my friends and neighbors, both white and colored, for three lifetimes."

Long disclosed that he was preparing a speech he intended to deliver to a joint session of the Texas Legislature, although that body had not invited him to appear and, in fact, would continue to avoid him.

For a man who had reviled the press a scant twelve hours before, Earl underwent a remarkable transformation. Soon he was barreling deep into his thoughts. The main purpose of his trip, he revealed, was to "get some rest." At the same time, however, he wanted to get away for a long look at the home scene, to determine for himself who the "scalawags" in his administration were.

"When I get back," he told newsmen, "hell's going to break loose."

Earl said he didn't want to get specific about skulduggery now, but that he planned to investigate reports of it nonetheless. "We have given away a hundred million acres of state land in Louisiana and 90 per cent had oil on it," said Earl. "Some of it went at four cents an acre."

To the amazed newsmen, Long cheerfully revealed that he had gambled money and won on the campaigns in which he had run for office.

"As far as campaigns go," he said, "I'm a super-duper. I outslick the slickers. I hope to take some money [in the coming campaign] from those who are well able to lose it. I won't take any money from anybody who has less than a million dollars. With that kind of money, I should be able to use it like I want to. Of course, I'll have a big set-to with the federal government after I win it."

It had never occurred to him, Earl confessed, that his campaign winnings had any relation to his income taxes.

"It never dawned on me you'd owe income tax on gambling money, because all my life my losses were greater than my gains. And that's true with the average American who is sucker enough to try to beat the horses and bingo and the lottery and slots."

In the next breath, Earl disclosed that he would have been financially fixed for eternity if Blanche hadn't "taken me" for several hundred thousand dollars when she decided to divorce him. Still, he mused, he had that $300,000 left, and that was enough.

What, a newsman asked, would Earl tell the Texas Legislature if he went to Austin?

Well, said Earl, one of the areas he hoped to cover was the problem of an old man taking a young wife.

"Now, I don't know what you could do for a substitute, but I'm sure going to find out and let you know," he grinned.

Finally, having just confessed that he had gambled on his

past campaigns, and would gamble again on his forthcoming campaign, Earl promised that when he returned to Louisiana gamblers there would come under closer supervision. Solemnly raising a hand, Earl predicted, "I'll guarantee the people of Louisiana that gambling in the state will be looked after better and with a more wide-awake attitude than it has in the past. I'll take an oath on this."

That afternoon, jaunty as a peacock, Earl ventured into the streets of Fort Worth. He visited a factory where he ordered twenty pairs of cowboy boots, pressed the hand of a pretty receptionist and asked if she was married, then invited a quartet of singers to his room. There he joined one of them in a rendition of "The Old Rugged Cross." Having sung, Earl sat down with tears in his eyes.

That night, after having maintained his sweetest disposition in weeks for better than six hours, Earl Long changed again as he sought to elude newsmen who followed him to a dinner date. But there was method in the old man's madness. When an aide cautioned him about losing his temper, Earl responded heatedly, "Damn it, when I get angry I get angry for a purpose. I swear I don't know why you bastards haven't learned that yet."

Earl's antics went far from unnoticed in Texas and elsewhere. In Texas, for example, a big majority of the press called on the governor to quit the ridiculous clowning and go home. Earl responded to these invitations by saying that he'd go home when he felt like it, but not sooner.

In Tyler, Texas, that city's two newspapers got into something of an editorial tug of war, one taking Earl's side, the other opposing him. The Tyler *Courier-Times* urged the Texas Legislature not to invite Long to address it and asked the governor to go home to Louisiana.

The Tyler *Star,* however, maintained that "every man is allowed to speak his beliefs, whether they be good or bad." Regardless of Earl's behavior, said the *Star,* the American system of fair play dictated that he be considered "legally sane until proven insane, and his actions, although certainly not to be condoned, do not take away his title as governor of Louisiana." Added the *Star:* "Governor Earl Long, next-to-last man on the Louisiana Long regime totem pole, is sick, sick, sick physically and, perhaps, mentally.... Let's not kick a man in the teeth after he is down."

In Pennsylvania, the little Lehighton *Evening Leader* defended Long's successful fight to free himself from mental institutions. Intimating that Earl had been railroaded into the asylums, the editorial pictured him as "an old man [who] stands alone." Earl, after reading the editorial, called it a "brilliant piece of work."

"Put me in a room for forty years," said Earl, "and I couldn't write anything as good. Anything as truthful as this you can't question."

But these were voices from afar, while in Houston another voice added perhaps more authority to the debate that raged about Earl's physical and mental well-being.

Said Dr. Alton Ochsner, head of the hospital to which Earl had come for treatment after leaving Galveston, "The governor definitely is not in his right mind." But, he added, that didn't mean that Long would be removed from office.

"Long," said Dr. Ochsner, "will remain as governor of Louisiana until he dies. They couldn't impeach him if they tried. You don't realize how popular the Long family is in Louisiana. It's like a dynasty—they believe anything he tells them." But, said Ochsner, "you know the man is sick, not in his right mind, when he pulls things like he has been doing. His raging and raving is not the old Earl Long. He is much worse than he used to be."

Why did Earl come to Texas now? Answered Ochsner, "Who knows what his reason is for coming to Texas? I doubt if he knows himself."

For Earl, the sound and the fury around him was so much trivia. Bidding good-by to Fort Worth, he flew off to El Paso on the second leg of his western tour. By the time his three-day El Paso stay ended, his hotel, city officials and one of the city's newspapers were glad to see him go. Said Edward Pooley, in an editorial in the El Paso *Herald Post,* "The papers in this part of the country are disgusted with Long."

Little wonder that Earl generated displeasure when he rolled into El Paso. The first night he got there he left his room at the Hilton Hotel in a torrent of profanity while trying to dodge the ubiquitous newsmen. Shouting as he ducked out of the hotel, Long threatened to shoot the offending reporters.

"Goddam," raged Earl, "I'm going to shoot them sons of bitches. Why can't you leave me alone? Do you boys know what hot lead it? I've got plenty of it and I know how to use it. I'll shoot the lot of you. You sons of bitches want to see me well, but you won't leave me alone." Newsmen, mindful of reports that Earl had at least four pistols and some shells in his hotel room, had some wary moments.

El Paso's Hilton Hotel, of course, is a short walk from the International Bridge to Juarez, Mexico, and its myriad fleshpots. It was there that Governor Long steered himself as soon as he hit the border city.

In company with New Orleans physician Martin O. Miller, who hovered over him anxiously, Louisiana Racing Commissioner Pete Menefee, a state police lieutenant (who is a Boy Scout troop leader and a Baptist deacon), and his cousin, Dave Bell, Earl descended on a plush bawdyhouse named Irma's. Soon, in the spirit of the surroundings, he was passing out dollar bills to the girls, at the same time paying particular attention to a tall, striking blonde. As the others, particularly the deacon, blushed and groaned inwardly, Earl cavorted and, in his own expression, "raised hell."

There was comic relief aplenty. Spotting a group of perspiring *mariachis,* Earl beckoned them to his table. Did they know how to play "You Are My Sunshine"—ex-Governor Jimmie Davis' tune? The mariachis confessed they didn't know how to play it. Undaunted, Earl bellowed out a few bars of the melody and soon the players had the tune. Gleefully Earl sang along, remarking that the song might as well be played there as on the campaign trail back in Louisiana.

Earl's aides were no match for their "sick" chief. One by one, they drifted back to the hotel, unable to keep up with the carousing executive. When the governor returned, haggard, unkempt, bleary-eyed, at seven the next morning, the hotel door was locked from the inside, an affront Earl could not countenance.

Lifting a leg high in the air (a bellboy later described Earl as looking like a high jumper) Earl kicked at the door, yelling loudly for his cronies to wake up. Let in finally by a frightened bellboy, the governor upbraided his underlings for being a bunch of sissies. One state police captain was reduced to tears by the tongue-lashing.

"Sick," exclaimed the trooper as tears rolled down his cheeks, "why he could lick any fifty men in Texas."

Next day, as he prepared to leave for the horse races at Ruidoso, New Mexico, Earl darted into an elevator to escape newsmen and was lodged accidentally between hotel floors for forty minutes until he was helped out. El Paso, it is safe to say, was glad to see him leave.

The remainder of Earl's western trip was a kaleidoscope—with equal parts of nightmare, soap opera and pure buffoonery.

In New Mexico he bet thousands of dollars on the horses, claiming later that he "broke even." Once, he made the mistake of letting the Baptist-deacon-trooper place a large bet for him. The hapless trooper, unaccustomed to the intricacies of the track, placed the money on the wrong horse. When the horse originally designated by Earl romped home to an easy victory, Earl burst into gleeful chatter. Told about the mistake, he cursed softly, then subsided into crestfallen mumbling. Later, fancying that he had been insulted at the track, he labeled the local sheriff as a "goddam convict" before huffily heading west for Denver.

En route to Denver Earl had intended to stop at Albuquerque. But spotting an editorial in an Albuquerque paper that advised him to "check his guns" when he hit town, the governor stopped just long enough to telephone the paper's editor.

"You make me sound like Pancho Villa," Earl chided the editor. "Why," said the governor, who only the day before had threatened to pour hot lead into newsmen, "I never carried a gun six minutes in my life. I think a good run would beat a bad stand. I haven't had a fight in fifteen years." Still miffed at Albuquerque, however, he ordered the city bypassed in favor of Santa Fe where, in the higher atmosphere, he promptly suffered a mild heart attack and had to be attended by a nurse and doctor.

Pushing west, he stopped for lunch at a roadside grocery, had himself photographed in a supermarket shopping cart as he wheeled along munching on a cheese sandwich. Later, as he rode toward Denver, his entourage looked like something out of a Mack Sennett comedy as, at one juncture, a suitcase resting atop his official Cadillac jarred loose and clattered to the highway, scattering shorts, undershirts, socks and shirts over the countryside.

Before leaving New Mexico, Earl met briefly with Governor John Burroughs. Later, he kept that chief executive cooling his heels for two hours while he answered and made long-distance telephone calls. In Colorado he met Governor Steve McNichols, bet heavily at Denver's Centennial race track, then pushed on to Independence, Missouri, for a forty-five-minute visit with former President Harry Truman.

What, reporters asked, did Long and Truman discuss?

"Why," offered Earl, "I told him a lot of dirty jokes. But he didn't tell me any. He made out like he had not heard any of mine."

In addition, Earl volunteered, he and the former President had discussed possible presidential candidates for 1960 and had pretty well agreed that Missouri Senator Stuart Symington was the man both would endorse.

From Independence, Earl headed for the last stop on his trip, the mineral baths at Hot Springs, Arkansas. Arriving, he was greeted with the news that the Louisiana Association of Young Men's Business Clubs had called on him to resign because he had made the citizens of Louisiana "the butt of public ridicule." Earl said he had no intention of resigning.

In a trice, however, he forgot legislative and executive worries. Immersed in the baths, he soon struck up an acquaintance with an attractive Tennessee divorcee named Ann Billings.

"You got a husband?" inquired Earl. When Mrs. Billings confided that she had no husband at the moment, Earl promptly invited her to dinner that evening. Later, eluding spying newsmen, he and Mrs. Billings drove off and sat under the Arkansas moon for a half hour while Earl put his arm around her shoulder. Then he drove back to the hotel.

Two days later Mrs. Billings, who told newsmen that she thought the governor had "a brilliant mind," returned to Tennessee. Earl admitted sadly that he had been attracted to the lady, but that the difference in their ages (she was thirty-eight) ruled out romance.

In Louisiana, meantime, Committeeman Gravel pushed his

court case on behalf of Mrs. Schley. Rounding up witnesses by the score, Gravel announced ready for trial on the day Earl was due back in Louisiana, Wednesday, July 29. Then mysteriously the litigation ended.

On the morning of July 29, the attorney for the waitress-mother of the Schleys' adopted baby announced ready for trial. Witnesses began to converge on the courthouse for what would surely have been one of the most sensational hearings since Huey's impeachment proceedings in 1929.

Suddenly that afternoon—at about the same time Earl was re-entering Louisiana—the attorney appeared in court with a motion to discontinue the proceedings which he had originally instituted. There was no explanation for the attorney's action, nor was there any announced reason for the sudden shift in the attitude of the waitress-mother who had demanded the return of her baby. A satisfied Camille Gravel announced grimly, "We were ready to proceed, but somebody didn't want the facts in this thing to come out."

For the moment, at least, Earl had been spared the further indignity of appearing in the public courtroom to answer at least indirect charges that he had threatened a couple with the loss of their baby. But even as he rolled into Louisiana from Arkansas, political storm clouds were building up around him. More importantly, he was to come face to face with the saddest fact of his political life: Whatever the depth of his yearning, whatever price he had paid in physical and mental anguish to perpetuate himself in office, the people of Louisiana had made him their governor for the last time.

17

The Last Campaign

ON July 29, 1959, Earl Long re-entered Louisiana to prepare for the climactic showdown of his turbulent political career. Flying into Monroe in a borrowed private plane, rested but far from well, he was a man who alternately exuded good humor, gloom, hope or defiance, depending on his mood of the moment. Met at the airport by a small crowd, he spoke hopefully in a jesting vein about the difficulty of obtaining campaign contributions, then added, "We sure have a lot of big shots out here. Maybe we can raise some money."

He was solicitous and righteously indignant as he pondered the plight of airline stewardesses who could hold their jobs only if they remained unmarried. He would see to it at a special session of the Legislature, promised Earl, that this situation would be corrected. (Nobody pressed him about the interstate complications implicit in any such state law.) He spoke with determination of the need for legislation that would make it more difficult for a person to be committed to a mental institution against his will. He told newsmen he had "investigated" this unhappy state during his own confinement, then added, "I didn't have anything else to do, you know."

He was alternately defiant and apologetic when a newsman mentioned that there had been some talk of impeachment.

He bristled. "I wish they'd try it. I'll write it up for them. It ought to be a good showdown. You know, they tried to impeach my brother Huey and tried to accuse him of everything but the right thing. I don't doubt that I haven't been a little bit off all my life, but I guess everybody else has been off at one time or another. I know I've been busy talking out of both sides of my mouth, but if I ever got rid of my mouth those newspapers would burn me."

Earl had his first warning of things to come the next day when he strode into an Alexandria hotel for a meeting with a group of his legislative allies. Three who had been invited failed to appear, but Earl got right down to business.

Leveling his finger at Representative Buford Smith, whom newspapers had quoted as being opposed to a special session, Long asked, "Mr. Smith, you been popping off in the newspapers. Why are you opposed to the special session?" Smith told Earl he didn't think a special session was necessary.

"Now tell me this," said Earl, "who do you think knows the most—me or you?" Smith fell silent.

Another legislator suggested that the people didn't want a special session. Snorted Earl: "They've been brainwashed by the newspapers."

How would he finance the special session? another asked. Earl had a ready answer: "It won't cost a cent more than $148,000." If it did, he promised, he would cut the "deadheads" off the state payroll. Said Earl, "I'd hate to cut those deadheads off the payroll, but I will if I have to." He set the special session for August 10.

Soon, it was the same Earl who busily pranced around the state, energetically trying to convince the people that his illness was of the past. In New Orleans he underwent a well-publicized physical examination, then announced that the only thing doctors had discovered was that he was a bit tired. Earl conceded the doctors nothing. "I won't quit running unless I die," he announced. The doctors had advised him to slow down. He would follow their advice, said Earl, "when I like to."

The Air Force slapped him with a $4,251 bill, charging that his flights in a Louisiana Air National Guard plane to the Kentucky Derby, to Georgia and even to Galveston had constituted "misuse" of government property. Earl reacted predictably. He would pay as "little of the bill as possible," he said, then pointed out that congressmen used similar airplanes for "vacations in Europe." Said Earl jauntily, "When they pay, I'll pay. What's good for the goose is good for the gander."

Before leaving New Orleans Earl appeared at a rodeo, promised the crowd, "I'll die fighting for our people whether you vote for Uncle Earl or not." He declared that he would battle, as usual, the "big-shot millionaires."

"I got more backbone, more will power and more determination," he shouted. "I could hire out for more than you could pay me if I wanted to, but I never sold you out and I never will." His speech was short: "The main thing I want tonight is for you to look at me and see just how crazy I am." Speech over, he repaired to a night spot where he pumped nickels into a jukebox, joined in group singing and danced past midnight. "That," he told aides with relish, "got me more votes than any speech would."

In Franklinton, en route to Baton Rouge, Earl stood in a rainstorm, water dripping down his nose, roaring at a crowd, "I thought I would let you see how crazy I am." When the crowd cheered, Earl crackled, "I've got plenty of snap left." As the rain pelted him, Earl bore down again on corporation presidents, "big-shot millionaires," and "people who wouldn't give a nickel to see an earthquake." Soaked, Earl allowed himself to be led to his station wagon for the ride home. It was time to meet the Legislature.

Huey's successes with the Legislature had been astounding. In the memorable 1934–35 period his special sessions had been the work of an artist, sure of himself and his allies. The Legislature had delivered the state to the Kingfish to do with as he pleased.

Earl's legislative successes had been less spectacular, but no less heady. The Kingfish had always had a small but adamant core of opponents. At times Earl's opposition was virtually nonexistent, as he pushed through legislation by counts of 90–3 in the House, or 23–2 in the Senate. Occasionally he stubbed his toe, as, for example, in the special session he had tried to call following his defeat at the hands of Sam Jones in 1940. Earl sought to hamstring his successor with as much Long-directed legislation as possible. The Legislature, wary over post-Scandal voter reaction, had rebuffed Earl on that occasion. A quorum of legislators simply failed to show up, forcing Earl to cancel the call. Now, with twenty-one bills drawn up and ready for the lawmakers, Earl's tactics were obvious. He would try to use the Legislature as a vehicle to regain some of his lost prestige.

The special session was destined to become a turning point

for Earl. If, prior to this time, he had held any illusions about recapturing his prestige, the special session washed them away. If, in terms of power and prestige, Earl had been going downhill slowly, the special session accelerated the descent.

The session was scheduled to begin at five o'clock, Monday evening, August 10. It was twenty minutes late in convening. By six it had adjourned—the shortest legislative session in Louisiana's history.

Ironically, it was one of Earl's former floor leaders in the House, Representative Ben Holt, who took charge immediately after the lawmakers were gaveled to order. Calling on his colleagues to adjourn forthwith to "save the state a lot of embarrassment and harassment," Holt said the special session could serve no good purpose. It was all the argument that was needed. The House voted 71–25 to adjourn. A few minutes later the Senate followed with a 26–9 vote.

Earl, who had not yet made an appearance, rushed to the Senate when he heard what had happened. As he readied himself before the microphone, the lawmakers settled back, expecting another typical Long tongue-lashing. Instead, it was a conciliatory and forgiving Earl who delivered a short speech.

"I'm not mad at anybody," said Earl hoarsely. "There will be no repercussions. If that's the way you look at it, I don't know much I can do. I'm going to carry my fight to the people. If I was ever crazy, then I'm still crazy." Added Earl, who seemed actually to be relieved at the course of events: "Maybe it's a good thing. It might be the difference in life or death for me. It'll give me a chance to get a little better." Minutes after the adjournment, Earl was joking and laughing with the legislators who had led the adjournment move.

The laughter was short-lived. Speaking to a crowd of 10,000 in New Orleans the following night, Earl once again found himself face to face with ugly political reality. "Be careful in whom you vote for senator or representative," Earl exhorted the crowd. "You have just seen a legislature refuse to act to benefit the people of this state." He called for election of a legislature "that won't stab me in the back." There was a sprinkle of applause and Earl, encouraged, followed by denouncing New Orleans Mayor deLesseps Morrison, who had already announced as a candidate for governor.

"Boooo," roared the crowd. "Boooo, boooo, boooo . . ." Earl stood there, perspiring, shaking slightly, a look of bewilderment on his face. The boos, catcalls and heckling continued, followed by a rising chant of "We want Chep [Morrison]. We want Chep."

Angered, Earl pointed a shaky finger at the hecklers. "You're so damn silly you stink," he cried, "you go to Texas." The heckling increased. There were more "booos," and—suddenly—they were laughing at Earl, who could only stand and shout back, "Either go take a bath or shut up. You stink so bad I can't think. Go take a bath please." Then Earl, a weary old man, his anger spent, collapsed into a chair and stared straight ahead. The crowd began to melt away while a few staunch friends came forward to shake hands. "Hoodlums," rasped a plainly hurt Earl, as he watched the others go.

Earl returned to Baton Rouge to lick his wounds, but there he faced more pressures. There had been talk that the Internal Revenue Bureau had called off its investigation of Earl's finances. Senator Ellender had announced in Washington that he thought this was so. In New Orleans, a succinct Bureau announcement debunked the rumor. The investigation would continue, as before.

The Air Force pressed for payment of its bill, intimating that Louisiana's Air National Guard would be deprived of Air Force planes and facilities if a settlement was not made. Earl relented, settling the $4,251 bill for $1,260. The Air Force announced that it was satisfied. Earl turned again to the campaign, announcing that he would resign as governor by October 15, then head a ticket in an attempt to govern the state for another four years. He pressed home a twin theme: He was as he had always been—that is, not mentally ill; and his friends, family and hostile legislators had sabotaged the program intended to benefit the people.

In DeQuincy he spelled it out. "The people will censure them," Earl said of the legislators who had been "foolish enough" to adjourn his special session. "If you vote for Uncle Earl, don't vote for some sapsucker who will stab me in the back." In Kinder he blasted his old enemy, the newspapers: "They said they want an honest man; they want anything but an honest man. They'd like to close my mouth—and they darned near did when they drug me around to them crazy houses." His wife? Blanche, said Earl, was the "most jealous woman that God ever let live on this earth." She had wanted to run the state herself. Russell? He wanted "to be governor worse than a Chinaman needs a bath." Wasn't he fearful of losing the Chinese vote? a reporter laughed. "There aren't enough to count," said Earl. In Washington, Russell announced a hands-off attitude toward the campaign.

Earl announced that he would go to New Orleans again. Why? "Just to raise hell," he told reporters. "Maybe," he added slyly, "I'll do a little courtin'."

The real reason for the trip came out at once. Behind closed doors at the Roosevelt Hotel, Earl met with his old friend Bob Maestri and leaders of the "Old Regulars," the Regular Democratic Organization, successor to the old New Orleans Ring. For two days reporters, parked outside in hallways, could hear Earl threaten, rant, yell at the top of his lungs, as he accused RDO members of ingratitude, of running out on him when he needed them most. Suddenly he left New Orleans in a huff and the RDO quickly revealed the candidate it would support in the December 5 primary: ex-Governor Jimmie Davis. Back in Baton Rouge, the Old Regulars felt the ax as Earl began a systematic dismissal of RDO members who held state jobs. How many would go? Said Earl, "Man, give me time. He [any RDO member with a state job] won't be there long if he ain't classified."

These were the long, lonely nights for Earl Long. The hectic traveling had ended and there was no Legislature in session. He occupied the executive mansion in solitary splendor. Blanche, together with a sister, stayed in the new house she and Earl had built.

Earl called frequently, always ready to discuss the possibility of reconciliation. He kept Blanche on the telephone for hours, calm at first, sometimes losing his temper, shouting into the telephone, exhausting himself with a steady flow of dialogue. Once, Blanche met Earl at the New Orleans home of a relative. They talked calmly at first, then Earl grew angry again. Their talks always boiled down to the same terms: Blanche would be willing to come back—for a price. Earl had to promise to leave politics and rest. Consistently Earl refused, and Blanche, too, was adamant. It was not that Blanche didn't understand politics. It was that she understood too well the stresses and strains Earl underwent when he had a political program to sell.

Earl first met Blanche while he worked as a salesman and attended law school at Tulane. Dark-haired and pretty, Blanche had been born in Covington, the daughter of Mr. and Mrs. Robert Revere. When she was two, her parents brought her to New Orleans, where she attended public schools, studied briefly at Tulane, then took a secretary's course at Soule Business College. Earl met her at the cigar counter of the Monteleone Hotel.

Six years Earl's junior, impressed by this brother of Governor Huey, Blanche dated Earl for a year, then married him on August 17, 1932, in Sister Caledonia Long's home in Estes Park, Colorado. When they returned to Louisiana, Earl plunged into his first race for office as a candidate for lieutenant governor.

In some ways Blanche proved to be the perfect choice for Earl. He was hearty, bluff, as rough as a corncob. Blanche was quiet, refined, industrious, gracious. Earl spat on the floor when the spirit moved him. Blanche kept a spotless house, took to reading and needle point and became an expert at the latter. She winced when Earl spat, begged off trips to the pea patch, went in for riding horses, especially a favorite Palomino, Lady Buff, a gift from Earl. If "Miz Blanche," as Earl called her, sometimes irritated Earl with her quiet refinement, he never lost sight of the fact that she balanced his erratic behavior and minimized his rough-and-tumble ways. As the good, devoted wife, she was a distinct political asset.

"I guess," Blanche had told reporters during Earl's 1948 campaign for governor, "all the Longs just naturally take to politics, and even though I'm a Long by marriage, I guess I take to it too."

During Earl's first, brief term as governor, Blanche had stayed mainly in the background, content to let her husband take the limelight. By 1948, like the Long she had become, she took to politics with a will of her own. During that campaign Blanche bossed Earl's state campaign headquarters, made speeches, took in and dispensed campaign money. Despite the integral part she played in the successful campaign, she could tell the newspapers afterwards that Earl was the boss. "Earl's interests," she said in an interview, "are my interests." During the 1952–56 interim when Earl was again out of office, Blanche made the statement stand up as she dutifully followed Earl, played the role of ex-governor's wife, and made new friendships while cementing the old, in anticipation of the coming campaign. When a triumphant Earl swept back into office in 1956, Blanche again became the First Lady of Louisiana—but this time she had a new title to go with the old. She was elected Democratic National Committeewoman. Later, Earl was to rage from time to time about Blanche's effort to usurp his role as governor, about what he called "petticoat politics." But there is little if any evidence to show that Blanche had political designs of her own. New title or no, she continued to live, politically speaking, in Earl's shadow, just as she always had.

But Blanche had stretched the truth when she declared that Earl's interests were her own. They were, but only to a point. She cared nothing at all, for example, for slopping hogs and feeding chickens, and the thought of the dreary "shack" on the "pea patch" in rural Winn Parish gave her cold chills. She insisted on—and got—a house of her own, a rambling, air-conditioned modern structure with five bathrooms on Baton Rouge's most exclusive street. The value of the house has been variously estimated at from $60,000 to $150,000. (Part of the difficulty in pinning down the cost lies in the fact that it was built by Big George Caldwell, the massive ex-LSU construction superintendent.) But if Blanche was happy in the new home, Earl, from his statements, was not. He continually referred to it as "Miz Blanche's house," complained privately that it was a tactical political mistake to put on airs with a fancy house while he worked to convince voters that he was still the same old country boy at heart. When Earl got a chance, he spent a weekend at his shack. When that happened, Blanche stayed at home in Baton Rouge.

Earl's loneliness was aggravated for other reasons. He and Blanche were childless, a condition Earl plainly and acutely disliked. He always exhibited a great interest in and love for children, and if his childless state bothered him less after a time, he never completely got over it.

Meanwhile Earl's other relatives were scattered about the state. Russell, whom Earl had genuinely liked before their fallout, had proved to be a big disappointment to him. To the north, in Shreveport, Brother Julius kept to himself, making no secret of the fact that in the 1959 primaries he fully intended to support Segregationist Willie Rainach. Brother George had died at seventy-four on March 22, 1958, in the Bethesda Naval Hospital, victim of a heart attack. Although the two had rarely been close, and in his last years George had spent much of his time in Washington, Earl might have been able to turn to him at times. As it was, Earl was on his own.

So it was with him as the primary election drew near and decision making was at hand. The other candidates were already being heard from—some of them voices from the distant past, others new and untested.

In the lead stood ex-Governor Davis, whose unchallengeable virtue was that nobody could attack him too strongly on any issue. Able, popular, successful, Davis would command widely divergent voting segments in his bid for a second term. The smart money—the politicians with big backing and political savvy—turned to him.

Next came perhaps the most dramatic postwar figure in Louisiana politics, deLesseps "Chep" Morrison of New Orleans. He had come home an Army colonel with a fine war record and a penchant for public service. By 1946 New Orleans was ripe for change—gambling and vice were rampant, city services were spotty, the port was losing some of its prominence, the city lacked a forward-looking plan to ride with the postwar commercial and industrial surge.

A reform group put Chep Morrison up to run against Ring Mayor Maestri, a heavy favorite in the early betting. Morrison's prediction: "If I am elected, you can put me down as the most astonished and happiest mayor this city ever had." But campaigning in his Army uniform, promising reform and progress, Morrison conducted a vigorous and intelligent campaign to beat Maestri by little more than 4,000 votes (out of some 138,000 cast). In 1959, with a record of three successive re-elections as mayor, Chep Morrison could point to a sparkling record of civic achievement, in which New Orleans—boasting new libraries, public buildings, freeways, a revitalized port—had become a vigorous municipal leader in the South. Morrison had tried to become governor before, in 1956, when Earl had steamrollered him and all other opposition combined. Now Morrison once again organized his "broom brigade" (campaign workers with brooms), directed them to the stairs of the state capitol, and put them to sweeping out symbolically the entrenched order while they literally swept the capitol steps clean.

Behind Morrison and Davis stood Willie Rainach, the spokesman for the new southern voice, the segregationist, who billed himself as the "only real conservative" in the race—a man dedicated to preserving the separation of the races by any legal means at his command. Rounding out the big four was William Dodd, who had tried for the governership in 1952, only to have Earl back Carlos Spaht. Dodd's pitch was a fiscal one. He was, averred Dodd, the only man—by virtue of his experience as state comptroller—with the experience to administer Louisiana's modern budget. A campaign slogan that became identified with him was the catchy "In Dodd We Trust." Behind these widely known "front runners" stood a line of lesser candidates—a grocer, an insurance man, a music company executive, a public relations counselor, a New Orleans taxi driver. It was the largest gubernatorial field in modern Louisiana history.

On the face of it, the caliber of opposition might not have worried Earl too much under normal conditions. He had soundly beaten Morrison once before and, ranked alongside Earl, Bill Dodd was a rather minor threat. Rainach was an unknown quantity whose support would be vocal, but limited. Jimmie Davis was a cohesive influence, under whose roof widely divergent political interests could find asylum, but he had been out of office for eleven years and his gubernatorial record, although adequate, was hardly illlustrious. Under normal conditions, Earl could probably have beaten them all.

But for Earl conditions in the political year 1959 were far from normal. He was a demonstrably sick man and, indeed, a man whose very reason had been questioned. He was a man with a broken home—a drawback for any political candidate, even a Long. He was a man under investigation by the federal government. He was a man who, many felt, had reduced Louisiana and its highest office to a national laughingstock and himself to the status of an uninhibited clown. Under these conditions, it was a wonder that Earl chose to run at all. Even more curious was the way in which he ran.

Until the deadline for filing for office was upon him, Earl kept his own counsel, refusing to say exactly which office he would seek. Rumors variously had him resigning to run again for governor; running for lieutenant governor or attorney general; stepping out of active participation altogether, but lending his political influence to a hand-picked successor.

Earl answered all the questions by formally announcing that he would run not for governor, but for lieutenant governor. The ticket, he added, would be headed by Oilman Jimmy Noe, who had served briefly as governor during the halcyon days following the assassination of Huey and the death in office of Oscar Allen.

The announcement was anticlimactic. After months of loudly declaring that he would seek another term as governor, no matter what the obstacles or cost, Earl's sudden cognizance of political realities resulted in a spiritless fizzle. No less a letdown was the news that Noe would head the ticket. At sixty-eight, Noe was a voice from the ancient past. He had tried to step into the golden circle of heirs following Huey's assassination, only to be outmaneuvered by the Weiss-Maestri-Leche faction. In 1940 he had spelled the difference between victory and defeat in Earl's struggle with Sam Jones. Earl had denounced him as an "oil chisler" and a federal grand jury had indicted Noe along with Weiss for alleged income tax evasion of oil company profits. Weiss pleaded guilty to the charges, but Noe, electing to fight them, was acquitted.

But Noe and Earl forgot their differences, became friends and political allies. Noe had given blood to the dying Huey and even today keeps fresh flowers on the Kingfish's grave. He had backed Earl's political ambitions on several occasions after supporting Jones in 1940. Still, the public regarded Earl's choice as the dredging up of a lightweight. From all reports, Noe was reluctant to run in the first place, but did so to please Earl. Immediately the rumors spread, whipped along by Earl's opposition. In effect, said Earl's political opponents, Jimmy Noe was a blind; if he won, he would resign and let Earl, as the new lieutenant governor, take over Louisiana once more. Both denied the charge and Noe went so far as to offer to put up a $100,000 "performance bond" to guarantee that, if elected, he would serve his term. The idea, however, continued to gain some currency.

In all, eleven candidates formally ran for governor—a "bumper crop" as the newspapers described it; but from the beginning attention centered on the big five—Davis, Morrison, Rainach, Dodd and Noe. Earl usually followed Noe on the campaign stump as the chief crowd-getter, but the ticket's junior partner. It was a role he had not played since 1944.

The campaign proved to be the traditional Louisiana political binge. Invective and personal vilification, ridicule, charges of personal and official inadequacy, conflicting claims, promises, irrelevant observations, inaccurate estimates—few holds were barred, few rules observed as the campaigners warmed to the contest. For the most part, the candidates clothed themselves and their records in saintly dress; each, to hear him tell it, had been—and would be again—Louisiana's savior.

Noe, declaring the chief campaign issue was a clear-cut "Long against anti-Long" debate, kicked off his campaign on a light sporting tone. It was football time in Louisiana, with LSU's Tigers riding a long victory streak that had captured the imagination of sports partisans across the state. "The Go Team is the Noe Team," became the cry of the Noe-Long combine. "We're taking a page from the Tigers," said Noe. "If we can flatten the competition in Baton Rouge, we're going to be pretty close partners in the next four years."

In the early stages of the campaign, it was Earl that the crowds came to see, and the governor rarely disappointed.

"Davis was governor four years and just name me one constructive thing he did," challenged Earl. "I tell you it is a strange thing to see the cows, the polecats, the poodle dogs and the other dogs lying down together in the Davis campaign.

"Then there is that sweet little Morrison. He wears a toupee and puts on make-up. He says he won't vote taxes. Well, ask him what he will do to keep the schools open next spring [in the face of integration demands]."

Earl named Morrison as Noe's chief opponent, dismissing the others with a curt declaration that "the rest are so far behind the dust is smothering them." He declared, despite his heavy Negro vote in 1956, that he and Noe were "one million per cent" for segregation. "I'm for segregation, Jimmie Noe's for segregation—and we always have been. We've already done more for segregation than Willie Rainach will do in a lifetime."

Earl shifted his sights frequently, concentrating on the gubernatorial candidates. He rarely bothered with any of the candidates for lieutenant governor.

Davis, cried Earl, was "a sweet-smelling guitar player who's in North Louisiana Sunday morning singing 'Nearer My God to Thee' and Sunday night in South Louisiana singing 'Bed Bug Blues.' His pockets are lined with oil money, gambling money, and 'Bed Bug Blues' record money. He doesn't get excited over anything unless it's got to do with making money or filthy records or going out to Hollywood and appearing in those cheap, Grade B moving pictures." Strange testimony from Earl, who three years before had told his Legislature: "I respect Jimmie Davis . . . personally, I never had a better friend than Jimmie Davis. . . . I don't believe Jimmie Davis would harm a crawfish." But 1956 was a nonpolitical year.

When Earl cooled down Noe took up the slack. Davis has promised to increase old age pensions? "Jimmie must be crazier than a bumblebee on a wax flower" Noe campaigned. "When he was governor the largest pension check he ever mailed out was ten dollars and Senator Clements can tell you of an eighty-nine-year-old lady in his town who only got twenty-five cents."

Davis, campaigning with his band, singing "You Are My Sunshine," adopting a moderate tone, promised, once again, "peace and harmony," an end to factional bitterness, restoration of sound government. Cried Earl: Davis was "All Singin', Flingin' Jimmie," who had "nothing for a platform except sweetness and sunshine. He isn't saying anything about anybody or anything. He calls it 'peace and harmony.' But he knows when you're guilty, the best thing to do is to keep your mouth shut."

Sometimes it was difficult to tell whether it was Noe or Earl running against Davis. Cried Noe of Davis: "He was afraid that he might fall out with the big city corporations and the big city newspapers that controlled him. It took a man like Earl Long . . . to stand up against these big shots and put the taxes on the people who were able to best pay. And, for this, he's been persecuted ever since."

Earl took time from the local campaigning to view the national scene, declaring that he favored Stuart Symington for President, Senator Jack Kennedy for Vice-President. "That's my ticket," said Earl, who had supported Adlai Stevenson in 1952 and again in 1956. He took pains again to explain that he was fit, especially mentally, that his family—Russell in particular—had fabricated a story about his health while they tried to grab his office.

"Mentally, there wasn't anything any more wrong with me than there is now," said Earl. "It looks to me like Russell was just trying to launch his campaign for governor. Why, he even pulled out the mansion telephone wires—put this down—he took over. He tried to take over the Legislature while I was in Texas, but a lot of people wouldn't let him. . . . I guess they realized what he was up to." Grumbled Earl: "He had no more business taking charge at the mansion than I would have at the White House. Russell was very ungrateful, after all I've done for him. It beat me why he would want to leave Washington to run for governor."

Slowly, almost imperceptibly, the tenor of the campaign changed. The crowds at the Noe-Long "rallies" dwindled. Those meeting Candidates Morrison and Davis increased. Almost daily, imposing newspaper advertisements announced new group support for either Davis or Morrison. Earl, refusing as usual to take to television, grew strangely quiet at a time when he should have been making his most concerted pitch. Sometimes, after speaking briefly, the governor would slide heavily into a chair, a fixed smile on his face, obviously tired. During the last two weeks of the campaign he virtually gave up the race, concentrating instead on business at the capitol, while Noe went through the final gestures. By election eve there was little doubt about the verdict. With results streaming in from all corners of Louisiana, Earl took a brief automobile ride around Baton Rouge, returned to the mansion to retire early and refused to accept telephone calls.

ELECTION SPELLING DOOM TO DYNASTY, trumpeted the Dallas *News,* in an early postelection edition, as the results showed just how badly Earl had been beaten. Of 787,407 ballots cast, Earl could manage no better than third place in a six-man field for the lieutenant governor's post. In all, Earl received 157,452 votes—a paltry 20 per cent of the total. He trailed far behind the 227,758 votes received by the leading candidate, Alexandria Mayor W. George Bowdon, running on the Morrison ticket.

Earl's ticket leader, Noe, did even worse, coming in fourth—behind Morrison, Davis, and Rainach. In all, Noe could muster only 97,654 votes, far behind even Earl's poor total.

Earl's defeat was humiliatingly complete, almost completely personal. While he lost by a wide margin, his legislative leaders, with one exception, won re-election by substantial totals. In Alexandria his old political enemy, Camille Gravel, Jr., won another seat on the State Central Committee. Even Earl's Winn Parish neighbors registered their disapproval by refusing to return him to his local post as a delegate to the State Central Committee.

In historical terms the results were even more significant. For the first time since Huey's day, neither of the candidates in the ensuing runoff was a Long or a Long-backed choice. It was the first time since the Kingfish's heyday that a Long had received such a small percentage of the total vote. It was the first time that Longism and a Long had been so ignominiously repudiated by the vast majority of the electorate. Said a Baton Rouge *Morning Advocate* editorial, "Whether the magic [of the Long name] has been lost forever remains to be seen, but the political career of Gov. Long, which has been a remarkable one, may be near an end. The Long machine, as it existed until a few months ago, has been shattered by the dramatic events of the governor's illness and the outcome of the election."

For days Earl refused to comment on the election as the two winners—Morrison and Davis—lined up support among the defeated candidates. Jimmy Noe endorsed Morrison, as did Bill Dodd. But the two losers with the biggest backing—Rainach, with 143,000, and Earl—maintained a tactful silence. Conceivably, Rainach could be the key to the runoff if the people who voted for him followed whatever endorsement he might make.

Rainach's campaign leaders announced at first that they would steer a neutral course. Then Rainach announced his support of Davis. Soon, the "entire Rainach ticket" teamed up behind Davis.

Earl waited for the final week, then casually announced his

choice: Davis, the candidate he had colorfully denounced during the first campaign. "The reason I am voting for Mr. Davis," said Earl, "is that Mr. Davis is a kind man, a tolerant man, a Christian man, and I've always found him truthful . . . that means more to me than anything else." Added Earl: "My guess is a large, large percentage of my followers—if I have any—will vote for Davis." For Louisiana, it was not an inappropriate political gesture on Earl's part.

An all-time record number of voters—901,791—trooped to the polls to register their choices in the January 9 runoff primary. With the events of the turbulent summer still fresh in most minds, Louisiana's voters chose "peace and harmony" over the "clean sweep." Davis won handily by 73,771 votes, taking into office with him the entire Davis ticket. Chep Morrison, who had tried to become Louisiana's first Catholic governor in a hundred years, found that the maxim—Louisiana doesn't elect a Catholic governor—held true for him as well.

Even before Davis took office the "peace and harmony" he had pledged settled over Louisiana. The furor of the campaign was over, as was seemingly the turbulence of Earl's personal life. Russell returned to Washington for the Congressional session. Blanche stayed at the five-bathroom house, venturing out only occasionally, as she did, for example, to greet Presidential Hopeful Jack Kennedy. Alone again in the executive mansion, Earl said and did less than he had in thirty years of rough-and-tumble politicking.

Under Davis, Louisiana could, by past performance, expect easygoing, tolerant direction. There would certainly be no more TV "spectaculars," raging cross-country excursions, the slapdash behavior and red-hot language dear to the hearts of constituents and newsmen everywhere. Louisiana's politics, kept at the constant boiling point by thirty years of Longs and Longism, began to cool perceptibly even before Davis took office.

With the "peace and harmony" candidate in office, the cooling process would be even more pronounced. But even if it should heat up again, the odds are that new faces and new issues, such as segregation, will generate most of the heat. For better or worse, Earl Long, the self-styled "last of the red-hot poppas," will have left the political scene—probably for the last time.

EPILOGUE:

Dynasty in a Deep Freeze

IN THE thirty years since Huey launched his revolution and founded his dynasty, time and change have taken their inevitable toll in the Kingdom of the Kingfish.

An assassin's bullet shortened Huey's meteoric career. An aroused electorate, weary of his personal excesses, dismissed a saddened, physically spent Earl. A legislature that at first refused to hear him eventually listened in sullen silence while the dynasty's third member, Russell, sought to explain his uncle's erratic behavior. Twenty-five years after his death, the dynasty and the political machine that Huey fashioned are falling apart. Longism, once the bright symbol that magically commanded vast loyalty in Louisiana, has lost much of its sheen. Its luster, in fact, has been dulling progressively since Huey first gave it the new political look.

Huey was a revolutionary who appeared at a time when revolutions—economic, political and social—were fashionable. In different parts of the world—Germany, Italy, Central Europe—new orders had replaced the old. In Eastern Europe, Russia stood as the supposed shining example of a new and better way of life. Only in America, where a "new normalcy" stifled political progress and social reform, did the old political and economic *status quo* seem firmly embedded. In the South, in particular, the old order of "government by gentlemen," in cahoots with entrenched business interests, seemed secure, despite the early assaults of the Bilbos, the Talmadges and the Tillmans. If ever the South, including Louisiana, was ready for a change, it was when Huey approached political maturity.

Huey changed everything as he ushered in a new political

era. Government by gentlemen went out the window as government by corporate interest became his special target. No longer could political candidates campaign on the hazy anachronisms of Southern virtue and Confederate glory. With Huey, the issues were modernized, reduced to the simple realities of roads, bridges, schoolbooks, pensions and poll taxes. His opposition accused him of demagoguery and Huey pulled their goatees in return. "... He became a demagogue," wrote Gerald W. Johnson, but "when the choice lies between a demogogue and a political corpse, the voters who choose the demagogue may be degenerate, but I doubt that their choice proves it."

Huey revolutionized Louisiana's politics by the simple expedient of promising something, then delivering it. The people, so used to being promised little and getting less, were so grateful that they rarely stopped to inquire about the cost of what they were getting. That they were getting something was enough.

Under Huey, Louisiana saw its children get free schoolbooks and school bus service. Night schools became available to the illiterate and an estimated 200,000 learned to read and write. Huey built a new state capitol, medical and dental schools at the state university. The bed capacities of the state's biggest hospitals were doubled and the disgraceful mental institutions—supervised like medieval prison towers—were cleaned up. Tuition at LSU was put within the reach of every qualified student, but when a qualified student couldn't pay that, he was admitted anyway. The state was laced with a new and modern system of concrete and black-topped roads; toll bridges were virtually eliminated, replaced by free ones. The poll tax—that yoke around the neck of the poor southern voter—was removed once and for all and homestead exemptions for hard-pressed, lower-income families became a reality.

Hamilton Basso wearied of those who viewed Huey only as a power-mad dictator: "To wave aside his roads, his free schoolbooks, his school bus service, his new schoolhouses, his tax reductions, his debt moratorium, his abolition of the poll tax, is to wave aside some of the most important reasons for his continued success. It is to make the people of Louisiana absolute fools and idiots. After the control first of the plantation, banking, railroad and utility interests, then of the New Orleans Ring . . . Huey came as a welcome, even wholesome relief." [1]

Louisiana paid an exorbitant price for the blessings Huey bestowed. During his brief span he added or caused to be added thirty-five new taxes, many of them directed chiefly at the low-income consumer. The state's indebtedness leaped from forty-six million to one hundred and forty-three million dollars, and new taxes and new indebtedness were in the making when Huey was killed.

More importantly, the early Longism demanded—and got—complete subservience from its subjects. Government by dictatorship supplanted government by democratic process. The Legislature became the amenable arm of the dictator, and the courts an extension of his will. He ruled the state government like a family-owned corporation while he sought to extend his influence to the national level. Even after he had brought his enemies to their knees he continued to humiliate them, tightening his hold on the state, stamping out all opposition.

The Kingfish's assassination gave him a stature and a martyrhood that he might never have achieved had his program run its full course. His political heirs capitalized on his passing to take over the government, to loot the state. It was a logical outgrowth of despotism, but few linked the Scandals to the hallowed name of the departed Huey. He had become too entrenched as a legend, as a savior—indeed, in some quarters, as a political saint.

For eight years, 1940–48, the pendulum of political reaction swung away from Longism. The Scandals had disgusted the people, they wanted reform, but not an abandonment of the material fruits of Longism. The dividends, in the form of welfare services, continued, but not as dramatically or abundantly as under Huey and his heirs. Longism, as Allan Sindler put it, had ". . . set both the form and content of subsequent politics." But its adherents, unlike Huey, could not match its pace. The reform movement never came off as the grand crusade it was supposed to be. Cleanups began, then were abandoned; investigations of local officials suspected of corruption were stymied.

[1] *Mainstream*, copyright 1943, by Hamilton Basso, Harcourt, Brace and Company, Inc.

The reform movement ended with the beginning of the four years of "peace and harmony" envisaged by Jimmie Davis. But after the headiness of Huey, the excesses of the Scandals, the suspense of the reform movement, the "peace and harmony" regime settled like a stone in Louisiana stomachs—bulky, unmoving, indigestible, uninteresting.

By 1948 the pendulum was back again. The second of the Longs won office in a classic gesture of cynicism rivaling anything in modern Louisiana politics. Having little new to offer, Earl again offered the old package—that is, more of everything. To match Huey's schoolbooks Earl offered free hot lunches in the schools. To match Huey's new roads, Earl added his own wrinkle—wider roads. Huey had offered pensions; Earl vowed to increase them, and to add a veterans' bonus as well. Huey had offered homestead exemptions; Earl increased them.

But in outlining his programs, Earl differed in one important respect from his brother. Huey had rarely bothered to tell the people what the benefits would cost. In his day, it was enough that he promised and that they eventually received. In Earl's day, it was different. People became cost-conscious. Earl promised everything without new taxes. Despite the healthy budget surplus he inherited when he took office in 1948, Earl was forced to execute an abrupt about-face. As he doled out the benefits, he dug deeper for his taxes. But he was refreshingly frank about it.

"You know," he told the Legislature, "the [New Orleans] *Item* once said Ole Earl is coverin' up with one hand and cleanin' up with the other. Well, I'm not admittin' anything, but under that whisperin' they might have been right. You know, when they nail you with the truth it's hard to get around it. Maybe they were right."

Longism and the Longs were back with a vengeance, it seemed. Only an intrafamily division prevented a Long victory in 1952. By 1956, Longism was at its highest peak since Huey's days. One Long was governor, another a United States Senator, a third a congressman and a fourth National Democratic Committeewoman. The senior U. S. Senator was, by tradition and inclination, a staunch Long supporter, as were healthy segments of the Legislature and the Congressional delegation. Viewed in terms of the short span since 1956, Longism, far from waning, had flourished anew. Had it found a new magic to add to the old? Would it go on forever? The answer on both counts was no, and there were good reasons for the answer.

In the first place, the Longism of 1960 is hardly a call to revolution. In some respects, it is as outdated today as the philosophy it replaced. For twenty years it has offered Louisiana more of the same—but little that is new. Moreover, it has all but ignored the new issues that have stirred the South and the state.

"Huey," said F. Raymond Daniell, "was a reformer whose original motivation was a grievance against entrenched corporate wealth." Latter-day Longism has no such grievance. The reforms that Huey preached have all been won. One wondered, during the campaign of 1959, to whom Earl Long referred when he vowed that he would carry on his fight against the "big-shot millionaires."

Nor is Longism's appeal to welfare benefits unique in 1960. Huey's welfarism predated the New Deal and the Fair Deal. It largely predated Big Labor and modern pension plans, a realistic social security system, profit sharing, agricultural reform, and all the other accouterments of modern welfarism. Moreover, the wealth that Huey sought to distribute is being shared today, via a stiffly graduated income tax, to a degree that might have brought anguished cries from Huey himself. Huey gave Louisiana its welfare appetite, but the rest of the country has caught up with, if not surpassed, Louisiana. Welfarism is today too inextricably woven into the national fabric to show much of the Kingfish's stripe.

In the second place, the inheritors of Longism do not possess the genius of its founder. "Huey Long," said James Rorty as he assessed the Kingfish, "... [is] the most forceful, the most imaginative, the most daring, the ablest ... the most formidable politician the South has produced since the Civil War." [2] Neither Earl nor Russell can lay claim to such accolades. Earl admits that Huey was a genius, but reserves for himself more horse sense. Russell, plainly worshipful, calls his late father the "greatest man of his time." It is perhaps sufficient to note that Earl's programs have been further extensions of the programs laid down by Huey. Russell, although an able and conscientious

[2] "Callie Long's Boy Huey," by James Rorty, *Current History and Forum.*

legislator, has yet to introduce a major measure in the Senate. He has worked his way up the Senate committee ladder and one day may exert genuine influence in that body. But no one would seriously compare his doggedly earnest methods with the flash and fire that characterized the Kingfish's style.

There is still another reason for Longism's fading appeal. No longer is Louisiana as subject to dictatorship as it was in Huey's day. If the governor—be he Earl or someone else—is still the government's most powerful single figure, he in no respect can hope to command the awesome power that Huey exercised in the latter stages of his career. The Legislature, for one thing, is no longer a rubber stamp, to be shuffled like a deck of cards. Proof of this is the extreme length to which Earl was forced to go in dealing with it prior to his breakdown. Added proof is the summary manner in which a handful of legislators all but dismissed Russell when he appeared uninvited to plead his uncle's cause. In Huey's day, this would have been neither possible nor necessary.

The face of the government itself has undergone extensive remolding. Civil service, a joke under Huey, is today an accomplished fact. The governor can skirt it—as Earl did in the firing of a state police sergeant he branded as unloyal to him during his mansion confinement—but nowadays summary action on his part has a tendency to backfire. The police sergeant, along with a hospital attendant who was also dismissed by Earl, were reinstated on technical grounds. Earl chose not to press the issue. Finally, fewer of the important state jobs are "at the will and pleasure" of the governor. There are still many, of course, but an increasing trend is toward making higher posts elective. No longer, for example, would Earl dare to displace an attorney general by "discovering"—two years after the election—that he took the office illegally. Louisiana simply wouldn't stand for it today. In the last election, by way of comparison, Earl could only announce lamely that he would not support incumbent Attorney General Jack Gremillion for re-election. Gremillion took a place on the Davis ticket and won handily anyway.

Perhaps the most glaring failure of modern Longism has been its inability or its refusal to cope with Louisiana's most potentially explosive problem, the racial question.

Like the South, Louisiana is torn by ancient traditions that meet head on with modern realities. The state is strictly segregationist (except where preliminary inroads have been made in New Orleans) by tradition and by law. State legislation prohibits school integration, interracial athletic contests, interracial gatherings, and the like. Meanwhile, federal law demands racial equality and, as a condition, racial mixture. It is on this issue that most of the state's tensions center today.

The divisions inherent in the issue became clearly apparent only after Earl had already won his last election as governor, after Little Rock, and after the Legislature had formally reinforced—by law—the state's militant, no-integration stand. By the time of the 1959 election, the integration-segregation issue was a primary one, and the election results heightened its importance. State Senator Willie Rainach, a man who, without the issue, might not have commanded more than a local following, received an amazing 143,000 votes. In so doing, he lagged only about 7,000 votes behind Earl, an incredible showing for an essentially local politician without a demonstrable following. Ultimately, the racial issue became the single most important factor in deciding the runoff election between Jimmie Davis and Chep Morrison, who was repeatedly attacked for "allowing" integration of New Orleans' swimming pools and parks. If there was one candidate in the 1959 gubernatorial race who showed he could swing a hard core of votes to a candidate he chose to endorse, it was Rainach, the avowed segregationist.

Finally, there is the issue of Earl's health and his personal conduct. Earl is sixty-four. If he survives, he will be sixty-eight by the time Louisiana elects another governor and at sixty-eight there is no reason to suppose that his health will be any better than it was at sixty-four. Moreover, the segregationists under the leadership of Rainach view him as an enemy to the cause of racial separation, even though Earl professes to be "one million per cent" for continued segregation. Since it is the North Louisiana, hill-country voters who, themselves, are the chief proponents of continued segregation, Earl would have to do a magician's job of convincing them—on this issue alone—that he can be trusted. And if he succeeded in this, which is unlikely, he would still have to convince them all over again that his physical and mental health are up to another term in office. Again, his prospects here grow dim with the years.

What of the dynasty's future? It will survive, of course, as long as Russell holds high public office. And Russell has made no secret of the fact that he yearns some day to follow his father into the executive mansion.

Russell has several things in his favor. At forty-one, he need be in no hurry to make his bid. If he can win re-election to the U. S. Senate in 1962, he could easily come back to campaign for governor in 1963, yet still keep the Senate seat as a safety measure. In these respects, in short, he has both the advantage of time and an office in which he can succeed himself.

Russell's political conduct is another asset that may some day ride him to the governorship. He has repeatedly emphasized his dislike for Louisiana's bifactional, north-south, Long-anti-Long approach to politics. And he makes it clear that his political inclinations do not always coincide with those of his uncle. Says Russell, "My uncle and I have differed politically in the past. He has his following. I have mine." Russell, for example, has largely hewed to the liberal side of the Senate, but has been outspoken in his support of states' rights. He was, for example, a supporter of the move to limit the terms of U. S. Supreme Court Justice to twelve years, a states' rights reaction to the court's racial rulings.

Ultimately, Russell's greatest strength in perpetuating, perhaps modernizing, the dynasty will be the name he inherited from his father. Despite the criticism that has been heaped on Huey and his methods, his name is still genuinely revered by a large cross section of Louisianians. Even after the Scandals broke and became widely publicized, a Gallup Poll, taken in late 1939, showed that 55 per cent of those interviewed considered him a "good influence"; only 22 per cent thought him a "bad influence"; while 14 per cent of the "lower class" interviewed put Huey in the "good" category, and only 9 per cent of this group classified him as "bad." Twenty-five years after his death, the "bad" he did is largely obscured by the "good" he performed.

As a direct descendant of the dynasty's founder, Russell can command the prestige that naturally flows from father to son, but rarely from brother to brother. Moreover, Russell has publicly and repeatedly declared his complete allegiance to the ideals of his late father. And, unlike Earl, he has no record of having attacked the late Kingfish.

Not that Louisiana is apt to see anything like Huey or Earl again. Their breed is a thing of Louisiana's past now. The buccaneering political flavor that Huey introduced to Louisiana, a flavor that Earl sustained with his own brand of swashbuckling liberalism and personal dynamism, ended with Earl's political passing. That phase of the dynasty, at least, has ended.

But as long as Russell continues to occupy high political office in Louisiana the dynasty continues too, at least in name. It is with him that the dynasty's fate lies. It was Huey who so artfully built the political House of Long, Earl who occasionally refurbished it. To Russell goes the task of overhauling and remodeling it. If he fails, the dynasty may be ended in name, as well as in spirit.

The Dynasty

HUEY PIERCE LONG

Railroad Commissioner:	1918–1928
Governor:	1928–1930
U.S. Senator:	1930–1935

MRS. ROSE MCCONNELL LONG

Interim U.S. Senator:	1935

EARL KEMP LONG

Lieutenant Governor:	1936–1939
Governor:	1939–1940
Governor:	1948–1952; 1956–1960

MRS. BLANCHE REVERE LONG

National Democratic Committee Woman: 1956–

DR. GEORGE LONG

U.S. Representative	1952–1958

RUSSELL BILLIU LONG

U.S. Senator:	1948–

Acknowledgments

FOR aid and comfort above and beyond the call of either friendship or courtesy, the author is indebted to: Ed Clinton of the Baton Rouge *State Times,* whose willingness to help is exceeded only by his reputation as one of Louisiana's finest political analysts; to Arthur Folse of the Baton Rouge *Morning Advocate;* Barney Krebs of the New Orleans *Times-Picayune;* and John Wilds of the New Orleans *Item and States.* Thanks also to Bryce Miller of United Press International; to Camille F. Gravel, Jr., Democratic National Committeeman from Louisiana; Bill Bailey of the Alexandria *Town Talk.* Particular thanks are due the staff of the Howard Tilton Memorial Library at Tulane University, and to its counterpart in the Louisiana Room of the Louisiana State University Library.

The author gratefully acknowledges permission to quote from the following: *Mainstream,* copyright, 1943, by Hamilton Basso, Harcourt Brace and Co., Inc.; *Behind the Ballots,* by James A. Farley, Harcourt Brace and Co., Inc., copyright 1938; *Huey Long's Louisiana,* by Allan P. Sindler, Baltimore: Johns Hopkins Press, copyright 1956; *Louisiana Hayride,* by Harnett T. Kane, William Morrow & Company, copyright 1941; *American Messiahs,* by The Unofficial Observer, Simon and Schuster, Inc.; *We Saw It Happen,* by F. Raymond Daniell, edited by H. W. Baldwin and S. Stone, Simon and Schuster, Inc.; *Life* Magazine, New York: copyright Time Inc.; *The Story of Huey P. Long,* by Carleton Beals, Philadelphia: J. B. Lippincott Company, copyright 1935; *Huey Long—A Candid Biography,* by Forrest Davis, New York: Dodge Publishing Company, copyright 1935; *After Seven Years,* by Raymond Moley, New York: Harper & Brothers, copyright 1939; *The Kingfish,* by Thomas O. Harris, New Orleans: Pelican Publishing Co., copyright 1938; *You're The Boss,* by Edward J. Flynn, New York: Viking Press Inc., copyright 1945; "Callie Long's Boy Huey," by James Rorty, *Current History and Forum*; "Huey Long: American Dictator," by Hodding Carter, *The American Mercury; Forerunners of American Fascism,* by Raymond Gram Swing, New York: Julian Messner, Inc., copyright 1935; "The Governorship of Huey P. Long," by Leo Glen Douthit, Tulane University, Unpublished Master's Thesis; and to the New Orleans *Times-Picayune* and New Orleans *Item and States;* Baton Rouge *Morning Advocate* and Baton Rouge *State Times;* Shreveport *Times* and the Shreveport *Journal; The New York Times;* and the files of *Time* and *Life* magazines.

The map on the title page is reprinted by permission of the *Louisiana Almanac and Fact Book, Inc.,* and Stuart O. Landry, editor and owner of the copyright—305 Chartres Street, New Orleans, La.

My warmest thanks go to my wife, who typed the entire manuscript, and to Jim Shepley and Dick Clurman for their understanding and assistance.

INDEX